ROSE MURRAY'S

Comfortable

KITCHEN COOKBOOK

ROSE MURRAY'S

Comfortable

KITCHEN COOKBOOK

McGraw-Hill Ryerson
Toronto   Montreal

First published in 1991 by
McGraw-Hill Ryerson Limited
300 Water Street
Whitby, Ontario, Canada
L1N 9B6

Canadian Cataloguing in Publication Data

Murray, Rose, date
  Rose Murray's comfortable kitchen cookbook

Includes index.
ISBN 0-07-551295-5

1. Cookery, Canadian. I. Title. II. Title:
Comfortable kitchen cookbook

TX715.6.M88 1991   641.5971   C91-094827-5

Produced by B & E Publications Inc.
Suite 265
7025 Tomken Road
Mississauga, Ontario
L5S 1R6

Printed and bound in Canada

For Kent, Allen and Anne.

Contents

Food Facts and Tips

Introduction

"Comfortable" is a word you might normally associate with an old suit that you wear with ease time after time in a number of situations. Or, it might describe a friend with whom you can spend relaxing evenings without worrying about whose turn it is to talk. A comfortable room is one with which you feel completely familiar. It's soothing, calming—one whose contents provide a kind of quiet enjoyment.

I find my kitchen such a room. There's the equipment I use every day—my favorite whisk, those light stainless steel mixing bowls, my mini-food processor, the old black-handled fork of my mother's, the conical sieve and tiny ladle from Paris. In the corner, there's the radio that keeps me company on my solitary testing days. On the other days, there's plenty of room for someone else to work with me or for friends to gather while I whip up some appetizers. Often, these friends don't even need to get past the kitchen to eat them. It's like the farm kitchen when I was growing up. Everyone gathered there—and frequently didn't even see the parlor. It was my mother's good food that drew them to that room.

In terms of food, "comfort" means many things, too. It means food that tastes good, food that's soothing, like a hearty soup on a cold winter day, food like rice pudding that you remember with some nostalgia from bygone days.

A recipe becomes comfortable when you make it over and over again, knowing it will be good every time. Comfortable recipes are also easy to execute without always including a list of ingredients you don't have in the house.

A cookbook, in turn, becomes comfortable when it is well used—one that you will turn to time after time for easy recipes that become completely familiar.

I hope this book will be one with which you want to spend some relaxing time and one that you find a good source of reliable recipes, information and inspiration. My wish is that it will become an old friend. It's meant to be well used.

The recipes are all easy, but the emphasis is on good flavors for both family meals and entertaining. Since many of the old classics are simple and good, I've included a few as they have been cooked over the years in my own family. More often, I've updated traditional favorites by either simplifying the method or lightening the ingredients, or both. Sometimes, I've created a completely new version along the lines of an old favorite. Most of the recipes call for ingredients you can find in any supermarket, and even things you might have at home. (I've included further on a list of items you might like to consider when stocking your pantry.) Occasionally, however, I will introduce an ingredient that might not be so familiar—one that I think worthwhile knowing about for its good flavor contribution.

Some of the recipes are quick as well as easy, and many are quick-to-fix but long-simmering. There's great satisfaction in this type of simple sturdy cooking. It can be a soothing escape from the pressures of life.

Almost all the entertaining dishes are make-ahead—primarily because it is calming to have everything done before any guests arrive.

And if it isn't? Let everyone gather in your kitchen. My purpose with this book is to make yours as comfortable as mine.

Simple Snacks & Starters

One of life's great pleasures is getting together with good friends. Food is almost always part of this socializing.

The easy recipes in this chapter make great party food—either as simple starters to pique appetites when people come for dinner or nibbles to offer guests who drop in for an evening.

Dips and dippers, nibbles and bites, sit-down first courses—they're all approachable but impressive.

BLACK BEAN DIP

This easy, zesty dip will keep for days and can be the colorful focus of a casual party. Place it in a shallow bowl and garnish the top with rings of diced tomato, chopped green onion, grated Cheddar cheese with a dollop of sour cream in the middle. Surround the bowl with corn chips.

1	can (19 oz/540 mL) black beans, drained and rinsed	1
1/2 lb	cream cheese	250 g
1/4 cup	sour cream	50 mL
2	cloves garlic, minced	2
1 tsp	grated lime rind	5 mL
1/4 cup	fresh lime juice	50 mL
4 tsp	chili powder	20 mL
1 tsp	dried oregano	5 mL
1 tsp	hot pepper flakes	5 mL

In food processor, combine black beans, cream cheese, sour cream, garlic, lime rind and juice, chili powder, oregano and hot pepper flakes; process until smooth. Let dip sit, covered, in refrigerator for at least 2 hours for flavors to blend. Makes about 3 cups (750 mL).

LIGHT GUACAMOLE DIP

Surround this refreshing dip with a colorful selection of crisp seasonal vegetables for a light, but always popular appetizer or snack. Thinned with plain yogurt, it also makes a delicious sauce for sliced tomatoes, citrus fruit, cold roast beef or chilled seafood.

3	large sprigs fresh parsley	3
2	green onions, sliced	2
1	small clove garlic	1
1	ripe medium avocado	1
2 tbsp	fresh lime or lemon juice	25 mL
1/4 cup	*each* light mayonnaise and low-fat plain yogurt	50 mL
1/2 tsp	ground coriander (or 1 tbsp/15 mL chopped fresh)	2 mL
Pinch	cayenne pepper	Pinch
	Salt and pepper	

In food processor or blender, mince parsley with onions, dropping garlic through feed tube with motor running.

Reserving pit, peel and quarter avocado; add to processor and purée along with lime juice. Add mayonnaise, yogurt, coriander and cayenne pepper; season with salt and pepper to taste. Process until smooth.

Transfer to small serving bowl; push reserved pit into mixture to prevent browning. Cover and refrigerate until serving time or up to 4 hours. Makes about 1 1/2 cups (375 mL).

HOT AND CLASSY CRAB DIP

Serve this old favorite hot appetizer in the centre of a tray of crunchy raw vegetables and crackers.

1/2 lb	light cream cheese	250 g
1	can (6 oz/170 g) crab meat	1
2 tbsp	finely chopped shallots or onion	25 mL
1 tbsp	fresh lemon juice	15 mL
Dash	hot pepper sauce	Dash
1/4 cup	toasted sliced almonds	50 mL
1 tbsp	butter	15 mL

In medium bowl, beat cheese; mash in crab meat. Stir in shallots, lemon juice and hot pepper sauce.

Spoon into 3-cup (750 mL) baking dish. Sprinkle with almonds; dot with butter. (Recipe can be prepared to this point up to 1 hour ahead.)

Bake in 350°F (180°C) oven for about 30 minutes or until hot and bubbly. Makes about 1 1/2 cups (375 mL).

CREAMY POTATO GARLIC DIP

Don't be surprised if your guests ask for spoons to finish every bit of this Greek-style garlicky dip. Serve with assorted raw vegetables, grilled bread, pita triangles or fried eggplant sticks.

1 1/2 lb	red or yellow boiling potatoes (about 5)	750 g
8	cloves garlic, minced	8
1/2 tsp	coarse salt	2 mL
1/4 cup	olive oil	50 mL
2 tbsp	fresh lemon juice	25 mL
	Pepper	
1/2 cup	(approx) chicken stock	125 mL
	Olive oil	

Peel and quarter potatoes. In large saucepan, cover potatoes with salted water and bring to boil; reduce heat to medium-low and simmer, covered, for 20 to 30 minutes or until tender. Drain well and mash.

Meanwhile, place garlic and salt in medium bowl; mash with bottom of teaspoon against inside of bowl to release juices. Beat in mashed potatoes.

With fork or hand-held electric mixer, beat in oil, a few teaspoons (5 mL) at a time, until completely absorbed. Blend in lemon juice; season with pepper to taste. Taste and add more salt if desired.

Gradually blend in enough chicken stock to make smooth creamy mixture (like soupy purée). Transfer to serving bowl. (Recipe can be covered and refrigerated for up to 1 day.)

Serve at room temperature or slightly warmed in microwave. Just before serving, drizzle with a few drops olive oil. Makes about 3 cups (750 mL).

MIXED SPICED OLIVES

Keep these marinated olives on hand to serve with cheese and crackers for pre-dinner or late-night snacks.

1 cup	*each* green olives, black Greek olives and natural Niçoise olives	250 mL
1	jar (4¹/₂ oz/128 mL) whole pimientos	1
4	bay leaves	4
2	thin slices lemon	2
1 tsp	dried rosemary	5 mL
¹/₂ tsp	*each* dried thyme and ground coriander	2 mL
1 ¹/₄ cups	olive oil	300 mL

In jar, combine green, black and Niçoise olives. Drain pimientos and cut into circles. Add to jar along with bay leaves, lemon, rosemary, thyme and coriander. Pour in olive oil and cover tightly; shake to combine well.

Refrigerate at least 24 hours or up to 2 weeks before using, shaking occasionally. Bring to room temperature and drain well before serving, reserving oil for salad dressings. Makes 1¹/₂ lb (750 g), about 4 cups (1 L).

WILD MUSHROOM RISOTTO STARTER

On a wonderful trip to the north of Italy with a couple of other food writers, I had the chance to visit the oldest mushroom factory in the world in the mountain village of Borgotaro. The woodsy, orange-brown porcini mushrooms like the ones we saw that day give this simple first course a wonderful flavor, but use other dried wild mushrooms if porcini are unavailable. This very comforting dish is really quite easy.

1 oz	dried porcini mushrooms (or other dried wild mushrooms)	28 g
³/₄ cup	warm water	175 mL
¹/₂ cup	butter	125 mL
1	onion, chopped	1
2 cups	Arborio rice	500 mL
³/₄ cup	dry white wine	175 mL
5 cups	(approx) simmering chicken stock	1.25 L
¹/₂ cup	(approx) freshly grated Parmesan cheese Salt and pepper	125 mL

Soak mushrooms in warm water for at least 20 minutes or until water turns very dark. Strain through coffee filter or paper towel-lined sieve and reserve liquid. Rinse mushrooms in several changes of water until free of soil; chop and set aside.

In heavy-bottomed saucepan, melt three-quarters of the butter over medium heat; cook onion until softened, stirring often. Add rice and stir until well coated, about 3 minutes. Add wine and stir until absorbed.

Add hot stock, ¹/₂ cup (125 mL) at a time, stirring constantly and waiting until stock is absorbed before adding more; cook for 15 to 20 minutes or until rice is al dente (tender but firm) and very moist, adding more stock if necessary and adding mushrooms and reserved mushroom liquid halfway through cooking time.

Remove from heat; stir in remaining butter and cheese. Taste and season with salt if necessary and pepper. Serve immediately in warm shallow soup or pasta bowls. Sprinkle with more cheese. Makes 6 to 8 servings.

CAPONATA CUPS

These little mouthfuls of crisp toast and tangy, soft vegetable mixture will disappear from your appetizer tray in no time. You can even serve the caponata mixture on crackers or in little purchased crisp tart shells.

TOAST CUPS:

8	(approx) thin slices white bread	8
	Olive oil	

CAPONATA:

1 cup	diced peeled eggplant	250 mL
1/2 tsp	salt	2 mL
2 tbsp	(approx) olive oil	25 mL
1	onion, chopped	1
2	cloves garlic, minced	2
1/3 cup	chopped celery	75 mL
1 cup	drained canned tomatoes, chopped	250 mL
1/2 cup	chopped sweet red pepper	125 mL
1 tsp	granulated sugar	5 mL
1/4 tsp	*each* pepper, dried oregano and basil	1 mL
1 tbsp	chopped fresh parsley	15 mL
1/4 cup	chopped pitted black olives	50 mL
2 tbsp	drained capers	25 mL
2 tbsp	red wine vinegar	25 mL

TOAST CUPS: Cut crusts from bread. With rolling pin, roll out bread flat; cut into quarters. Press into greased miniature muffin cups. (Or, roll out enough bread to cut into rounds with cookie cutter to fit muffin or tart cups.) Brush lightly with oil. Bake in 350°F (180°C) oven for 5 to 7 minutes or until crisp and golden. Let cool. (Cups can be stored in airtight tin.)

CAPONATA: In colander, sprinkle eggplant with salt; let drain for 30 minutes. In skillet, heat half of the oil over medium-high heat; sauté onion and garlic for 5 minutes. Add celery and tomatoes; cook for 5 minutes. Remove from heat.

Rinse eggplant and pat dry. In separate skillet, fry eggplant in remaining oil until golden. Remove and drain on paper towel. Add red pepper to skillet; fry until wilted, adding teaspoon (5 mL) more oil if necessary.

Add eggplant, tomato mixture, sugar, pepper, oregano, basil, parsley, olives, capers and vinegar; cook for 15 minutes over low heat, stirring occasionally. (Caponata can be cooled and refrigerated in covered container for up to 3 days. Serve at room temperature.) Spoon into toast cups. Makes about 2 dozen hors d'oeuvres.

CHEVRE AND PESTO PATE

This pretty appetizer combines the piquancy of goat cheese and the distinctive flavor of pesto. To serve, accompany with slices of French bread for everyone to spread. You can use purchased pesto to make the pâté even faster, but be sure to drain off oil that is sometimes found on top of the jar.

¹/₂ lb	cream-style fresh chèvre (goat cheese)	250 g
¹/₄ lb	cream cheese (light if desired)	125 g
	Vegetable oil	
	Pesto (recipe follows)	
	Basil sprigs and walnut halves	

In food processor fitted with steel blade or in bowl with electric mixer, blend chèvre with cream cheese just until smooth but not liquid.

Brush 7- x 4-inch (750 mL) loaf pan or terrine with oil; line with waxed paper. Brush paper lightly with oil.

With rubber spatula, spread thin layer of chèvre mixture right to edges of pan, smoothing surfaces; cover with layer of pesto and smooth surface. Repeat with remaining mixtures, finishing with chèvre mixture. Cover and refrigerate for at least 1 hour or for up to 5 days.

To serve, invert onto serving plate; gently remove waxed paper. Garnish with basil sprigs and walnut halves. Makes 8 servings.

PESTO

1¹/₂ cups	lightly packed fresh basil leaves	375 mL
¹/₃ cup	freshly grated Parmesan cheese	75 mL
2 tbsp	olive oil	25 mL
2 tbsp	finely chopped walnuts	25 mL
2 tbsp	unsalted butter, softened	25 mL
¹/₄ tsp	pepper	1 mL

In food processor or blender, purée basil, Parmesan and oil; transfer to bowl. Stir in walnuts, butter and pepper. Makes about ³/₄ cup (175 mL).

QUICK COGNAC PATE

There are good prepared pâtés readily available these days, but this one is much less expensive, easy to prepare and goes a long way. Pass with French bread or crackers and Pickled Garlic (page 184) or cornichons.

1 lb	chicken livers	500 g
¹/₂ tsp	*each* celery seeds and peppercorns	2 mL
1 tsp	salt	5 mL
1 cup	unsalted butter, cut in bits	250 mL
1 tbsp	dry mustard	15 mL
¹/₄ tsp	*each* nutmeg and cayenne	1 mL
Pinch	cloves	Pinch
2	cloves garlic	2
¹/₄ cup	brandy or cognac	50 mL

In large saucepan of boiling water, simmer livers, celery seeds, peppercorns and half of the salt for 10 minutes or until livers are cooked but still slightly pink inside. Drain in sieve, reserving peppercorns.

In food processor, purée livers, peppercorns, remaining salt, butter, mustard, nutmeg, cayenne and cloves. With motor running, drop in garlic through feed tube. Blend in brandy.

Transfer to 3-cup (750 mL) terrine or other serving dish; cover and refrigerate at least overnight and for up to 3 days. Serve at room temperature. Makes 3 cups (750 mL).

HAM AND CHEESE SQUARES

These savory squares are easy, pretty, delicious to eat and can be made a day ahead. Be sure the ham and cheese slices are very thin and not too salty.

1	pkg (10 oz/284 g) spinach	1
2	eggs	2
1	pkg (411 g) frozen puff pastry, thawed	1
2 tbsp	Dijon mustard	25 mL
1¼ lb	sliced cooked ham	625 g
¾ lb	sliced Swiss cheese	375 g
1 tsp	milk or cream	5 mL

Remove stems from spinach. Wash spinach and shake off excess water. With just the water that clings to leaves, cook spinach until wilted, about 5 minutes. Drain very well and squeeze to remove any moisture. Set aside.

Separate one of the eggs; set yolk aside. Whisk together white with whole egg. Set aside.

Roll half of the pastry into rectangle to fit 17½ × 11½-inch (45 × 29 cm) jelly roll pan. Transfer to pan; spread with mustard.

Leaving 1-inch (2.5 cm) border all around, top with half of the ham, then half the cheese. Top with spinach and drizzle with egg mixture. Layer remaining meat and cheese slices on top. Fold edges of pastry over filling. Beat egg yolk with milk to make glaze; brush some over edges of pastry. Cover remaining glaze and refrigerate.

Roll remaining pastry into same-size rectangle; place on top. With tines of fork, press edges together to seal well. Cover with plastic wrap and chill at least 1 hour or up to 1 day.

About an hour before serving, brush with half the remaining glaze; let stand in refrigerator for about 30 minutes. Brush again with glaze, adding a bit more milk if necessary. With tip of sharp knife, cut shallow pattern in pastry top without going through pastry. Cut 2 or 3 vent holes for steam.

Bake in 425°F (220°C) oven for about 20 minutes or until puffed and golden brown. Let stand for 10 minutes before cutting into 1½ inch (4 cm) squares. Serve warm or at room temperature. Makes about 6 dozen squares.

BAKED HAZELNUT BRIE

Everyone will love this easy-to-make warm appetizer or snack. Provide butter knives so everyone can spread the warm cheese on the toast and apple slices.

¼ cup	olive oil	50 mL
⅓ cup	fresh whole wheat bread crumbs	75 mL
⅓ cup	finely chopped hazelnuts (filberts)	75 mL
1 lb	Brie cheese	500 g
	Watercress or lettuce leaves	
3	red apples (unpeeled), thinly sliced	3
	Fresh lemon juice	
	Hot toast triangles	

Pour oil into small bowl. In another small bowl, combine bread crumbs and hazelnuts. Cut Brie into serving-sized wedges; dip into oil and roll gently in bread crumb mixture. Place in shallow baking dish, leaving at least 1 inch (2.5 cm) between each wedge; drizzle with any remaining oil. Cover and refrigerate for at least 1 hour or overnight.

Uncover and bake cheese in 325°F (160°C) oven for 10 to 15 minutes or until brown on outside and soft and hot inside. (Don't worry if cheese starts to ooze.)

Meanwhile, arrange watercress on individual plates; fan apple slices over top. Sprinkle apple with lemon juice. Make toast triangles and arrange on each plate, leaving just enough room for cheese wedges.

With metal spatula, transfer cheese wedges to plates; serve immediately. Makes 8 servings.

SPICED ALMONDS

I needed to test these toasted nuts for an article I was doing with Elizabeth Baird; so I made them for a birthday party I was giving for my friend Sharon Boyd years ago. She's been making them ever since—and receiving rave reviews from guests.

2 tbsp	unsalted butter	25 mL
1 tbsp	Worcestershire sauce	15 mL
½ tsp	ground cumin	2 mL
Dash	hot pepper sauce	Dash
1½ cups	unblanched almonds	375 mL
1 tbsp	pickling salt	15 mL

In small saucepan, melt butter over low heat. Stir in Worcestershire sauce, cumin and hot pepper sauce; simmer gently for 5 minutes. Stir in almonds to coat well.

Spread nuts on baking sheet; bake in 325°F (160°C) oven, stirring occasionally, for 15 to 20 minutes or until toasted. Sprinkle with salt. Serve warm. (Nuts can be cooled and stored in airtight container for up to 2 weeks. Reheat in 325°F/160°C oven for about 4 minutes or just until warm.) Makes 1½ cups (375 mL).

SMOKED SALMON MOUSSE

This quick-to-make creamy mousse served with melba toast provides a very special first course.

6 oz	smoked salmon	175 g
3 tbsp	fresh lemon juice	50 mL
1/2 tsp	grated lemon rind	2 mL
1/3 cup	butter, melted	75 mL
1/2 cup	sour cream	125 mL
1/4 tsp	pepper	1 mL
	Capers and fresh dill sprigs	

Cut salmon into small pieces. In blender or food processor, combine salmon, lemon juice and rind. With motor running, gradually pour in butter and blend mixture to purée.

Transfer mixture to bowl; fold in sour cream and pepper. Pack into small bowl (or 8 individual ramekins if serving as sit-down starter).

Garnish with capers and dill sprigs. (Mousse can be covered and refrigerated for several hours or overnight.) Makes 8 servings.

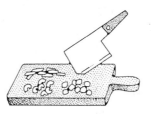

GRILLED PITA PIZZAS

Pita is good simply cut in two and brushed with olive oil before grilling. Or, add the following colorful topping, grill and cut into wedges for a quick, delicious outdoor appetizer.

2	pita breads (6 inch/15 cm)	2
1/4 cup	chopped sun-dried tomatoes (packed in olive oil)	50 mL
1 tbsp	finely chopped fresh oregano (or 1 tsp/5 mL dried)	15 mL
1/2 cup	feta cheese, rinsed and crumbled	125 mL
2 tbsp	coarsely chopped black olives	25 mL
1/2 cup	shredded mozzarella cheese	125 mL

Cut each pita in half to make 2 rounds. Drain tomatoes, reserving 2 tbsp (25 mL) oil; set tomatoes aside. Brush both sides of rounds with some of the oil; lay out on tray, outer sides down.

Sprinkle pitas with oregano; scatter with feta cheese. Scatter tomatoes, then olives, then mozzarella cheese over top. Drizzle with any remaining oil.

Place pitas on greased grill 4 inches (10 cm) from medium-hot coals or on medium-high setting; grill for 1 to 2 minutes or until undersides are golden brown and mozzarella is melted. Cut each circle into 4 wedges and serve hot. Makes 16 hors d'oeuvres.

QUICK POTATO SKIN SNACKS

When you're making mashed potatoes, prepare these nutritious snacks at the same time. Serve alone, with your favorite dip or as a garnish for Herbed Potato Soup (see page 26).

2 lb	baking potatoes (about 5)	1 kg
2 tsp	vegetable oil	10 mL
1	clove garlic, crushed	1
	Coarse salt	

Scrub potatoes well and dry. With small sharp knife, peel off skin lengthwise in ¾-inch (2 cm) wide strips, removing thin layer of flesh with each strip. Reserve potatoes in bowl of cold water for another use.

Place skins in small bowl. Combine oil and garlic; pour over skins and toss to coat.

Arrange strips, skin-side up, in single layer on baking sheet. Bake in 450°F (230°C) oven for 12 to 15 minutes or until crisp and golden. Toss with salt to taste.

Serve immediately or transfer to rack to let cool and store in airtight container. Serve at room temperature or reheat in 450°F (230°C) oven for 5 minutes. Makes 2 cups (500 mL).

GRILLED SHRIMP WITH CAPELLINI AND PESTO

For this elegant but easy starter or light lunch dish, use homemade (see page 16) or bottled pesto sauce. Sprinkle some lemon rind on the coals or lava rocks for even more flavor when you grill the shrimp. Be sure to soak the wooden skewers in water for 30 minutes beforehand to avoid charring. If you have one, use the side element of your barbecue for the pasta.

30	medium shrimp (1½ lb/750 g)	30
¼ cup	fresh lemon juice	50 mL
2 tsp	dry mustard	10 mL
2 tsp	grated lemon rind	10 mL
¼ tsp	*each* pepper, hot pepper flakes and dried oregano	1 mL
2	cloves garlic, minced	2
1	small anchovy, minced (or ½ tsp/2 mL anchovy paste)	1
⅓ cup	olive oil	75 mL
½ cup	pesto sauce	125 mL
½ lb	capellini, spaghettini or linguine	250 g
	Lemon slices and basil leaves	

Peel shrimp, leaving tails on; devein. Place in sturdy plastic bag set in bowl.

In measuring cup, whisk together 2 tbsp (25 mL) of the lemon juice, mustard, lemon rind, pepper, hot pepper flakes, oregano, garlic and anchovy; gradually whisk in oil. Pour over shrimp and close bag;

squeeze gently to coat shrimp well. Refrigerate for 30 minutes. (Do not marinate longer or shrimp will become mushy.)

Reserving marinade, thread shrimp onto soaked wooden skewers, pushing skewer through each end of shrimp but leaving centre free. (Recipe can be prepared to this point, covered and refrigerated for up to 4 hours. Cover and refrigerate marinade separately.)

Place shrimp on greased grill about 3 inches (8 cm) from medium-hot coals or on medium-high setting; grill, brushing often with marinade, for 2 to 3 minutes per side or until pink and firm to the touch. Do not overcook.

Meanwhile, stir together pesto sauce and remaining lemon juice; set aside. In large pot of boiling salted water, cook capellini until al dente (tender but still firm). Drain well and return to pot; toss with three-quarters of the pesto mixture.

Arrange pasta on 6 heated plates; place shrimp skewers on top. Drizzle remaining pesto on shrimp. Garnish plates with lemon slices and basil leaves. Makes 6 first-course servings.

EASY PORK PATE

This simple version of a coarse, delicious pâté is made with chunks of lean pork cooked for hours until it falls apart and combined with just enough fat to make it nicely spreadable. Accompany with cornichons, Pickled Garlic (page 184) and slices of my easy No-Knead French Bread (page 38).

1	small onion, halved	1
2	whole cloves	2
12	sprigs fresh parsley	12
1	bay leaf	1
1 tsp	dried thyme	5 mL
1½ lb	pork shoulder, cut into 1-inch (2.5 cm) cubes	750 g
½ lb	pork back fat, cut into 1-inch (2.5 cm) cubes	250 g
2	cloves garlic, halved	2
½ tsp	salt	2 mL
¼ tsp	pepper	1 mL
Pinch	*each* cinnamon and allspice	Pinch

Stick onion halves with a clove each. Tie parsley, bay leaf and thyme in square of rinsed cheesecloth to make bouquet garni.

In large heavy saucepan, combine pork, pork fat, onion halves, bouquet garni, garlic, salt, pepper, cinnamon and allspice. Pour in 4 cups (1 L) cold water; bring to boil. Reduce heat, cover and simmer for 2½ to 3 hours or until meat is falling apart.

Remove and discard onion and bouquet garni. With slotted spoon, remove meat to food processor, reserving liquid and fat. Shred meat but don't purée. Reduce liquid by cooking, uncovered, over medium heat for 20 to 30 minutes or until fat is slightly transparent. Let fat cool a little, then mix in shredded meat well. Taste and adjust seasoning.

Pack into 3-cup (750 mL) terrine or other suitable dish. Cover and refrigerate at least overnight or for up to 3 days. Bring to room temperature to serve. Makes 3 cups (750 mL).

SATISFYING SCOTCH EGGS

This is one of my favorite picnic foods, especially if I'm packing just finger food. They're also great for brown baggers, but be sure that wherever you carry them, you do so in an insulated bag with a small freezer pack or frozen box of juice.

1/2 lb	pork sausage meat	250 g
1/4 tsp	dried thyme	1 mL
Pinch	dried sage	Pinch
4	hard-cooked eggs, peeled	4
1	egg, beaten	1
1/2 cup	dry bread crumbs	125 mL
2 tbsp	(approx) vegetable oil or butter	25 mL

In bowl, mash sausage meat with thyme and sage; divide into 4 portions.

Wrap each portion of meat mixture evenly around egg, sealing well. (Moist hands will make this easier.) Dip into beaten egg; roll in bread crumbs.

In medium skillet, heat oil over medium-low heat; fry coated eggs, turning frequently and adding more oil if necessary, until sausage meat is cooked and browned on all sides, about 10 minutes. Makes 4 servings.

CHEESE PITA TOASTS

These quick and easy toasts are great with a dip or as an accompaniment to soup.

1/2 cup	olive oil	125 mL
2 tbsp	chopped fresh parsley	25 mL
2	large cloves garlic, crushed	2
6	large pita breads	6
3/4 cup	freshly grated Parmesan cheese	175 mL

In small bowl, stir together oil, parsley and garlic. Let stand for a few minutes for flavors to develop.

Cut each pita bread in half to make 2 rounds. Brush interior sides with oil mixture; sprinkle with cheese. Cut each round into 8 wedges; place on baking sheets. (Bread can be prepared to this point, covered and left at room temperature for 2 hours.)

Toast, uncovered, in 350°F (180°C) oven for 7 to 9 minutes or until lightly browned and crisp. Serve hot or at room temperature. Makes 8 dozen.

FOOD PROCESSOR GOUGERE RING

One of the most delightful French picnics I've had was in Burgundy, France, on a sunny Sunday in May with a couple of friends. We stopped at a tiny village to buy delicious ham, fruit and vegetables from the farmers' market and small shops. But it was the gougère, a rough cheese bread that we bought at the local boulangerie that I remember most.

Gougère has become one of my favorite company appetizers to serve along with cucumber pickles or Pickled Cherries (page 184). This easy recipe I developed for a series of classes I was doing in Toronto for Canadian writer, Helen Gougeon.

6 or 7	eggs	6 or 7
³/₄ tsp	salt	4 mL
5 oz	Gruyère cheese	150 g
4¹/₂ tbsp	unsalted butter	100 mL
1¹/₄ cups	water	300 mL
1 tsp	*each* Dijon mustard and granulated sugar	5 mL
¹/₂ tsp	dry mustard	2 mL
¹/₄ tsp	pepper	1 mL
Dash	hot pepper sauce	Dash
1¹/₄ cups	all-purpose flour	300 mL

With fork, beat together one of the eggs and pinch of the salt; set aside.

Using shredding disc in processor or by hand, grate cheese; set aside.

In medium saucepan, bring butter, water, Dijon mustard, sugar, remaining salt, dry mustard, pepper and hot pepper sauce to boil, stirring to melt butter. Remove from heat and immediately add flour all at once; beat with wooden spoon for 1 minute or until mixture is well combined and leaves side of pan. Cook over medium heat for 2 minutes, stirring constantly.

Transfer mixture to processor fitted with metal blade. Cool for 1 or 2 minutes. Add 5 remaining eggs and process, stopping once to scrape down side of bowl, until eggs are completely incorporated and mixture is very thick, smooth and shiny, about 30 seconds. If not shiny, process in another egg for 10 seconds. Add three-quarters of the reserved cheese and process for 5 seconds.

Grease baking sheet and sprinkle with water, shaking off excess. Using your finger, draw 9-inch (23 cm) circle for guide when forming ring.

Using 2 large spoons, drop dough by spoonfuls onto circle so that rounds touch to form ring. With any remaining dough, form another ring of smaller rounds on top. Brush with egg glaze. Sprinkle with remaining cheese. (This can be done up to 30 minutes ahead and covered with inverted bowl.)

Place in 425°F (220°C) oven and immediately reduce temperature to 400°F (200°C); bake for 25 minutes. Reduce temperature to 375°F (190°C) and bake for another 20 minutes or until golden brown. Carefully remove ring to rack and cool for 5 minutes before placing on large plate to cut into wedges and serve warm. Makes 6 servings.

CAVIAR MUSHROOMS AND TOMATOES

A little caviar provides a special start to a dinner or sparkle to a tray of finger cocktail food. Use whichever kind of caviar that suits your taste and budget.

16	large mushrooms	16
	Fresh lime juice	
20	cherry tomatoes	20

FILLING:

¼ lb	light cream cheese	125 g
2 tbsp	plain yogurt or light sour cream	25 mL
1 tsp	grated shallots or onion	5 mL
1 tsp	fresh lime juice	5 mL
¼ tsp	pepper	1 mL
2 oz	caviar	50 g
	Watercress or parsley sprigs	
	Additional caviar for garnish (optional)	

Clean mushrooms and remove stems, reserving for another use. Sprinkle caps with lime juice; set on plate lined with paper towels. Cover tightly with plastic wrap and refrigerate.

Using small sharp knife, cut stem end from tomatoes; hollow out by removing seeds. Drain upside down on plate lined with paper towels. Refrigerate.

FILLING: In small bowl, beat cream cheese; blend in yogurt, shallots, lime juice and pepper. Cover and refrigerate if making ahead.

Shortly before serving, gently stir caviar into cheese mixture; spoon into mushroom caps and tomatoes. Arrange on thick bed of watercress on serving plate. Garnish each appetizer with additional caviar (if using). Makes about 36 appetizers.

FIERY TEX-MEX POPCORN

Popcorn is enjoying a definite revival with more people staying at home to watch videos and everyone knowing that it's a good healthy snack. New hot-air poppers produce lovely light kernels without the aid of any oil. Here, I've added just a bit of melted butter along with some interesting and fun seasoning. Great with beer!

½ cup	popcorn kernels	125 mL
2 tbsp	butter, melted	25 mL
1 tsp	chili powder	5 mL
½ tsp	ground cumin	2 mL
¼ tsp	hot pepper flakes	1 mL
⅓ cup	freshly grated Parmesan cheese	75 mL

Pop popcorn. Stir together butter, chili powder, cumin and hot pepper flakes; drizzle over hot popcorn and toss to coat well.

Sprinkle with cheese; toss to coat and serve immediately. Makes about 8 cups (2 L).

Soothing Soups

When I was a child, I studied music with a blind pianist who lived in a huge house in Collingwood, Ontario. Except for the light by the piano, the interior of that house was dark and gloomy indeed. I can still remember with great vividness that the only comforting thing about it was the pervading aroma of homemade vegetable soup the housekeeper would make every Saturday morning.

I never saw the housekeeper nor had any of her soup, but I always thought of it when my mother filled one of her big kettles with delicious, steaming vegetables and broth that she would always make from scratch.

There is something wonderfully soothing about soup—whether it's hot or cold. In this chapter, you'll find hearty main course soups to warm family and friends on the coldest winter's day, as well as a couple of quick and refreshing combinations to comfort a heated brow.

If you don't have homemade broth like my mother used to have, use bought canned beef or chicken broth...not the powdered kind which could render a soup very salty. A bit of powdered stock is all right for sauces when you need just a little, however.

Stock and broth are basically made the same way, but broth is the term usually used to apply to the liquid used in soups, and stock refers more to the base of sauces.

HEARTY BEEF VEGETABLE SOUP

Quick chowders and soups are great, but sometimes it's very satisfying to throw chopped vegetables and beef together in a big pot and forget about them while they simmer for hours into an old-fashioned stick-to-your-ribs soup. The preparation time is next to nothing, but the enjoyment is great while the aroma pervades not only your kitchen but also the whole house. This thick soup reheats and freezes well, too.

2 lb	beef shank	1 kg
12 cups	water	3 L
1	can (19 oz/540 mL) tomatoes (undrained), chopped	1
4	carrots, coarsely chopped	4
2	leeks, sliced	2
2	*each* parsnips and stalks celery with leaves, coarsely chopped	2
2	cloves garlic, chopped	2
½ cup	pot barley	125 mL
2 tsp	salt	10 mL
1 tsp	*each* granulated sugar, dried savory, marjoram and thyme	5 mL
½ tsp	pepper	2 mL

In large kettle, combine beef shank, water, tomatoes, carrots, leeks, parsnips, celery, garlic, barley and salt. Bring to boil, skimming off any froth.

Stir in sugar, savory, marjoram, thyme and pepper; reduce heat and simmer, partially covered, for 4 hours. Skim fat from surface. Remove beef shank. Dice meat and return to pot, discard bone. Serve in heated bowls. Makes 8 servings.

HERBED POTATO SOUP

Potato soup was so popular with early Canadian settlers that it was eaten even for breakfast. This hearty soup made from ingredients you have on hand will dispel winter chills at any time of the day.

6	potatoes, peeled and diced	6
2 cups	chicken broth	500 mL
1 tsp	dried marjoram	5 mL
5	slices smoked side bacon, diced	5
1	onion, coarsely chopped	1
2	cloves garlic, minced	2
2 tbsp	all-purpose flour	25 mL
4 cups	hot milk	1 L
½ cup	whipping cream	125 mL
	Salt and pepper	
½ cup	chopped fresh parsley	125 mL

In large saucepan over medium heat, cook potatoes, broth and marjoram for 10 to 15 minutes or until potatoes are tender. Without draining, coarsely mash in pan. Set aside.

Meanwhile, in medium skillet, fry bacon over medium heat until crisp. Remove with slotted spoon and let drain on paper towel.

Pour off all but 2 tbsp (25 mL) drippings in skillet. Add onion and garlic; cover and cook over low heat until softened but not browned, about 5 minutes. Stir in flour and cook; stirring, for 2 minutes. Add to potatoes and stir well to combine.

Gradually add hot milk to potato mixture; bring to boil, stirring constantly. Boil gently for 1 minute.

Reduce heat to low and stir in cream. Season with salt and pepper to taste. Stir in parsley. Ladle into heated bowls. Garnish with reserved cooked bacon. Makes 6 to 8 servings.

QUICK CHUNKY MINESTRONE

For an interesting touch, omit the Parmesan cheese and top each serving with a big dollop of pesto (see page 16). Serve with garlic toast: rub thick slices of Italian bread with cut side of garlic and toast under broiler or in toaster oven. If you don't have fresh green beans on hand, use 1 cup (250 mL) frozen.

4	slices side bacon, diced	4
2	stalks celery, sliced	2
1	onion, chopped	1
1	carrot, thinly sliced	1
1	clove garlic, minced	1
5 cups	chicken broth	1.25 L
1	can (19 oz/540 mL) tomatoes (undrained)	1
1/4 tsp	*each* crumbled dried sage and thyme	1 mL
1	can (19 oz/540 mL) chick-peas, drained and rinsed	1
1/4 lb	green beans, sliced	125 g
1/3 cup	macaroni	75 mL
	Salt and pepper	
	Freshly grated Parmesan cheese	

In large saucepan, cook bacon over medium heat, stirring often, until crisp. Remove with slotted spoon and set aside; pour off all but 1 tbsp (15 mL) drippings.

In same pan, cook celery, onion, carrot and garlic for 5 minutes. Stir in broth, tomatoes, sage and thyme, breaking up tomatoes with back of spoon. Bring to boil; reduce heat, cover and simmer for 5 minutes.

Add chick-peas, green beans and macaroni; cook, uncovered, for about 10 minutes or until beans are tender and macaroni is tender but firm. Return bacon to pot. Season with salt and pepper to taste. (Soup can be cooled, covered and refrigerated for up to 2 days or frozen for up to 3 months.)

Ladle into heated bowls with lots of cheese. Makes 4 to 6 servings.

ROBUST ITALIAN VEGETABLE SOUP
WITH FRESH SPINACH

Instead of cooking the spinach for the last few minutes with the soup, an interesting way to serve it is as a garnish. Using only part of a bag, chop the spinach finely and sprinkle some over top of each serving.

2 cups	Northern or white navy (pea) beans	500 mL
1	pork hock or meaty ham bone	1
2	bay leaves	2
2 tbsp	olive oil	25 mL
1	*each* sweet yellow and red pepper, finely diced	1
2	*each* stalks celery and carrots, chopped	2
1	onion, chopped	1
4	cloves garlic, minced	4
1	can (28 oz/796 mL) Italian tomatoes, (undrained), chopped	1
8	fresh sage leaves (or 1 tsp/5 mL crumbled dried)	8
1/2 tsp	*each* salt and granulated sugar	2 mL
1 tsp	balsamic or red wine vinegar	5 mL
1/4 tsp	pepper	1 mL
1	pkg (10 oz/284 g) spinach, chopped	1
1/2 cup	freshly grated Parmesan cheese	125 mL

Sort and rinse beans. In large saucepan, cover beans with 6 cups (1.5 L) water and let soak overnight in refrigerator. (Or, cover with water and bring to boil; boil for 2 minutes. Remove from heat; cover and let stand for 1 hour.)

Drain beans and return to saucepan. Add pork hock, bay leaves and 16 cups (4 L) cold water; bring to boil. Reduce heat to low; cover and simmer for 1 hour.

Meanwhile, in large skillet, heat oil over low heat; cook yellow and red peppers, celery, carrots, onion and garlic, covered, for 15 minutes, stirring occasionally. Add to soup along with tomatoes, sage, salt and sugar; simmer for 30 minutes. Stir in vinegar and pepper. Remove bay leaves.

Add spinach to soup; cook for 5 minutes. Taste and adjust seasoning. Serve immediately in heated bowls with sprinkling of Parmesan. Pass remaining cheese separately. Makes about 10 servings.

ELEGANT LEEK AND POTATO SOUP
WITH CREME FRAICHE AND CAVIAR

Without the caviar, this is a lovely quick-and-easy soup to enjoy as an easy family supper with warm crusty bread, cheese and cold cuts. The same soup can be an exciting first course for a dinner party with the addition of a small amount of caviar. You don't have to use expensive imported Iranian or Russian. A dab of rinsed lumpfish, Spanish mullet or a bit of Canadian golden whitefish is quite acceptable.

¹⁄₄ cup	butter	50 mL
4	leeks, thinly sliced	4
5 cups	chicken broth	1.25 L
4	potatoes, peeled and sliced	4
	Salt	
2 cups	coarsely chopped trimmed watercress	500 mL
	Black pepper	
¹⁄₄ cup	crème fraîche (see recipe on this page) or sour cream	50 mL
4 tsp	caviar (optional)	20 mL

In large heavy saucepan, melt butter over low heat; cook leeks, stirring occasionally, for about 8 minutes or until softened but not browned.

Stir in chicken broth, potatoes, and salt to taste; bring to boil. Reduce heat and simmer partially covered, for about 10 minutes or until potatoes are tender.

Using fork, mash most of the potato slices against side of pan. Stir in watercress and simmer, uncovered, for 1 minute longer. Season with lots of pepper.

Ladle into heated bowls. Garnish each serving with dollop of crème fraîche. Place mound of caviar (if using) on top of cream. Makes 4 to 6 servings.

CREME FRAICHE

A cultured heavy cream that is sometimes available for sale in plastic tubs in the dairy counter, crème fraîche adds a tart and delicious accent to fruit or savory dishes.

If you cannot find it for sale, whisk together equal quantities of whipping cream and sour cream, cover and let sit in the refrigerator for a day or two or until thickened. Crème fraîche will keep in the refrigerator for 2 weeks.

RAINBOW SALMON CHOWDER

On a gray, misty day, a version of this quick and colorful soup dispelled any chills from the whale-watching boat I boarded with members of the British Columbia Fisheries Council.

2 tbsp	butter	25 mL
1/2 cup	chopped red or yellow onion	125 mL
1/2 cup	diced celery	125 mL
1	clove garlic, minced	1
3	potatoes, peeled and diced	3
2	carrots, diced	2
2 1/2 cups	chicken broth	625 mL
	Salt and pepper	
1	can (7 1/2 oz/213 g) salmon	1
1	can (14 oz/398 mL) cream-style corn	1
1 cup	milk	250 mL
1 tsp	lemon juice	5 mL
1/2 tsp	Worcestershire sauce	2 mL
1/4 cup	chopped fresh parsley	50 mL

In large saucepan, melt butter over medium heat; cook onion, celery and garlic for 5 minutes, stirring often.

Add potatoes, carrots, broth, and salt and pepper to taste; bring to boil. Cover and reduce heat; simmer for 15 to 20 minutes or until vegetables are tender.

Drain salmon and flake, mashing bones and reserving liquid; add to chowder along with liquid. Stir in corn, milk, lemon juice and Worcestershire sauce; heat through. Stir in parsley. Serve in heated bowls. Makes 4 to 6 servings.

SIMPLY SUPERB OYSTER STEW

This thin stew (actually a soup) has been one of the most popular ways of enjoying oysters since the 19th century. Thick chowders laden with vegetables and pork are appropriate for more strongly flavored shellfish, such as clams, while oysters taste best in this simple preparation.

1/4 cup	butter	50 mL
2 cups	oysters in their liquor	500 mL
3 cups	milk, scalded	750 mL
1/2 cup	whipping cream	125 mL
1/4 tsp	white pepper	1 mL
Pinch	nutmeg	Pinch
	Salt	
	Paprika	

In large heavy saucepan, melt butter over low heat; simmer oysters with their liquor until edges begin to curl, about 3 minutes.

Stir in scalded milk, cream, pepper, nutmeg, and salt to taste. Heat through but do not boil.

Ladle into heated bowls. Sprinkle with paprika. Serve immediately. Makes 4 servings.

SPLIT PEA AND LENTIL SOUP
WITH SPICED YOGURT GARNISH

Instead of the usual ham, beef short ribs lend an extra heartiness to this nourishing soup that's almost like a stew. Warming and comforting, it's perfect to come home to on a cold winter's night. Although great as is, a little garnish of golden spiced yogurt turns it into a terrific casual party fare.

2 lb	beef short ribs	1 kg
3 tbsp	olive oil	50 mL
1 tbsp	butter	15 mL
2	parsnips, diced	2
1	*each* celery stalk, onion and carrot, diced	1
1	can (19 oz/540 mL) tomatoes (undrained)	1
1 cup	green lentils, rinsed	250 mL
1 cup	split peas, rinsed	250 mL
8 cups	beef broth	2 L
½ tsp	ground cumin	2 mL
Pinch	*each* dried oregano and thyme	Pinch
	Salt and pepper	
	Spiced Yogurt (recipe follows)	

In shallow roasting pan, drizzle short ribs with 1 tbsp (15 mL) of the oil. Roast in 450°F (230°C) oven for about 20 minutes or until browned all over, turning occasionally.

Meanwhile, in large pot, heat remaining oil and butter over medium-high heat; sauté parsnips, celery, onion and carrot until golden brown. Add tomatoes, breaking up with back of spoon; reduce heat to low and simmer, uncovered, for 20 minutes. Stir in lentils and peas.

Drain ribs well and add to pot along with broth, cumin, oregano, thyme, and salt and pepper to taste. Bring to boil; reduce heat and simmer, covered, for about 1½ hours or until lentils, split peas and ribs are tender. Taste and adjust seasoning.

Remove ribs and cut off meat in small cubes; return meat to soup. Serve in heated bowls; garnish with dollop of Spiced Yogurt. Makes about 8 servings.

SPICED YOGURT

½ cup	plain yogurt	125 mL
½ tsp	*each* paprika and ground cumin	2 mL
¼ tsp	turmeric	1 mL
Pinch	cayenne	Pinch

In small bowl, whisk together yogurt, paprika, cumin, turmeric and cayenne. Cover and refrigerate for up to 3 days. Makes ½ cup (125 mL).

ITALIAN COUNTRY PASTA AND BEAN SOUP
(PASTA E FAGIOLI)

There are many versions of this healthy and hearty Italian soup, which is a staple of Tuscany. I've used Romano beans, but white or pink and white cranberry beans are also good. If using dried beans, use 6 cups (1.5 L) of their cooking liquid instead of chicken broth and purée half the beans with ¼ cup (50 mL) of cooking liquid.

1	can (19 oz/540 mL) romano beans, drained and rinsed	1
6 cups	chicken broth	1.5 L
2 tbsp	olive oil	25 mL
1	*each* onion, stalk celery and carrot, chopped	1
2	cloves garlic, minced	2
Pinch	hot pepper flakes	Pinch
1 cup	chopped drained canned plum tomatoes	250 mL
½ tsp	(approx) salt	2 mL
¾ cup	short tubular macaroni (tubetti or ditali)	175 mL
	Chopped fresh parsley	
	Freshly grated Parmesan cheese	

Purée half the beans with ¼ cup (50 mL) of the broth; set aside.

In large saucepan, heat oil over medium-low heat; cook onion, celery, carrot, garlic and hot pepper flakes for 10 minutes or until softened, stirring often. Add tomatoes and salt; cook for 10 minutes.

Add puréed and whole beans; cook for 3 minutes. Stir in remaining stock and bring to boil; add macaroni and cook until tender but still firm, 10 to 15 minutes. Taste and add more salt if necessary. Serve immediately in heated bowls. Sprinkle with parsley and lots of cheese. Makes 4 to 6 servings.

HUNGARIAN GOULASH SOUP

Long simmering with interesting spices and herbs gives this hearty soup lots of flavor that is improved even more if the soup is made one day and reheated another. This is one of our family's all-time favorites.

2 tbsp	lard, shortening or vegetable oil	25 mL
1½ lb	cubed (¾-inch/2 cm) lean beef	750 g
2	onions, sliced	2
½ lb	mushrooms, sliced	250 g
2 tbsp	caraway seeds, crushed*	25 mL
1 tbsp	sweet paprika	15 mL
½ tsp	(approx) salt	2 mL
1	can (19 oz/540 mL) tomatoes (undrained), chopped	1
1¼ tsp	dried basil	6 mL
2	sweet green peppers, diced	2

¹/₄ cup	water	50 mL
4	potatoes, peeled and diced	4
7 cups	beef broth	1.75 L
1¹/₄ tsp	dried marjoram	6 mL
³/₄ tsp	pepper	4 mL
¹/₄ lb	egg noodles	125 g

In large heavy-bottomed kettle, melt lard over medium-high heat; cook meat until browned all over. Add onions and mushrooms; cook until onions are softened.

Remove from heat; stir in caraway seeds, paprika and salt. Return to low heat; cover and cook for 20 minutes, stirring occasionally.

Stir in tomatoes, basil, green peppers and water; bring to boil. Reduce heat, cover and simmer for about 1 hour or until meat is almost tender, adding a little water if necessary to prevent sticking.

Add potatoes and broth; bring to boil. Reduce heat, cover and cook until potatoes and meat are tender, about 30 minutes. Taste and add more salt if necessary. Stir in marjoram and pepper; cook for 2 minutes. (Recipe can be prepared to this point, cooled, covered and refrigerated. Reheat slowly, stirring often.)

Stir in noodles; cook for about 7 minutes or until tender but firm. Ladle into heated bowls. Makes 8 generous servings.
*Crush caraway seeds with a mortar and pestle or place in sturdy plastic bag and roll firmly with rolling pin.

FAMILY-STYLE TURKEY CORN SOUP

For this quick and easy soup, use leftover turkey and stock from a big weekend dinner or substitute cooked chicken and chicken broth. Either corn kernels cut from cooked ears or frozen corn kernels may be used.

5 cups	turkey stock	1.25 L
3	stalks celery with leaves, chopped	3
2	*each* onions and carrots, chopped	2
¹/₂ tsp	dried marjoram	2 mL
	Salt and pepper	
1 cup	diced cooked turkey	250 mL
1 cup	cooked corn kernels	250 mL
¹/₄ cup	chopped fresh parsley	50 mL
6 oz	mozzarella cheese	175 g

In large saucepan, bring stock to boil. Add celery, onions, carrots, marjoram, and salt and pepper to taste; return to boil. Reduce heat, cover and simmer for 10 minutes or until vegetables are tender.

In batches, purée in food processor or blender; holding down lid or feed tube. Return to saucepan. Stir in turkey, corn and parsley. (Soup can be prepared to this point, covered and refrigerated.) Simmer until heated through.

Meanwhile, finely dice or crumble cheese; place in heated bowls and pour hot soup on top. Makes about 6 servings.

CHILLED RED PEPPER AND MUSHROOM BISQUE

Your guests may not guess what's in this flavorful soup, but they'll certainly find it appealing. It's perfect as a starter at a dinner party on a warm fall evening.

¹/₄ cup	butter	50 mL
4	medium sweet red peppers, chopped	4
1 lb	mushrooms, finely chopped	500 g
1	onion, chopped	1
2	cloves garlic, minced	2
3 cups	chicken broth (homemade or canned)	750 mL
2 tsp	paprika	10 mL
1 tsp	granulated sugar	5 mL
2 tbsp	fresh lemon juice	25 mL
¹/₄ tsp	cayenne	1 mL
	Salt and pepper	
	Mushroom or lemon slices	

In large saucepan, melt butter over medium-low heat; cook red peppers, mushrooms, onion and garlic, stirring often, for 10 minutes or until softened.

Stir in broth, paprika and sugar; bring to boil. Reduce heat and simmer, uncovered, for 20 minutes.

Purée in batches in blender, holding down lid; strain through sieve into large bowl. Or pass through food mill into bowl. (A blender makes smoother soup.) Stir in lemon juice, cayenne, and salt and pepper to taste. Chill, covered, at least 4 hours or overnight.

Taste and adjust seasoning. Serve in chilled bowls; garnish with mushroom or lemon slice. Makes 4 to 6 servings.

QUICK GAZPACHO

This quick refreshing soup, using some of fall's bounty, is great to carry to the office in a thermos with melba toast, cheese and fruit packed alongside. To share or have extra on hand in the refrigerator, double the recipe.

Quarter	cucumber, peeled and seeded	Quarter
Quarter	*each* small onion and sweet green pepper	Quarter
Half	small clove garlic	Half
²/₃ cup	cocktail vegetable juice (V-8)	150 mL
2 tsp	white wine vinegar	10 mL
1 ¹/₂ tsp	olive oil	7 mL
Dash	hot pepper sauce	Dash
	Salt and pepper	

In food processor or blender, process cucumber, onion, green pepper and garlic until chunky.

Blend in juice, vinegar, oil, hot pepper sauce, and salt and pepper to taste. Serve immediately or refrigerate until chilled. Makes 1 serving.

Breads, Muffins & Breakfast Stuff

When the only bread I could buy was the sponge-like cellophane-wrapped supermarket kind, I made all the bread for our family. I would find great satisfaction in kneading the soft dough and letting it rise like magic into a yeasty mountain. Then, as it baked, the aroma alone would be worth the few minutes spent preparing the bread.

Now, with such a vast choice of good bread around, I can buy soft crusty loaves of Portuguese or Italian white or corn bread, and a whole variety of multi-grain loaves without travelling far in even the small city where we live.

It's such an easy matter to round out a menu of homey stew with a purchased loaf of good bread that I have included only one of these yeast breads here—No-Knead French Bread (Page 38) because you can produce an extremely good loaf with only five minutes work.

I still find such tremendous enjoyment in making pizzas and focaccia and smelling their wonderful homey fragrance as they bake, that I could not resist including a few recipes for these.

The remainder of the chapter is made up of soda bread, quick breads or biscuits that would make happy companions to my vast array of soups and stews, or breakfast treats that are always a most welcome way to greet houseguests on weekend mornings.

PUFFED PANCAKE WITH FRESH PEARS AND CARDAMOM

Serve this unique pancake with tiny pork sausages for a satisfying but easy family breakfast.

1/4 cup	unsalted butter	50 mL
2	pears, peeled, cored and thinly sliced	2
2/3 cup	granulated sugar	150 mL
1/2 cup	*each* all-purpose flour and milk	125 mL
2	eggs	2
1/2 tsp	*each* vanilla and cardamom	2 mL
1/4 tsp	salt	1 mL
	Maple syrup or Remarkable Low-Fat Cream (see page 185), optional	

In heavy ovenproof 8-inch (20 cm) skillet, melt butter over medium heat; cook pears, stirring often, for about 5 minutes or just until softened.

Meanwhile, in large bowl, combine 1/2 cup (125 mL) of the sugar, all of the flour, milk, eggs, vanilla, 1/4 tsp (1 mL) of the cardamom and salt; whisk just until blended. Mix together remaining sugar and cardamom; set aside.

Pour batter over pears in skillet; bake in 425°F (220°C) oven for about 15 minutes or until batter sets.

Remove skillet and reduce temperature to 350°F (180°C). Run thin spatula around edge of skillet; invert pancake onto large plate and slide back into skillet.

Sprinkle with reserved sugar mixture; bake for 10 to 15 minutes longer or until puffy and golden brown and tester inserted in centre comes out clean. Cut into wedges to serve. Pass syrup if using. Makes 4 servings.

FIESTA CORNBREAD

This spicy cornbread is very moist but still light in texture.

1 1/4 cups	cornmeal	300 mL
3/4 cup	all-purpose flour	175 mL
1/2 tsp	*each* salt and baking soda	2 mL
1 cup	shredded old Cheddar cheese	250 mL
3	eggs, beaten	3
1	can (10 oz/284 mL) cream-style corn	1
3/4 cup	buttermilk	175 mL
1/3 cup	vegetable oil	75 mL
2 tbsp	chopped pickled jalapeño pepper	25 mL

In large bowl, stir together cornmeal, flour, salt and baking soda. Stir in cheese.

In medium bowl, stir together eggs, corn, buttermilk, oil and pepper. Add to dry mixture and stir only enough to combine.

Pour into greased 8-inch (2 L) square cake pan; bake in 400°F (200°C) oven for about 35 minutes or until golden and cake tester inserted in middle comes out clean. Makes 8 generous servings.

MIKE'S MOM'S IRISH SODA BREAD

For years, I had such fond memories of the thick, buttered slices of warm soda bread I had every morning on a visit to Ireland, that I spent much time trying to reproduce that bread. I came to the conclusion that the flour was different here and left it for a time. Just recently, armed with an authentic recipe from an Owen Sound friend's Irish mother-in-law, I made this version for a St. Patrick's Day party and it was a hit. It goes really well with soup or stew.

2 cups	whole wheat flour	500 mL
3/4 cup	all-purpose flour	175 mL
1/3 cup	granulated sugar	75 mL
1/4 cup	rolled oats	50 mL
1 1/2 tsp	baking soda	7 mL
1 tsp	baking powder	5 mL
3/4 tsp	salt	4 mL
1 1/4 cups	(approx) buttermilk	300 mL

In large bowl, stir together whole wheat and all-purpose flours, sugar, rolled oats, baking soda, baking powder and salt. Stir in buttermilk to make soft dough. Form into ball.

On greased baking sheet, flatten dough with floured hands to circle about 2 inches (5 cm) high; cut cross 3/4 inch (2 cm) deep in centre. Place in 475°F (240°C) oven; immediately reduce heat to 350°F (180°C) and bake for 45 minutes. Wrap in damp clean tea towel and let cool on rack for at least 5 hours to allow to set. Makes 1 loaf.

FRESH MINT QUICK BREAD

Nothing could be more refreshing than tiny slices of this pretty bread spread with Lemon-Apricot Butter (see page 178) and served with tea. Easy to make, the loaves can be refrigerated for one week or frozen for three months.

1/2 cup	butter, softened	125 mL
2	eggs	2
2 1/4 cups	all-purpose flour	550 mL
2 tbsp	granulated sugar	25 mL
1 tbsp	baking powder	15 mL
1 tsp	ginger	5 mL
1/2 tsp	salt	2 mL
1/2 cup	fresh mint leaves	125 mL
3/4 cup	milk	175 mL

In large bowl, beat butter and eggs together well.

Sift or stir together flour, sugar, baking powder, ginger and salt. Chop mint and stir into flour mixture. Add to butter mixture alternately with milk.

Spoon into four greased 4 1/2- × 2 1/2-inch (250 mL) loaf pans. Bake in 350°F (180°C) oven for 30 minutes or until cake tester inserted in middle comes out clean. Makes 4 loaves (about 16 slices each).

BANANA BREAD WITH TOASTED COCONUT

I purposely let bananas get overripe just for an excuse to make this delicious quick bread. Toasting the coconut and walnuts gives it an exceptional flavor.

1 cup	shredded coconut	250 mL
1/2 cup	chopped walnuts	125 mL
2/3 cup	butter, softened	150 mL
1/2 cup	*each* packed brown sugar and granulated sugar	125 mL
1 tsp	vanilla	5 mL
2	eggs	2
1 cup	mashed banana (3 medium)	250 mL
2 tsp	grated lemon rind	10 mL
1/4 cup	sour cream	50 mL
2 cups	all-purpose flour	500 mL
1 tsp	baking powder	5 mL
1/2 tsp	*each* baking soda and salt	2 mL

Spread coconut and walnuts on baking sheet; toast in 350°F (180°C) oven for about 5 minutes or just until golden, watching carefully.

In large bowl, cream butter with brown and granulated sugars until fluffy. Beat in vanilla and eggs, 1 at a time. Stir in banana, lemon rind and sour cream.

Sift or stir together flour, baking powder, baking soda and salt; stir into creamed mixture just until blended. Stir in coconut and nuts.

Pour into greased and floured 9- × 5-inch (2 L) loaf pan; bake in 350°F (180°C) oven for about 1 hour and 15 minutes or until cake tester inserted in middle comes out clean. Let stand for 10 minutes in pan; remove to let cool on rack. Makes 1 loaf.

NO-KNEAD FRENCH BREAD

Through the years, I have had great fun teaching cooking in various schools and colleges throughout Ontario. Although I no longer have time to teach, I still enjoy the recipes generous students have shared with me. Lew Short, one of my students in Owen Sound, gave me the idea for this extremely easy bread. Although they take only 5 minutes of actual work, the loaves are beautiful and delicious.

Use a large stationary electric mixer with a dough hook if you have one. If not, use the mixer attachment, but use a rubber spatula to help get the dough up from the bottom edges and sides of the bowl.

3 cups	(approx) all-purpose flour	750 mL
4 tsp	granulated sugar	20 mL
1 tsp	salt	5 mL
1	pkg active dry yeast (or 1 tbsp/15 mL)	1
2 tbsp	vegetable oil	25 mL
1 1/4 cups	very hot tap water	300 mL
1/3 cup	cornmeal	75 mL

Combine 1 cup (250 mL) of the flour, sugar, salt and yeast in large mixer bowl; mix very well at low speed. Add oil, then drizzle in water, mixing constantly at low speed. Increase to medium speed and mix for 3 minutes, scraping sides of bowl once.

Return to low speed and add 1 cup (250 mL) flour. Beat at highest speed for 4 minutes, scraping bowl occasionally. At lowest speed, very gradually add enough of the remaining flour to make soft dough that leaves sides of bowl and starts to become a ball. Remove bowl from machine; cover tightly with plastic wrap held on by elastic band to secure wrap while dough rises. Let rest for 45 minutes.

With floured hands, remove dough to heavily floured surface and shape into smooth oblong form. (Dough will be sticky.) Divide into two and form into long, thin tapered loaves. Grease baking sheet and sprinkle with cornmeal. Place loaves on sheet leaving plenty of room between them. Cover with dry clean tea towel and let rest in warm place (a heating pad on low works well) for 45 minutes or until doubled in bulk.

With razor blade or very sharp knife, make 5 or 6 shallow diagonal cuts in tops of loaves, being careful not to press down on loaves. Bake in 400°F (200°C) oven for about 25 minutes or until loaves sound hollow when tapped on the bottom. Remove to cool on wire racks. Makes 2 loaves.

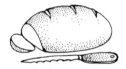

MAKE-AHEAD FULLY LOADED FRENCH TOAST

This peanut-banana version of French toast will be a big hit with kids of all ages.

³⁄₄ cup	unsalted peanuts	175 mL
3	large bananas	3
4	eggs	4
1	egg white	1
1¹⁄₂ cups	milk	375 mL
1 tsp	vanilla	5 mL
9	(approx) slices French bread, ³⁄₄ inch (2 cm) thick	9
	Cinnamon and honey	

In food processor or blender, process peanuts until coarsely chopped. Remove half, cover and set aside.

Coarsely chop 1 of the bananas; add to processor along with eggs, egg white, milk and vanilla. Process until well blended. Transfer to shallow dish.

Dip bread slices into egg mixture, pressing and turning until thoroughly soaked. Place on greased baking sheets. Spoon any remaining mixture over top; sprinkle with cinnamon. Cover with plastic wrap and refrigerate overnight.

Next morning, bake in 475°F (240°C) oven for 5 to 10 minutes on each side or until golden brown. Transfer to warmed plates. Slice remaining bananas and arrange around toast; sprinkle with reserved peanuts. Drizzle with honey. Makes 4 to 6 servings.

RASPBERRY-WALNUT MUFFINS

Use whatever jam (or marmalade) you have on hand for these easy muffins. No need to butter them either!

1 1/2 cups	all-purpose flour	375 mL
1/2 cup	finely chopped toasted walnuts	125 mL
1/4 cup	packed brown sugar	50 mL
1 tbsp	baking powder	15 mL
1/2 tsp	*each* baking soda and salt	2 mL
1	egg	1
1 cup	milk	250 mL
1/4 cup	butter, melted	50 mL
1/4 cup	raspberry jam	50 mL

In large bowl, stir together flour, walnuts, sugar, baking powder, baking soda and salt; make a well in centre.

Lightly beat together egg, milk and butter; pour into centre of dry ingredients and stir lightly just to combine, being careful not to overmix.

Spoon just enough batter into each of 12 greased muffin cups to cover bottom. Top each with scant teaspoonful (5 mL) jam; spoon in remaining batter to fill cups about three-quarters full.

Bake in 400°F (200°C) oven for 18 to 20 minutes or until tops are firm to the touch. Let cool in pan for 3 to 4 minutes. Remove and serve warm or let cool completely on rack. Store in airtight container. Makes 12 muffins.

MARY LOU'S BLUEBERRY STREUSEL MUFFINS

These moist, blueberry-rich muffins are the best you'll ever taste. From her family collection of recipes, Mary Lou Ruby Jonas makes them often for morning guests at her farm house or cottage. If using frozen blueberries, do not thaw first.

1/2 cup	butter, softened	125 mL
1 1/4 cups	granulated sugar	300 mL
2	eggs	2
1 tsp	grated lemon rind	5 mL
4 cups	all-purpose flour	1 L

4 tsp	baking powder	20 mL
1/2 tsp	salt	2 mL
1 1/4 cups	milk	300 mL
4 cups	blueberries	1 L

STREUSEL TOPPING:

1/4 cup	*each* granulated sugar and all-purpose flour	50 mL
1/2 tsp	cinnamon	2 mL
1/4 cup	butter	50 mL

STREUSEL TOPPING: In small bowl, combine sugar, flour and cinnamon; cut in butter until crumbly. Set aside.

In large bowl, cream butter with sugar until fluffy; beat in eggs, 1 at a time. Add lemon rind.

Stir together flour, baking powder and salt; add alternately with milk to creamed mixture, stirring just to combine but not overmix. Gently stir in blueberries.

Spoon into 24 greased muffin cups. Sprinkle with Streusel Topping. Bake in 375°F (190°C) oven for 25 to 30 minutes or until tops are firm to the touch. Makes 24 muffins.

MAPLE-ALMOND GRANOLA

Maple syrup adds a subtle sweetness to this easy, healthy breakfast treat. The recipe is easily doubled if you want to have lots on hand to sprinkle over yogurt or ice cream for snacks, in addition to the usual morning bowl with milk.

3 1/2 cups	rolled oats	875 mL
1 1/2 cups	coarsely chopped unblanched almonds	375 mL
1 cup	raw sunflower seeds	250 mL
1 cup	wheat bran	250 mL
1/2 cup	oat bran	125 mL
3/4 cup	maple syrup	175 mL
1/4 cup	vegetable oil	50 mL
1/2 tsp	vanilla	2 mL
2 cups	coarsely chopped dried apricots or golden raisins or a combination	500 mL

In large bowl, stir together oats, almonds, sunflower seeds, wheat bran and oat bran.

In small saucepan, heat together maple syrup and oil to boiling; boil for 1 minute without stirring. Remove from heat and stir in vanilla. Drizzle over rolled oat mixture and toss well to coat.

Spread mixture on jelly roll pan; bake in 350°F (180°C) oven for 15 minutes. Stir and reduce temperature to 325°F (160°C); bake for 30 minutes longer or until evenly golden, stirring every 10 minutes.

Return to bowl and stir in fruit. Let cool, stirring occasionally. Store in airtight container for 2 weeks at room temperature or freeze for up to 2 months. Makes about 10 cups (2.5 L).

CLASSIC TEA BISCUITS

When my mother disappeared with a cup and came back with cream from the basement, we knew there would be flaky, hot tea biscuits for lunch. These aren't made with cream, but they are nice and tender. They're great with stews or on top of potpies instead of pastry. If you wish, add your own favorite chopped herb or some grated cheese.

2 cups	all-purpose flour	500 mL
4 tsp	baking powder	20 mL
1 tbsp	granulated sugar	15 mL
1/2 tsp	salt	2 mL
1/2 cup	shortening	125 mL
1	egg, beaten	1
2/3 cup	(approx) milk	150 mL

In large bowl, sift or stir together flour, baking powder, sugar and salt; cut in shortening until mixture is like fine meal.

Stir together egg and milk; add to flour mixture all at once, stirring with fork until dough follows fork around bowl. (If too dry, add a bit more milk for soft, sticky dough.)

Turn out onto lightly floured surface; knead gently 20 times. Pat or roll to even 1/2-inch (1 cm) thickness. Using cookie cutter, cut into 2-inch (5 cm) circles.

Bake on ungreased baking sheets in 450°F (230°C) oven for about 10 minutes or until golden brown. Makes about 20 biscuits.

APPLE CHEDDAR MELT

For a quick and different lunch, enjoy this enlightened version of an old classic. The recipe can easily be halved or doubled for other numbers.

4	large slices rye bread, toasted	4
1	apple, peeled and minced	1
1 cup	shredded Cheddar cheese	250 mL
1/4 cup	light mayonnaise	50 mL
2 tbsp	liquid honey	25 mL
2 tsp	Dijon mustard	10 mL

Place toast on baking sheet. In small bowl, stir together apple, cheese, mayonnaise, honey and mustard; spread over toast, mounding in centre.

Broil 4 inches (10 cm) from heat for 2 to 3 minutes or until bubbly. Or, cooking 2 slices at a time, place on paper towel and microwave at Medium (50%) power for 1 to 2 minutes. Makes 4 servings.

Comforting Main Courses

"What's for supper?" When this question comes through the door with hungry children from school or a tired spouse from work, look to this chapter for comfort.

Because many people run out of ideas for family suppers, I have, in fact, made this section the bulk of the book.

There are fast stir-frys, one-skillet sautés, quick pasta dishes, so that whole meals can materialize in minutes—often in one dish. While most of these meals centre around poultry, meat or seafood, there are some vegetarian ideas as well.

But don't pass over the quick-to-fix but long-simmering dishes that to me constitute the easiest cooking of all. My baked beans or updated pot roast may take hours to cook, but only minutes to put together. And there is the added advantage of savoring their aroma throughout the afternoon if you happen to be in the house.

Included in this section, too, are several easy ideas for casual entertaining—make-ahead, dressed-up stews and casseroles, incredibly easy roasts, simple but fancy grills.

Whether it's family fare or company food, this section puts forth a myriad of easy answers to the question "What's for supper?"

Chicken

HOW DO YOU TELL A YOUNG CHICK FROM AN OLD HEN?

In the poultry world, it's not a matter of wrinkles, but it is a matter of weight.

Broilers are 2⅓ to 3 pounds (1.17 to 1.5 kg) and are best broiled, fried or braised. Fryers, weighing in at 3 to 4 pounds (1.5 to 2 kg) are basically used the same way as broilers.

Roasters, on the other hand, at 4 to 6 pounds (2 to 3 kg), are the big males with more meat per pound than smaller birds and can be used for roasting, too.

Now capons, at 6 to 9 pounds (3 to 4.2 kg) are interesting. They are cocks or males that were desexed when young. They grow big and fat and are therefore delicate and tender, with lots of white meat and a mild flavor. Higher in price per pound than chicken and sometimes hard to find, they are worth seeking out at farmers' markets and delicatessens because they're perfect for stuffing and roasting.

Stewing hens are just that. These older 3 to 7 pound (1.5 to 3.1 kg) gals are only good for stew or soup because they're tough without long braising.

Free-range chickens are raised outside any confines and are generally firmer with richer chicken flavor, but they may not be quite as tender as supermarket poultry because of the extent of their travels and unpredictable food.

SPICY PEANUT-CITRUS GRILLED CHICKEN

You can use the same marmalade and method if eight thick pork chops take your fancy instead of chicken.

8	large chicken breasts (4½ lb/2 kg)	8
1	small onion	1
1	clove garlic	1
¾ cup	Seville orange marmalade	175 mL
¼ cup	peanut butter	50 mL
2 tbsp	*each* lemon juice, vegetable oil and low-salt soy sauce	25 mL
Pinch	hot pepper flakes	Pinch

Wipe chicken breasts and place in shallow baking dish just big enough to hold them in single layer.

Into food processer or blender, drop onion and garlic, processing until finely chopped. Add marmalade, peanut butter, lemon juice, oil, soy sauce and hot pepper flakes; process until smooth.

Pour sauce over chicken and coat well. Cover and refrigerate for at least 6 hours or overnight, turning breasts occasionally. Remove from refrigerator 30 minutes before cooking.

Bake, uncovered, in 350°F (180°C) oven for 30 minutes. Remove chicken from marinade, reserving marinade in small saucepan; bring to boil and boil for 1 minute. Meanwhile, place chicken on greased grill about 4 inches (10 cm) from medium-hot coals or on medium-high setting; grill, basting often with marinade, for 15 to 20 minutes or until chicken is no longer pink near bone. Serve with remaining sauce. Makes 8 servings.

ELEGANT CHICKEN BREASTS WITH SUN-DRIED TOMATO STUFFING

This impressive dish is easy to execute, and can be made ahead, might be doubled or tripled and is delicious served hot or cold. Sun-dried tomatoes are now available in many grocery stores. If you can only find dried, let them sit for a day or two in oil before using. Reserve oil to use in the recipe.

6	chicken breast halves	6
	Salt and pepper	
	Paprika	

STUFFING:

1/2 lb	low-fat ricotta cheese (drained if necessary)	250 g
1	egg, lightly beaten	1
1	clove garlic, minced	1
1/3 cup	chopped drained sun-dried tomatoes (reserving oil)	75 mL
2 tbsp	chopped fresh basil (or 2 tsp/10 mL dried)	25 mL
1 tbsp	lemon juice	15 mL
1 1/2 tsp	chopped fresh oregano (or 1/2 tsp/2 mL dried)	7 mL
	Salt and pepper	

STUFFING: In bowl, blend together cheese, egg, garlic, tomatoes, basil, lemon juice, oregano, and salt and pepper to taste.

Remove bones from chicken, but leave skin on.

Loosen skin from one side of breast, leaving edge of skin attached on other side. Spoon scant 1/3 cup (75 mL) stuffing into pocket, spreading with spatula. Tuck skin and meat neatly under breast, covering stuffing completely. Form breast into neat even round. Place, skin side up, in greased shallow baking dish just big enough to hold them in single layer.

Brush chicken lightly with some of the oil from tomatoes and sprinkle with salt, pepper and paprika. (Breasts can be covered and refrigerated for a few hours or overnight. Remove from refrigerator 30 minutes before baking.)

Bake in 400°F (200°C) oven for 25 to 30 minutes or until meat is no longer pink inside, basting once or twice after 15 minutes. Makes 4 to 6 servings.

SPICY WINGS WITH MANGO MUSTARD

Because they're cooked at an unusually high temperature, these tangy wings are crusty on the outside, juicy and tender within. Watch them carefully for the last few minutes. They're great with beer. Just be sure to have lots of serviettes on hand.

3 lb	chicken wings	1.5 kg
4	cloves garlic, minced	4
2 tsp	*each* dry mustard and paprika	10 mL
1 tsp	*each* dried thyme and ground coriander	5 mL
½ tsp	*each* cayenne pepper, black pepper, salt and ground cumin	2 mL
2 tbsp	(approx) lemon juice	25 mL
2 tbsp	brandy	25 mL
MANGO MUSTARD:		
1 cup	sweet mango chutney	250 mL
¼ cup	Dijon mustard	50 mL

Cut tips from wings and reserve for stock; separate wings at joint.

In small bowl, stir together garlic, dry mustard, paprika, thyme, coriander, cayenne pepper, black pepper, salt and cumin; blend in lemon juice and brandy to make paste.

Brush over wings and arrange, meaty side down, on lightly greased foil-lined baking sheets. Add 1 tsp (5 mL) more lemon juice to paste if it becomes too dry. Refrigerate for at least 30 minutes or up to several hours.

MANGO MUSTARD: Meanwhile, in food processor or blender, purée chutney with mustard. Heat in small saucepan until chutney melts, stirring often; let cool.

Bake wings, uncovered, in 475°F (240°C) oven for 20 to 30 minutes or until brown and crisp, turning after 15 minutes. Serve hot with Mango Mustard for dipping. Makes 8 appetizer servings or 4 main-course servings.

HONEY-CURRIED FAST FAMILY CHICKEN

This quick and delicious chicken dish can be prepared just before baking or early in the morning. Add more curry powder for a hotter dish. Accompany with rice and colorful stir-fried vegetables.

3 lb	chicken breasts (6 or 7 halves)	1.5 kg
⅓ cup	liquid honey	75 mL
¼ cup	Dijon or deli-style mustard	50 mL
2 tbsp	butter, melted	25 mL
4 tsp	curry powder	20 mL
Pinch	cayenne pepper	Pinch

In greased shallow 13- x 9-inch (3.5 L) baking dish, arrange chicken in single layer, skin-side down.

Combine honey, mustard, butter, curry powder and cayenne; stir until smooth and blended. Pour over chicken. Cover and refrigerate if preparing ahead.

Bake chicken, uncovered, in 375°F (190°C) oven for 20 minutes, basting once. Turn chicken over and baste again; bake for 20 minutes longer or until chicken is no longer pink inside, basting once more. Makes 4 to 6 servings.

COUNTRY ROAST CAPON
WITH DRIED FRUIT STUFFING

In this fast-moving world, we yearn for comfort foods like the plump roast chicken that was so often the focus of Grandmother's Sunday supper. It's worth seeking out a capon for this updated version.

1	capon (about 8 lb/3.5 kg)	1
Half	lemon (cut crosswise)	Half
2 tbsp	butter, melted	25 mL
2 tbsp	Dijon mustard	25 mL
1 tsp	paprika	5 mL
2	cloves garlic, minced	2
1/2 tsp	crushed dried sage	2 mL

FRUIT STUFFING:

1 cup	coarsely chopped dried fruit (pears, apples, apricots, prunes, etc.)	250 mL
1 cup	hot chicken stock	250 mL
2 tbsp	butter	25 mL
2	onions, chopped	2
1 cup	chopped celery	250 mL
6 cups	cubed slightly stale bread	1.5 L
1/4 cup	chopped fresh parsley	50 mL
1/2 tsp	*each* crushed dried sage and salt	2 mL
1/4 tsp	pepper	1 mL

FRUIT STUFFING: Soak fruit in stock for at least 30 minutes.

In large skillet, melt butter over medium heat; cook onions and celery for 5 minutes, stirring often. Remove from heat; stir in bread, parsley, sage, salt, pepper and fruit with stock. Let cool.

Remove neck and giblets from capon; pat dry inside and out. Rub with lemon half inside and out. Stuff with Fruit Stuffing and truss bird.

In small bowl, stir together melted butter, mustard, paprika, garlic and sage; spread over capon.

Place capon on its side on rack in shallow roasting pan; roast in 325°F (160°C) oven for 1 hour. Using oven mitts protected with foil, turn onto other side; roast for 1 hour longer. Turn onto back and roast for 30 to 60 minutes longer or until juices run clear when thigh is pierced with skewer and meat thermometer registers 185°F (85°C).

Transfer capon to cutting board. Cover loosely with foil and let stand for 15 minutes before carving. Remove stuffing to heated bowl. Makes about 8 servings.

HOISIN-ORANGE CHICKEN LEGS

*An easy, flavorful glaze gives a dark mahogany appearance to chicken.
Serve with fried rice and snow or sugar snap peas.*

4	chicken legs	4
¹⁄₄ cup	hoisin sauce*	50 mL
1 tsp	granted orange rind	5 mL
¹⁄₄ cup	orange juice	50 mL
2	cloves garlic, minced	2
1 tbsp	*each* minced fresh ginger and vegetable oil	15 mL
1 tbsp	bitter orange marmalade	15 mL

Wipe chicken dry; place in shallow glass dish or sturdy plastic bag.

In small bowl, stir together hoisin sauce, orange rind, orange juice,
garlic, ginger and oil; pour over chicken. Cover and refrigerate for at least
3 hours or up to 8 hours, turning occasionally. Remove from refrigerator
30 minutes before cooking.

Remove chicken from marinade, reserving marinade in small saucepan; bring to boil and boil for 1 minute. Stir in marmalade; set aside on
edge of grill.

Meanwhile, place chicken on greased grill 6 inches (15 cm) from
medium-hot coals or on medium-high setting; grill for 15 minutes,
turning often. Brush marinade liberally over chicken and grill, turning
often and brushing with marinade, for 10 to 20 minutes longer or until
juices run clear when chicken is pierced with fork. Makes 4 servings.

*Available at most supermarkets and all Chinese food stores.

THAI THIGHS

*An easy marinade and a quick coating keeps these sprightly thighs nice
and moist during baking. Accompany with rice and snow peas.*

8	chicken thighs	8
1 cup	plain low-fat yogurt	250 mL
2 tbsp	fresh lime juice	25 mL
2	cloves garlic, minced	2
1 tbsp	minced fresh ginger	15 mL
1 tsp	ground coriander	5 mL
¹⁄₄ tsp	cayenne	1 mL
1 ¹⁄₂ cups	finely chopped peanuts	375 mL

Wipe chicken dry; pierce in several places with fork.

In shallow dish just big enough to hold thighs in single layer, stir
together yogurt, lime juice, garlic, ginger, coriander and cayenne. Add
chicken and roll to coat evenly. Cover and refrigerate for at least 2 hours or
up to 6 hours. Remove from refrigerator 30 minutes before cooking.

Place peanuts in shallow dish. Remove thighs from marinade and let
excess drip off. Roll each thigh in nuts patting to coat well. Place, meaty
side up, on greased baking sheet; bake, uncovered, in 350°F (180°C)
oven for 40 to 45 minutes or until juices run clear when chicken is
pierced. Makes 4 servings.

ELIZABETH BAIRD'S CHORIZO AND CHICKEN PAELLA

My long-time friend Elizabeth Baird, food director of Canadian Living Magazine, *and I have gone on so many cooking, eating and food-learning explorations together that my book would not be complete without one of her favorite recipes. This one she describes as ''A welcome dish for a buffet or dinner party. . .a paella that slips away from the traditional mix of seafood and meat.''*

¼ cup	all-purpose flour	50 mL
½ tsp	salt	2 mL
¼ tsp	pepper	1 mL
2 lb	chicken legs (about 5)	1 kg
2 tbsp	olive oil	25 mL
1 lb	smoked chorizo sausages	500 g
1	large onion, chopped	1
2	large cloves garlic, minced	2
2	zucchini (preferably yellow), coarsely chopped	2
1	*each* large sweet red and green pepper, cubed	1
1 tsp	paprika	5 mL
¼ tsp	dried thyme	1 mL
Pinch	cayenne pepper	Pinch
½ tsp	saffron threads	2 mL
3 cups	hot chicken stock	750 mL
3 cups	chopped peeled tomatoes	750 mL
2 cups	parboiled long-grain rice	500 mL
1 cup	frozen peas	250 mL
¼ cup	minced fresh parsley	50 mL
2 tbsp	chopped green onion or chives	25 mL
1	lemon	1

In plastic bag, combine flour, salt and pepper. Separate each chicken leg at joint. Add to bag and shake to coat; shake off excess.

In wide heavy shallow saucepan or large skillet, heat half of the oil over medium-high heat; brown chicken well on all sides. Remove and set aside.

Cut sausages into 2-inch (5 cm) lengths; add to pan and cook until browned. Set aside with chicken. Pour off and discard all fat.

Add remaining oil to pan and heat over medium heat; cook onion, garlic, zucchini and red and green peppers until softened, about 5 minutes. Stir in paprika, thyme and cayenne; cook, stirring, 2 minutes.

Meanwhile, steep saffron in stock for 5 minutes. Add to vegetable mixture along with tomatoes and rice; bring to boil. Nestle chicken and sausages into rice mixture. Cover and cook over medium-low heat until rice is tender and liquid absorbed, about 30 minutes. Sprinkle with peas; cover and cook for about 2 minutes or until heated through.

To serve, sprinkle with parsley and green onion. Cut lemon lengthwise into wedges and arrange attractively on paella. Makes 6 generous servings.

LIGHT CHICKEN CHILI

On a recent trip to Texas, I discovered chili of every description, and there was much talk of "white chili" made with chicken and white beans instead of the usual beef and red beans. I came home to recreate this quick chicken chili, but I'm afraid I still like to use some chili powder, which does render the dish less than white. Serve with rice or tortillas and a green salad. You might like to accompany it with bowls of sour cream, salsa and grated Monterey Jack or mild Cheddar cheese.

2 tbsp	olive oil	25 mL
1	onion, chopped	1
1	stalk celery, sliced	1
1 lb	boneless skinless chicken, cubed	500 g
2	cloves garlic, minced	2
1	can (4 oz/125 g) chopped mild green chilies, drained	1
1 tbsp	chili powder	15 mL
1 tsp	*each* ground cumin and crushed oregano	5 mL
Pinch	black pepper	Pinch
Pinch	(approx) hot pepper flakes	Pinch
2 cups	chicken stock	500 mL
1	can (19 oz/540 mL) white kidney beans (undrained)	1
1/3 cup	chopped fresh coriander	75 mL

In large saucepan, heat half of the oil over medium heat; cook onion and celery for 5 minutes. Push to one side of pan. Heat remaining oil on other side of pan over high heat; brown chicken on all sides, about 5 minutes.

Stir in garlic, chilies, chili powder, cumin, oregano, black pepper and hot pepper flakes; cook, stirring for 1 minute. Stir in stock and beans; bring to boil. Cover and reduce heat; simmer for 15 minutes.

Uncover and simmer for 15 minutes longer. Taste and adjust seasoning, adding more hot pepper flakes if desired. Serve sprinkled with coriander. Makes about 4 servings.

CHICKEN POTPIE WITH PARTY PHYLLO CRUST

A crisp light phyllo crust gives chicken potpie a new twist. Serve with a crisp green salad for a quick make-ahead company meal.

1/3 cup	butter	75 mL
1/4 lb	mushrooms, quartered	125 g
1	onion, chopped	1
1	clove garlic, minced	1
1/4 cup	all-purpose flour	50 mL
3 cups	hot chicken stock	750 mL
	Salt and pepper	
1/4 cup	chopped fresh parsley	50 mL
1 tsp	dried marjoram	5 mL
6 cups	diced cooked chicken	1.5 L

4 cups	cooked cubed parsnips or carrots	1 L
1 cup	fresh or frozen peas	250 mL
5	sheets phyllo pastry	5

In large saucepan, melt 2 tbsp (25 mL) of the butter over medium heat; cook mushrooms, onion and garlic for 3 minutes. Stir in flour and cook, stirring, for 2 minutes.

Gradually stir in stock and bring to boil, stirring constantly; cook for about 3 minutes or until thickened. Season with salt and pepper to taste; stir in parsley and marjoram. Remove from heat.

Stir in chicken, parsnips and peas. Pour into ungreased 13- × 9-inch (3 L) baking dish. Refrigerate until cooled.

Melt remaining butter. Cover phyllo sheets with waxed paper and damp tea towel to prevent drying out while you work. Place one phyllo sheet over chicken mixture, folding under excess pastry around edges to fit inside dish. Lightly brush sheet with butter. Repeat with remaining sheets and butter, making sure to brush top sheet. (Recipe can be prepared to this point, covered and refrigerated for up to 12 hours. Remove from refrigerator 30 minutes before cooking.)

Bake in 375°F (190°C) oven for 25 to 30 minutes or until pastry is golden and filling bubbly. Makes 4 to 6 servings.

TERIYAKI CHICKEN WITH CHUNKY TROPICAL SALSA

If you wish to serve this interesting chicken and its quick, fresh sauce for one, merely cut the marinade and salsa in half.

2 tbsp	low-salt soy sauce	25 mL
1/4 tsp	*each* granulated sugar and ginger	1 mL
2	cloves garlic, crushed	2
1 lb	boneless skinless chicken breasts (about 4)	500 g

CHUNKY TROPICAL SALSA:

1	small mango, peeled and diced	1
1	kiwifruit, peeled and diced	1
2 tbsp	rice wine vinegar	25 mL
1	banana, diced	1
1	green onion, sliced	1
2 tbsp	diced sweet red pepper	25 mL
	Salt, pepper and hot pepper flakes	

In sturdy plastic bag, combine soy sauce, sugar, ginger and garlic; add chicken breasts and turn to coat. Let stand at room temperature for 20 minutes or refrigerate for up to 4 hours. Remove from refrigerator 30 minutes before cooking.

Broil chicken 6 inches (15 cm) from heat for about 12 minutes, turning once, or until chicken is no longer pink inside.

CHUNKY TROPICAL SALSA: Meanwhile, in bowl, combine mango, kiwifruit and vinegar; stir in banana, green onion and red pepper. Season with salt, pepper and hot pepper flakes to taste. Serve with chicken. Makes 2 servings.

ONE-DISH STIR-FRIED CHICKEN WITH ORIENTAL NOODLES

In this satisfying and simple main-dish stir-fry, the contrast of crisp green broccoli and soft egg noodles is a treat for both eye and palate.

2 tbsp	peanut or vegetable oil	25 mL
4	cloves garlic, minced	4
1 lb	fresh Chinese egg noodles	500 g
1 lb	boneless skinless chicken breast halves, cut across grain in thin strips	500 g
1/2 lb	broccoli florets, cut in narrow lengths	250 g
1/2 cup	chicken stock	125 mL
1 tsp	cornstarch	5 mL
1 tbsp	cold water	15 mL
2 tbsp	oyster sauce	25 mL
1 tbsp	fish sauce (nam pla)*	15 mL
1/2 tsp	granulated sugar	2 mL
	Salt and pepper	

In wok or large skillet, heat oil over high heat; stir-fry garlic and noodles for 1 minute to flavor noodles. With slotted spoon, remove to large bowl and set aside.

Add chicken and broccoli to wok; stir-fry for 2 to 3 minutes or until chicken is no longer pink inside. Add stock and bring to boil; reduce heat to low, cover and simmer for 2 minutes or until broccoli is tender-crisp. Stir in noodles for last few seconds.

Meanwhile, dissolve cornstarch in water. Increase heat to high and stir in cornstarch mixture, oyster sauce, fish sauce, sugar, and salt and pepper to taste; cook, stirring, until well blended and shiny. Serve immediately. Makes 6 servings.

*Fish sauce is a thin, salty, brown liquid indispensable in Southeast Asian cooking. It's milder than soy sauce and available in Oriental grocery stores.

QUICK HONEY-GARLIC CHICKEN WINGS

I've been doing chicken wings like this for many years, and no matter how else I prepare wings, my family likes these best. Serve these quick and easy braised wings with rice and green peas for a Friday night treat.

3 lb	chicken wings	1.5 kg
2 tbsp	peanut or vegetable oil	25 mL
1/3 cup	soy sauce	75 mL
2 tbsp	*each* liquid honey and dry sherry	25 mL
2	cloves garlic, crushed	2
1 tbsp	minced ginger	15 mL

Remove tips from wings and reserve for stock. Separate wings at joint.

In wok or skillet, heat oil over high heat; stir-fry wings for 3 to 4 minutes or until browned.

Stir together soy sauce, honey, sherry, garlic and ginger; pour over wings and stir to coat well.

Reduce heat to low; cover and simmer for about 30 minutes or until tender, stirring often near end of cooking to make sure glaze doesn't burn. Makes 4 servings.

NEW-STYLE CHICKEN WITH PARSLEY DUMPLINGS

This is an updated version of my mother's chicken and dumplings, for which she always used a large stewing hen. Chicken breasts are much more tender and far less greasy. Be sure to use a pot large enough to allow 3 inches (8 cm) of space for dumplings to rise.

4	bone-in chicken breast halves	4
	Salt and pepper	
	All-purpose flour	
1 tbsp	*each* butter and vegetable oil	15 mL
4	small red potatoes, quartered	4
2	*each* parsnips, carrots and onions, quartered	2
2	stalks celery, diagonally sliced	2
1/2 tsp	*each* dried thyme and salt	2 mL
1/4 tsp	crushed dried sage	1 mL
2	bay leaves	2
1 cup	frozen peas	250 mL

PARSLEY DUMPLINGS:

2 cups	sifted cake-and-pastry flour	500 mL
4 tsp	baking powder	20 mL
3/4 tsp	salt	4 mL
2 tbsp	chopped fresh parsley	25 mL
2 tbsp	shortening	25 mL
2/3 cup	(approx) milk	150 mL

Sprinkle chicken with salt and pepper; dust lightly with flour.

In large saucepan, melt butter with oil over medium heat; brown chicken on all sides and remove to plate.

Add potatoes, parsnips, carrots, onions and celery to pan; cook for 5 minutes. Cover with about 4 cups (1 L) water; bring to boil, scraping up any brown bits from bottom of pan.

Return chicken to pan; add thyme, salt, sage and bay leaves. Return to boil; reduce heat, cover and simmer until chicken is no longer pink inside, about 25 minutes. Remove and discard bay leaves. Stir in peas.

PARSLEY DUMPLINGS: Meanwhile, mix or sift together flour, baking powder and salt in large bowl; stir in parsley. Cut in shortening until texture of meal. Stir in milk, adding a few more drops if necessary to make sticky dough.

Evenly dust large plate with flour. With tablespoon, cut out dumplings and drop onto floured plate. Quickly drop dumplings onto gently simmering stew, spacing evenly; cover pan tightly and simmer, without lifting lid, for 15 minutes or until dumplings are cooked. Makes 4 servings.

EASY GRILLED CHICKEN-RICE SALAD

Everything, except grilling the chicken, can be done ahead for this full-flavored main-course salad. Serve with Cheese Pita Toasts (page 22) and sliced tomatoes. Both hoisin sauce and rice vinegar are readily available in most supermarkets today.

½ cup	rice vinegar	125 mL
¼ cup	hoisin sauce	50 mL
2 tbsp	rice wine or sherry (optional)	25 mL
1	clove garlic, minced	1
1 tbsp	minced fresh ginger	15 mL
4	boneless, skinless chicken breast halves (about 1 lb/500 g total)	4
1 cup	parboiled long-grain rice	250 mL
⅓ cup	vegetable oil	75 mL
2 tbsp	chopped fresh coriander or parsley	25 mL
1 tsp	curry powder	5 mL
½ tsp	*each* salt and granulated sugar	2 mL
½ cup	sliced fresh or dried apricots	125 mL
3	green onions, sliced	3
1 cup	cooked green peas	250 mL
	Coriander or parsley sprigs	

In bowl, stir together ¼ cup (50 mL) of the vinegar, hoisin sauce, rice wine (if using), garlic and ginger; add chicken and toss to coat well. Cover and refrigerate for at least 4 hours or overnight, turning twice. Remove from refrigerator 30 minutes before cooking.

Cook rice according to package instructions. In large bowl, stir together oil, remaining rice vinegar, coriander, curry powder, salt and sugar. Add hot cooked rice; toss with fork to coat well. Gently stir in apricots and green onions. Cover and refrigerate for up to 2 days. Bring to room temperature before proceeding.

Just before serving, remove chicken from marinade, reserving marinade. Place chicken on greased grill 6 inches (15 cm) from medium-hot coals or on medium-high setting; grill for 6 to 7 minutes per side or until no longer pink inside, basting often with marinade and turning once. (Alternatively, broil 4 inches/10 cm from heat for about 5 minutes per side.)

Stir peas into rice mixture; mound on large platter. Cut each hot chicken breast into 3 strips; arrange around rice mixture. Garnish with coriander sprigs. Makes 4 servings.

LEMONY SAUTEED CHICKEN AND GREEN PEPPER

Ready in less than 30 minutes, this easy dish is impressive enough to serve to guests. You could add two more chicken breasts for six servings if appetites are hearty. Accompany with rice pilaf, dilled carrots, broccoli vinaigrette and fresh fruit.

6	chicken breast halves, boned and skinned	6
1	lemon	1

	Salt and pepper	
¹/₄ cup	**all-purpose flour**	**50 mL**
¹/₄ cup	**pecan halves**	**50 mL**
¹/₄ cup	**unsalted butter**	**50 mL**
3	**large cloves garlic, minced**	**3**
1	**large sweet green pepper, cut in strips**	**1**
¹/₂ cup	**chicken stock**	**125 mL**

On cutting board, pound chicken to flatten slightly. Grate rind from lemon and set aside. Cut lemon in half and rub over chicken. Squeeze juice from one half over both sides of breasts. Sprinkle both sides with salt and pepper to taste, flour and grated lemon rind.

In large heavy skillet, toast pecans over medium heat, stirring often, for 3 minutes. Remove and reserve.

In same skillet, melt butter; cook garlic over low heat for 3 minutes until softened; remove with slotted spoon and reserve.

Increase heat to medium-high and add chicken; cook just until golden brown on both sides, 3 to 4 minutes. Remove to warm platter. In pan drippings, sauté green pepper for 2 minutes. Remove with slotted spoon.

Drain off all fat and add stock; bring to boil, stirring to scrape up brown bits from bottom of pan. Return garlic and chicken with any accumulated juices; cover and cook over low heat for about 10 minutes or until chicken is no longer pink inside. Return green pepper and pecans to pan; heat through.

Arrange chicken, green pepper and pecans on heated platter. Pour pan juices over top and serve immediately. Makes 4 to 6 servings.

OVEN-FRIED GOLDEN CRISP CHICKEN LEGS

This is my favorite everyday way to cook chicken. I always pop potatoes (and perhaps some squash) into the oven to bake alongside. Accompany with Cider-Baked Applesauce (page 155) and green beans. If you don't have cornmeal in the house, use all flour.

1 tbsp	***each* butter and vegetable oil**	**15 mL**
¹/₄ cup	***each* all-purpose flour and cornmeal**	**50 mL**
2 tsp	**paprika**	**10 mL**
¹/₄ tsp	***each* salt and pepper**	**1 mL**
¹/₂ cup	**milk**	**125 mL**
4	**chicken legs**	**4**
2 tbsp	**lemon juice**	**25 mL**

In 13- x 9-inch (3.5 L) baking dish, melt butter with oil in 375°F (190°C) oven; tilt dish to evenly coat bottom.

In plastic bag, combine flour, cornmeal, paprika, salt and pepper. Pour milk into shallow dish. Shake chicken in flour mixture, dip in milk, then shake again in flour mixture.

Place chicken, skin side down, in baking dish; drizzle with lemon juice. Bake for 20 minutes; turn chicken over. Bake for 20 to 25 minutes longer or until juices run clear when chicken is pierced. Makes 4 servings.

Variation: *Sesame Oven-Fried Chicken:*
Substitute sesame seeds for the cornmeal.

MAKE-AHEAD MEDITERRANEAN PARTY CHICKEN WITH SAFFRON

Even better after reheating, this sunny French dish with its Mediterranean flavors is perfect for casual entertaining. Serve with noodles, rice or just good crusty bread and a green salad.

2	large chickens (fryers or roasters, 3 to 4 lb/1.5 to 2 kg each)	2
	Salt and pepper	
2 tbsp	(approx) olive oil	25 mL
1 cup	diced bacon	250 mL
2	onions, chopped	2
12	cloves garlic, minced	12
Pinch	crumbled saffron	Pinch
1 cup	dry white wine	250 mL
2	cans (28 oz/796 mL each) plum tomatoes, drained and chopped	2
2 cups	chicken stock	500 mL
1/3 cup	finely chopped fresh parsley	75 mL
2 tsp	anchovy paste	10 mL
2	bay leaves	2
1/2 tsp	dried thyme	2 mL
1/4 tsp	cayenne pepper	1 mL
2	strips (3- x 1-inch/8 x 2.5 cm) orange zest (outer rind)	2
30	good-quality pitted black olives	30

Cut up chickens and pat dry; season with salt and pepper to taste.

In heavy casserole, heat half of the oil over medium-high heat; brown chicken, in batches and adding more oil as necessary. Remove chicken and keep warm.

Pour off all but 2 tbsp (25 mL) pan drippings; cook bacon, onions and garlic over medium heat, stirring, for 3 to 4 minutes or until onion is softened. Do not let garlic brown.

Sprinkle with saffron; pour in wine and cook over medium-high heat, stirring often, for about 5 minutes or until most of the wine evaporates. Stir in tomatoes, stock, half of the parsley, anchovy paste, bay leaves, thyme, cayenne and orange zest.

Return chicken to pan and bring to boil; reduce heat and simmer, covered, for 20 to 30 minutes or until chicken is no longer pink inside and juices run clear when chicken is pierced. Remove chicken; cover and keep warm.

Increase heat and boil sauce until desired thickness, about 15 minutes. Remove and discard orange zest and bay leaves. Stir in olives; taste and adjust seasoning.

Return chicken to pot and warm through if serving immediately. Or, cover and refrigerate overnight; reheat gently in sauce. Garnish with remaining parsley to serve. Makes 8 servings.

MAKE-AHEAD JAMBALAYA

A rice dish descended from Spanish paella, jambalaya is seasoned with chili powder as well as cayenne and, in view of its name (probably coming from the French 'jambon' for ham), should aways contain some ham. The rest of the ingredients can be varied—sausage, shrimp, crawfish, oysters, pork. This make-ahead, easy version of the classic Creole stew has more sausage and chicken than anything else and is just right for casual entertaining. Accompany with a green salad and crusty bread.

1 tbsp	vegetable oil	15 mL
6 oz	cooked ham, cubed	175 g
1 lb	hot Italian or chorizo sausage, cut in ½-inch (1 cm) thick slices	500 g
10	chicken thighs (about 2 lb/1 kg)	10
3	onions, coarsely chopped	3
1	*each* sweet red and green pepper, chopped	1
¼ cup	chopped fresh parsley	50 mL
4	cloves garlic, minced	4
4	stalks celery, sliced	4
2	bay leaves	2
1 tsp	dried thyme	5 mL
½ tsp	*each* chili powder, salt, pepper and dried oregano	2 mL
¼ tsp	cayenne	1 mL
1	can (28 oz/796 mL) tomatoes (undrained), chopped	1
2 cups	beef stock	500 mL
2 cups	parboiled long-grain rice	500 mL
6	green onions, sliced	6
12	large shrimp, peeled and deveined	12

In large heavy saucepan, heat oil over medium-high heat; brown ham and sausage for 8 to 10 minutes. With slotted spoon, transfer to bowl. Brown chicken, in batches; remove to bowl.

Pour off all but 2 tbsp (25 mL) drippings. Reduce heat to medium and cook onions, red and green peppers, parsley, garlic and celery for 5 minutes. Stir in bay leaves, thyme, chili powder, salt, pepper, oregano and cayenne; cook, stirring for 2 minutes.

Return chicken and meat to pan along with any accumulated juices. Stir in tomatoes and stock; bring to boil. Reduce heat to medium-low; cover and simmer for 35 to 45 minutes or until juices run clear when chicken is pierced, stirring occasionally. Remove and discard bay leaves. (Recipe can be prepared to this point, covered and refrigerated for several hours or overnight.)

In large pot of lightly salted boiling water, cook rice for 6 minutes; drain through fine sieve. Place rice in 16-cup (4 L) Dutch oven or shallow casserole; fluff with fork.

Stir green onions into chicken mixture; spread over rice. Cover and bake in 350°F (180°C) oven for 25 minutes. Stick shrimp down into mixture; bake for 10 to 15 minutes or until shrimp are pink and casserole is bubbly. Makes about 8 servings.

MUSTARD-BAKED CHICKEN

This quick and delicious chicken dish can be prepared just before baking or early in the morning, then covered and refrigerated. If you wish, use one chicken, cut up, instead of breasts. In that case, you may have to bake the dish longer and turn pieces at half time.

8	chicken breast halves	8
¼ cup	*each* lemon juice and Dijon mustard	50 mL
2 tbsp	butter, softened	25 mL
2	cloves garlic, minced	2
1 tsp	*each* dried marjoram and paprika	5 mL

Wipe breasts dry; arrange in single layer, skin side up, in shallow baking dish.

Stir together lemon juice, mustard, butter, garlic, marjoram and paprika; spread over chicken. Bake, uncovered, in 375°F (190°C) oven basting once or twice, for about 40 minutes, or until no longer pink inside. Serve with pan juices. Makes 6 to 8 servings.

$\mathbb{P}$ork

MAPLE APRICOT CHOPS

When I want something easy but a bit special, I put these in the oven. Serve with a wild and white rice mixture and lemony green beans.

12	dried apricots	12
4	pork chops, loin or butt	4
	Salt and pepper	
½ tsp	dried thyme	2 mL
⅓ cup	maple syrup	75 mL

Soak apricots in ½ cup (125 mL) warm water for 20 minutes.

Meanwhile, remove any fat from chops and render it in large ovenproof skillet over medium-high heat to coat pan well; discard solid fat. Brown chops on both sides; sprinkle with salt and pepper to taste.

Sprinkle chops with thyme; top with apricots, reserving soaking liquid. Stir maple syrup into liquid; pour around chops in pan.

Cover and bake in 350°F (180°C) oven for 35 minutes. Uncover and bake for 10 minutes longer or until chops are tender and no longer pink inside. Makes 4 servings.

PORK MEDALLIONS IN DOUBLE-MUSTARD SAUCE

Serve this easy but impressive sauté with buttered fettuccine, green beans and tiny glazed carrots.

1 1/2 lb	pork tenderloin	750 g
	Salt and pepper	
	All-purpose flour	
2 tbsp	butter	25 mL
1 tbsp	vegetable oil	15 mL
3 tbsp	white wine vinegar	50 mL
3/4 cup	chicken stock	175 mL
1/2 cup	whipping cream	125 mL
2 tbsp	Dijon mustard	25 mL
Pinch	dry mustard	Pinch
	Watercress	

Cut tenderloin into 3/4-inch (2 cm) thick slices; flatten between 2 sheets of waxed paper until 1/2 inch (1 cm) thick. Sprinkle with salt and pepper to taste; dust with flour.

In large skillet, melt half of the butter with oil over medium heat; cook pork, in two batches, for 4 to 5 minutes per side or until golden and tender, turning once. Transfer to heated platter and keep warm.

Add vinegar to pan; bring to boil, stirring to scrape up any brown bits in pan. Add stock and cream; simmer, stirring, for 5 minutes or until thickened.

Remove from heat; gradually stir in remaining butter, cut in pieces. Gradually blend in Dijon and dry mustards. Taste and adjust seasoning. Spoon over pork; garnish with watercress. Makes 4 servings.

GRILLED BASIL CREAM PORK CHOPS

Cover pork chops with fresh basil and then marinate them in a little cream for wonderfully moist, flavorful meat. Serve with buttered new potatoes, tiny fresh green beans and sliced tomatoes.

6	pork loin chops, 1-inch (2.5 cm) thick	6
1/4 cup	chopped fresh basil (or 2 tbsp/25 mL dried)	50 mL
1/4 tsp	pepper	1 mL
1/4 cup	whipping cream	50 mL

Rub pork chops with basil until well coated; sprinkle with pepper.

Arrange chops in single layer in plastic bag; place in shallow dish. Pour cream over chops and turn to coat well. Tie bag closed and let stand at room temperature for 30 minutes, turning occasionally. (Or, refrigerate for at least 4 hours or overnight; remove from refrigerator 30 minutes before grilling.)

Place chops on greased grill 5 inches (12 cm) from medium-hot coals or at medium setting; grill, turning frequently, for about 20 minutes or until meat is no longer pink inside. Makes 4 to 6 servings.

HOMEY APPLE-BAKED SAUSAGE

Apples bake to a soft applesauce consistency alongside crisp, brown sausage. Serve with an oven potato dish (like Baked German Potato Salad, page 125) and baked beets.

2 lb	Italian or farmer's sausage	1 kg
3	apples (Spy or Ida Red), peeled and cut in 8 wedges each	3
Half	small Spanish onion, thinly sliced	Half
1/2 cup	apple cider or apple juice	125 mL
1	sweet green pepper, slivered	1

If sausage is in links, separate; if not, cut into serving lengths. Prick in several places and place in large shallow baking dish. Arrange apple wedges around sausage; sprinkle with onion slices. Pour in cider.

Bake, uncovered, in 375°F (190°C) oven for 40 to 50 minutes or until sausage is cooked through and browned, turning sausages and apples once. Scatter with green pepper; bake for 5 to 10 minutes or until tender but still bright green. Makes 6 servings.

ONE-DISH MEXICAN PASTA AND PORK CHOPS

Kids will love this easy pork chop casserole. Serve it right away or make it ahead of time for an instant answer when everyone rushes home with ''What's for supper?'' If chops are small, you might like to use six.

2 tbsp	vegetable oil	25 mL
1	onion, chopped	1
1	sweet green pepper, diced	1
2	cloves garlic, minced	2
1	can (19 oz/540 mL) tomatoes (undrained)	1
1 tbsp	chopped fresh parsley	15 mL
2 tsp	chili powder	10 mL
1 tsp	ground cumin	5 mL
1/2 tsp	dried oregano	2 mL
Pinch	hot pepper flakes	Pinch
4 cups	boiling water	1 L
1/2 lb	spaghetti, broken in half	250 g
4	large pork chops	4
	Salt and pepper	
3/4 cup	shredded Cheddar cheese	175 mL
	Parsley sprigs	

In large saucepan, heat half of the oil over medium heat; cook onion, green pepper and garlic for 3 minutes or until softened. Add tomatoes, breaking up with fork. Stir in parsley, chili powder, cumin, oregano and hot pepper flakes.

Stir in boiling water; bring to boil and add spaghetti. Reduce heat to medium-low; cover and simmer, stirring occasionally, for 20 to 25 minutes or until most of the liquid has been absorbed.

Meanwhile, trim fat from chops. In large ovenproof skillet, heat remaining oil over medium-high heat; cook chops, without turning, for 10 minutes. Turn chops over and sprinkle with salt and pepper to taste; cover and cook for 5 minutes longer or until no longer pink inside but still moist.

Remove chops from skillet and drain off any fat. Spread spaghetti mixture in skillet; top with chops. (Recipe can be prepared to this point, covered and refrigerated for up to 6 hours. Heat, covered, in 350°F/180°C oven for 20 minutes before continuing.) Sprinkle cheese over chops; bake, uncovered, in 350°F (180°C) oven for 5 to 10 minutes or until cheese melts. Garnish with parsley. Makes 4 servings.

BARBECUED SPARERIBS WITH APPLE-SAGE GLAZE

Cook the spareribs, apply the flavorful rub to them and make the tangy-sweet sauce a day ahead for a carefree and irresistible barbecue. Accompany with New-Way Old-Fashioned Potato Salad (page 128) and a platter of crisp raw vegetables.

9 lb	meaty pork spareribs	4 kg
4	cloves garlic, minced	4
2 tbsp	minced fresh sage (or 2 tsp/10 mL crumbled dried)	25 mL
1 tbsp	dry mustard	15 mL
1/2 tsp	salt	2 mL
1/4 tsp	pepper	1 mL
1	jar (500 mL) apple butter	1
1/2 cup	water	125 mL
1/4 cup	cider vinegar	50 mL
1 tbsp	*each* Dijon mustard, horseradish and brown sugar	15 mL
1/4 tsp	cayenne pepper	1 mL

In large saucepan, cover ribs with water and bring to boil; reduce heat, cover and simmer for 45 to 60 minutes or until meat is tender. Drain well and let cool slightly.

Meanwhile, stir together garlic, sage, dry mustard, salt and pepper; rub all over cooked ribs. Place in sturdy plastic bag, tie closed and refrigerate for up to 1 day. Remove from refrigerator 30 minutes before cooking.

In small saucepan, stir together apple butter, water, vinegar, Dijon mustard, horseradish, brown sugar and cayenne; bring to boil. Reduce heat and simmer, uncovered, for 15 minutes, stirring often. (Glaze can be cooled, covered and refrigerated for up to 1 day. Reheat before continuing.)

Place ribs on greased grill over slow coals or on low setting; place glaze on side of grill. Barbecue ribs for 30 to 45 minutes or until heated through, turning every 10 to 15 minutes and brushing with glaze during the last 15 minutes. Cut between bones to serve. Pass remaining glaze as sauce. Makes 8 servings.

SAUSAGE SKILLET DINNER

Beer gives a simple everyday dish a special flavor. Accompany with Colcannon (page 111) and steamed whole green beans. Follow with a warm Pear Gingerbread (page 165).

1 lb	farmer's sausage	500 g
	Boiling water	
1 tbsp	vegetable oil	15 mL
2 cups	thinly sliced onions	500 mL
1 cup	sliced apples	250 mL
2 tbsp	all-purpose flour	25 mL
½ tsp	paprika	2 mL
1	bottle (340 mL) lager or ale	1
1 tbsp	Worcestershire sauce	15 mL
6	peppercorns	6
1	bay leaf	1
	Salt	

Pierce sausage and pour boiling water over to remove some of the fat; drain well and dry with paper towels. In large skillet, heat oil over medium-high heat; brown sausage and remove to warm platter.

Drain off all but 3 tbsp (50 mL) drippings; cook onions over medium heat for 3 minutes. Add apples and cook for another 2 minutes. With slotted spoon, transfer onions and apples to platter.

Stir flour and paprika into pan; cook, stirring, for 2 minutes. Remove from heat and gradually stir in beer; cook, whisking constantly, until smooth and thickened. Stir in Worcestershire sauce, peppercorns and bay leaf.

Return sausage, onions and apples to pan. Cover tightly and cook over low heat for about 20 minutes or until sausage is cooked through. Taste and add salt if necessary. Discard bay leaf. Makes 4 servings.

GINGER-GRILLED PORK LOIN

I devised this flavorful marinade many years ago and still use it when I grill pork sirloins to keep them moist as they cook. Sirloins are the fresh form of cured back bacon and can only be found at certain farmers' markets—particularly in this Waterloo area of Ontario, where I live. Since these great cuts are not available country-wide, this recipe is for a centre loin boneless roast. If you do happen to find sirloins, cook two for eight people, omitting the searing step and grilling about 1 hour, turning and basting often.

3 tbsp	finely chopped fresh thyme (or 1 tbsp/15 mL crumbled dried)	50 mL
1 tbsp	dry mustard	15 mL
1	pork centre loin boneless roast (about 5 lb/2.5 kg)	1
½ cup	*each* green ginger wine* and low-salt soy sauce	125 mL
¼ cup	vegetable oil	50 mL
3	large cloves garlic, crushed	3

In small bowl or mortar, crush together thyme and mustard with tip of spoon or pestle to form paste; rub all over pork.

Place pork in plastic bag set in shallow dish. Stir together wine, soy sauce, oil and garlic; pour over pork. Seal bag and turn to coat meat well; refrigerate several hours or overnight, turning occasionally. Remove from refrigerator 30 minutes before cooking.

Reserving marinade, remove pork and pat dry with paper towel. Sear pork on greased grill 4 inches (10 cm) from medium-hot coals or on high setting, turning often, for 15 minutes.

Raise grill 2 inches (5 cm) or reduce setting to medium. Cover with lid or tent pork with foil; grill, turning often and basting occasionally with reserved marinade, for about 2 hours or until meat thermometer inserted in thickest part registers 160°F (70°C) and juices are no longer pink. (If cooking on rotisserie, omit searing and baste often.)

Transfer roast to carving board; cover loosely with foil and let stand for 10 minutes before slicing thinly. Makes about 8 servings.

*Green ginger wine is available from a liquor store.

CURRANT-GLAZED COMPANY PORK ROAST

For an elegant company meal, accompany this succulent roast with Scalloped Potatoes (page 112), Gingered Squash and Pear Purée (page 116) and Simple Garlic-Sautéed Green Beans (page 118).

1 tsp	dry mustard	5 mL
1 tsp	crumbled dried basil	5 mL
1/4 tsp	pepper	1 mL
2 tbsp	*each* sherry and soy sauce	25 mL
2	cloves garlic, crushed	2
1	boneless pork loin, rolled and tied (4 lb/2 kg)	1
1/4 cup	red currant jelly	50 mL
1 tbsp	cornstarch	15 mL

In small bowl, stir together mustard, basil and pepper, crushing basil finely with back of spoon. Stir in half of the sherry and half of the soy sauce to make runny paste. Add garlic.

Place pork on rack in shallow roasting pan; spread paste all over roast. Cover and refrigerate for at least 2 hours and up to 6 hours. Remove from refrigerator 30 minutes before cooking.

Roast pork, uncovered, in 325°F (160°C) oven for about 2 hours or until meat thermometer registers 160°F (70°C).

Meanwhile, in small saucepan, stir together remaining sherry and soy sauce with red currant jelly; heat over medium heat, stirring, until jelly melts. Spoon some of the mixture over meat 2 or 3 times during last 30 minutes of roasting.

Remove pork to carving board; cover loosely with foil and let stand for 10 minutes before carving.

Remove and discard excess fat from pan; stir in about 1 cup (250 mL) water and bring to boil, stirring to scrape up any brown bits from bottom of pan. Stir cornstarch with 2 tbsp (25 mL) cold water; add to pan, stirring constantly, and cook over medium heat until smooth and thickened. Pass in heated sauceboat with pork. Makes 8 servings.

SPLENDID BAKED GLAZED HAM

"Fully cooked" smoked hams are greatly improved by a short cooking time to finish them off. A spicy fruit-honey mixture goes on for the last few minutes to give a seductive and delicious glaze to a ham that would be a perfect focus to any festive dinner table. Accompany with a mustard sauce, Sweet Potato Party Flan (page 114) and Three-Ingredient Creamy Coleslaw (page 134).

1	**fully cooked bone-in smoked ham (about 7½ lb/3.3 kg)**	1
	Whole cloves	
½ cup	**peach or apricot jam**	125 mL
¼ cup	**liquid honey**	50 mL
2 tbsp	**lemon juice**	25 mL
1 tbsp	**cornstarch**	15 mL
¼ tsp	**ground cloves**	1 mL
Pinch	**cinnamon**	Pinch

With sharp knife, remove any rind and excess fat from ham. Place, fat side up, on rack in shallow pan.

With sharp knife, score outside layer of fat diagonally in both directions to make 2-inch (5 cm) diamonds. Do not cut too deeply. Insert whole cloves at corners or in centre of diamonds. Bake in 325°F (160°C) oven for 2 to 2½ hours or until meat thermometer registers 130°F (55°C).

Meanwhile, in small saucepan, stir together jam, honey, lemon juice, cornstarch, cloves and cinnamon; bring to boil over medium heat, stirring. During last 30 minutes of cooking ham, spoon some of the glaze on ham 2 or 3 times until all glaze is used, basting with pan juices too. Makes about 10 servings.

HARVEST PORK STEW

This flavorful stew would be good company fare with crusty bread and a crisp green salad. Oven-browning the meat is not only easier but cuts down considerably on fat in the recipe.

3 lb	**lean pork, cut in 1½-inch (4 cm) cubes**	1.5 kg
¼ cup	**all-purpose flour**	50 mL
½ tsp	**salt**	2 mL
¼ tsp	**pepper**	1 mL
1 cup	*each* **dry white wine and chicken stock**	250 mL
12	**cloves garlic, peeled**	12
1	**large sweet red pepper, finely diced**	1
1 tbsp	*each* **Dijon mustard and cider vinegar**	15 mL
½ tsp	*each* **crushed dried sage and thyme**	2 mL
Half	**rutabaga, cut in ¾-inch (2 cm) cubes**	Half
2	**apples, peeled and thickly sliced**	2
	Chopped fresh parsley	

In paper bag or bowl, toss pork with flour, salt and pepper. Spread pork in big shallow pan; roast in 500°F (260°C) oven for about 15 minutes or until browned, stirring occasionally. Remove and reduce oven temperature to 350°F (180°C).

Meanwhile, in large Dutch oven or flameproof casserole, combine wine, stock, garlic, red pepper, mustard, vinegar, sage, thyme, rutabaga and apples; bring to boil. Add browned meat; cover and return to boil.

Transfer to oven and bake, stirring occasionally, until meat is fork-tender, about 1½ hours. Taste and adjust seasoning. Sprinkle with parsley to serve. Makes 6 to 8 servings.

IMPRESSIVE CHILLED PORK TENDERLOIN STUFFED WITH PISTACHIO NUTS AND FRUIT

This elegant make-ahead meat course is attractive to look at and delicious to taste. Serve with marinated asparagus and crusty French bread.

½ cup	dry white wine or white grape juice	125 mL
¼ cup	chopped dried mixed fruits	50 mL
2 lb	pork tenderloin	1 kg
1	small clove garlic, cut in half	1
2 tbsp	*each* butter, minced onion and diced celery	25 mL
½ cup	finely diced stale bread	125 mL
2 tbsp	coarsely chopped pistachios	25 mL
2 tbsp	chopped fresh parsley	25 mL
¼ tsp	dried thyme	1 mL
Pinch	dried sage	Pinch
	Salt and pepper	
2 tsp	Dijon mustard	10 mL
1½ tsp	curry powder	7 mL
	Watercress	

In small bowl, combine wine and fruits; set aside.

Slice meat lengthwise through half its thickness; open like a book and flatten with edge of cleaver. Rub with cut side of garlic; set aside.

In large skillet, melt butter over medium heat; cook onion and celery for 3 minutes or until softened. Remove from heat; stir in bread, nuts, parsley, thyme, sage, and salt and pepper to taste. Drain fruits, reserving wine; stir fruits into bread mixture.

Spread stuffing evenly over meat; roll up meat. Using trussing or darning needle and thin cord, sew all edges of meat closed. Place, seam side down, on rack in shallow roasting pan; brush with mustard. Sprinkle with ½ tsp (2 mL) curry powder, and salt and pepper to taste. Pour in reserved wine. Roast, uncovered, in 350°F (180°C) oven for 40 to 50 minutes or until meat thermometer registers 160°F (70°C), basting with pan juices and sprinkling with ½ tsp (2 mL) remaining curry powder twice during roasting. Remove to plate and let cool in refrigerator until steaming stops. Wrap tightly in foil and refrigerate overnight.

To serve, remove cord; carve into thin slices and arrange on platter garnished with watercress. Makes 4 to 6 servings.

BEER-GLAZED PICNIC SHOULDER

This easy smoked picnic shoulder is delicious hot. Barbecue foil packets of sliced potatoes and onions to serve along with green peas that have been cooked in the kitchen or on a side element on the barbecue. Any leftover meat is good cold in sandwiches.

²/₃ cup	packed brown sugar	150 mL
¹/₄ tsp	ground cloves	1 mL
1	boneless fully cooked smoked picnic shoulder (3 lb/1.5 kg)	1
¹/₂ cup	beer	125 mL
1 tbsp	all-purpose flour	15 mL
1 tbsp	dry mustard	15 mL
2 tbsp	vinegar	25 mL

In small bowl, stir together brown sugar and cloves. Place picnic shoulder on piece of heavy-duty foil large enough to enclose it, set in foil pan. Press half the sugar mixture on top and drizzle with beer.

Wrap meat completely with foil and set pan on grill over medium-hot coals or on medium-high setting. Cover with barbecue lid and cook for 1 hour, turning wrapped meat once.

Meanwhile, stir flour and mustard into remaining sugar mixture. Blend in vinegar. Set aside for glaze.

Remove ham from foil and pan and place right on greased grill. Brush with some of the glaze and cook another 15 minutes, brushing often with glaze and turning once.

Makes 6 to 8 servings.

EASY PORK SCALOPPINE
WITH FRESH RED PEPPER RELISH

Where I live, all the local taverns feature pork schnitzel as one of their specialties. It's traditionally served with applesauce and sauerkraut—two great accompaniments if you don't have a red pepper on hand. This relish, however, is a bright, fresh tart-sweet sauce that particularly complements the meat. It would also go along happily with veal, chicken or turkey scaloppine if you cooked them like this. The relish can also be made ahead and reheated.

1 lb	pork cutlets	500 g
	Salt and pepper	
¹/₄ cup	all-purpose flour	50 mL
2	eggs	2
³/₄ cup	dry bread crumbs	175 mL
2 tbsp	(approx) vegetable oil	25 mL
	Lemon wedges	

RED PEPPER RELISH:

1 tbsp	olive oil	15 mL
1	large sweet red pepper, finely diced	1

1	clove garlic, minced	1
1/4 cup	red wine vinegar	50 mL
2 tsp	granulated sugar	10 mL
	Salt and pepper	
1 tbsp	chopped fresh parsley	15 mL

RED PEPPER RELISH: In small skillet, heat oil over medium heat, cook red pepper for 7 to 10 minutes or until softened. Stir in garlic, vinegar, sugar, and salt and pepper to taste; bring to boil. Reduce heat and simmer, uncovered and stirring often, for 10 minutes or until thickened. Stir in parsley.

Meanwhile, if cutlets are not already thin, pound between two pieces of waxed paper as thinly as possible. Sprinkle with salt and pepper to taste; dust with flour.

With fork, beat eggs in shallow dish. Place crumbs on waxed paper. Dip floured cutlets in egg, then coat well with crumbs. (Cutlets can be covered and refrigerated for up to 3 hours. Remove from refrigerator 30 minutes before cooking.)

In large skillet, heat oil over medium-high heat; cook cutlets, in batches and adding more oil if necessary, for about 2 minutes per side or until golden brown, turning once. Drain on paper towels. Serve immediately with lemon wedges and Red Pepper Relish. Makes 4 servings.

MAPLE-GLAZED BACK BACON

For a special brunch, a glazed roast of back bacon is a nice change from baked ham, especially with this tangy glaze. Accompany with a crisp green salad and poached eggs on toasted French bread. It's also great for a family supper with Old-Fashioned Scalloped Potatoes (page 112) and green peas. Any leftovers make nice sandwiches.

1	back bacon roast (3 lb/1.5 kg)	1
1/2 cup	boiling water	125 mL
1/2 cup	maple syrup	125 mL
2 tbsp	all-purpose flour	25 mL
1 tbsp	*each* Dijon mustard and lemon juice	15 mL
Pinch	ground cloves	Pinch

Place bacon on rack in small shallow roasting pan or baking dish. Pour boiling water into pan and roast, uncovered, in 325°F (160°C) oven for 1 1/2 hours.

In small saucepan, stir together maple syrup, flour, mustard, lemon juice and cloves; bring to boil over medium heat, stirring constantly. Pour and spread over bacon; roast for 20 minutes longer, basting occasionally with glaze, until meat is tender and nicely glazed. (For a darker glaze, increase oven temperature to 375°F/190°C for last 20 minutes of baking.) Remove from oven and cover loosely with foil; let stand for a few minutes before carving. Makes 8 servings for brunch.

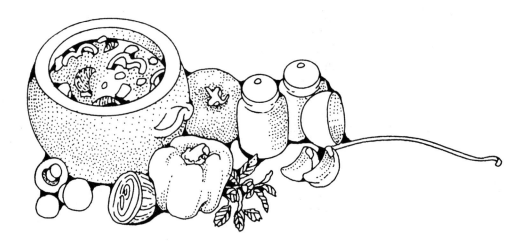

ONE-POT FAMILY SUPPERS

As time goes on, I find myself preparing simpler food for both family meals and entertaining. I don't rely on sodium- or chemical-laden mixes; nor do I think that everything that comes out of a microwave oven is marvellous. (Mind you, it's great for countless things and will make life much easier if you have one.) I don't know why everyone wants something quick. Quick is good, but easy is great.

Somehow, I prefer a long-simmered or roasted meal in the oven or on top of the stove—one that I can pop in and go off and forget while I read the evening paper. I guess I don't care how long it takes to cook as long as it's easy to make.

There's a certain satisfaction, too, in cooking sturdy real food in your own kitchen, rather than heading for the nearest fast food place or running to the telephone to order in. Long simmered food is a comfortable kind of cooking, a soothing escape from the pressures of life.

Sociologists refer to this decade as one of cocooning—a term used to describe the art of staying at home and talking to your family, surely a good excuse to enjoy an easy home-cooked meal.

I particularly like one-pot suppers. They're very easy to prepare and serve both to family and good friends.

OVEN-BAKED PARTY BEEF STEW

Serve this flavorful make-ahead beef dish with Three-Ingredient Creamy Coleslaw (page 134) and a full-bodied red wine.

1/4 cup	(approx) vegetable oil	50 mL
10	small pearl onions	10
8	carrots, quartered	8
4	stalks celery, cut in large pieces	4
1/2 lb	button mushrooms	250 g
2	large cloves garlic, minced	2
2 1/2 lb	lean boneless beef	1.25 kg
1/3 cup	all-purpose flour	75 mL
1/2 tsp	*each* salt and pepper	2 mL
2 1/2 cups	hot beef stock or consommé	625 mL
2/3 cup	dry red wine	150 mL
2 tbsp	*each* tomato paste, tarragon vinegar and Worcestershire sauce	25 mL
2	bay leaves	2

PIQUANT CRUST:

1/3 cup	unsalted butter	75 mL
3	large cloves garlic, minced	3
	French bread slices (1/2-inch/1 cm thick) to cover casserole	
1 tbsp	Dijon Mustard	15 mL

In large heavy skillet, heat half of the oil over medium-high heat; cook onions, carrots, celery, mushrooms and garlic until onions are golden brown, about 5 minutes. With slotted spoon, remove vegetables to large bowl.

Trim and cut meat into 1-inch (2.5 cm) cubes. In plastic bag, combine flour, salt and pepper. In batches, shake cubes in flour mixture, then brown in skillet, adding remaining oil as needed. Transfer to separate bowl.

Add any remaining flour mixture to skillet; cook, stirring, until browned. Gradually stir in hot stock, stirring to scrape up brown bits from bottom of pan; bring to boil. Stir in wine, tomato paste, vinegar, Worcestershire sauce and bay leaves. Taste and adjust seasoning.

In 12-cup (3 L) casserole, layer meat and vegetables alternately; pour hot sauce over all. Cover and bake in 300°F (150°C) oven for 3 hours or until beef is very tender. Remove and discard bay leaves. (Stew can be prepared to this point and refrigerated or frozen. Thaw in refrigerator before proceeding. Heat in 350°F/180°C oven for 20 minutes before adding crust.)

PIQUANT CRUST: In large skillet, melt butter over low heat; stir in garlic. Spread bread with mustard; arrange in garlic butter. Heat gradually, turning slices over, until butter is absorbed; arrange on top of baked stew. Bake, uncovered, in 350°F (180°C) oven for about 30 minutes or until stew is bubbly and crust is golden. Makes 6 servings.

SUPER EASY ONE-DISH SPAGHETTI

Family supper couldn't be easier and better. Everyone's favorite meal cooks in one pot. My friend Jean Medley makes it often for her family, but she calls it "Glop." Enjoy with a green salad and crusty bread.

1 lb	ground beef	500 g
1	clove garlic, minced	1
1 tsp	*each* dried basil, oregano, paprika and granulated sugar	5 mL
1/2 tsp	salt	2 mL
1/4 tsp	*each* pepper and hot pepper flakes	1 mL
2 cups	water	500 mL
1	can (14 oz/398 mL) tomato sauce	1
1	can (14 oz/398 mL) tomatoes (undrained)	1
1/4 cup	chopped fresh parsley	50 mL
3/4 cup	(approx) freshly grated Parmesan cheese	175 mL
1/2 lb	spaghetti, broken	250 g

In large deep skillet or shallow Dutch oven, combine beef, garlic, basil, oregano, paprika, sugar, salt, pepper and hot pepper flakes; cook over medium heat, breaking up beef with wooden spoon, for about 5 minutes or until browned.

Stir in water, tomato sauce, tomatoes, parsley and 1/4 cup (50 mL) of the Parmesan cheese; bring to boil. Reduce heat; cover and simmer for 45 minutes. (Recipe can be prepared to this point, covered and refrigerated or frozen. Bring to simmer before continuing.)

Stir in spaghetti, making sure all pasta is covered with sauce. Cover and simmer, stirring occasionally, for 10 to 15 minutes or until pasta is tender but firm. Serve in bowls. Pass remaining Parmesan cheese separately. Makes about 4 servings.

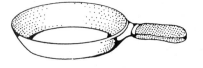

SASSY SKILLET SHEPHERD'S PIE

On a cold night, don't you sometimes yearn for a steaming, comforting helping of old-fashioned shepherd's pie? This one, which cooks in a matter of a few minutes on top of the stove, uses raw ground beef instead of leftover roast beef, but it still relies on mashed potatoes left over from the night before. Roasted red peppers are available in jars in most supermarkets.

2 tsp	vegetable oil	10 mL
1	onion, chopped	1
1 lb	lean ground beef	500 g
2/3 cup	beef stock	150 mL
2 tbsp	tomato paste	25 mL
4 tsp	chili powder	20 mL
1/2 tsp	*each* dried oregano and ground cumin	2 mL

1	can (10 oz/284 mL) kernel corn, drained	1
	Salt and pepper	
1 cup	coarsely diced roasted red peppers	250 mL
3 cups	mashed potatoes	750 mL
¼ cup	milk	50 mL
1	egg	1

In 10-inch (25 cm) ovenproof skillet, heat oil over medium heat; cook onion for 3 minutes. Add beef, breaking up with wooden spoon; cook for 5 minutes or until browned. Drain off any fat.

Stir in beef stock, tomato paste, chili powder, oregano, cumin and corn; cook for 5 minutes. Season with salt and pepper to taste. Spread out in pan evenly; sprinkle with roasted red peppers.

Beat potatoes with milk and egg; spoon over meat mixture. Place in bottom third of oven and broil for 7 to 8 minutes or until potatoes are golden. Makes 3 or 4 servings.

BEEF CHEESE CASSEROLE

Everyone loves lasagna, but there isn't always time to make it. This easy casserole, somewhat like lasagna in flavor, can be prepared ahead, then reheated. Serve with crusty Italian bread and a salad of Romaine lettuce and avocado with lemon vinaigrette.

2 lb	lean ground beef	1 kg
2	large onions, chopped	2
1	can (14 oz/398 mL) tomato sauce	1
1 tsp	dried basil	5 mL
	Salt and pepper	
½ lb	broad egg noodles (about 6 cups/1.5 L)	250 g
¾ lb	mozzarella cheese, cubed (about 3½ cups/875 mL)	375 g
1	sweet green pepper, chopped	1
½ cup	sour cream or plain yogurt	125 mL
¾ cup	freshly grated Parmesan cheese	175 mL

In large skillet over medium-high heat, cook beef and half of the onion until beef is browned, breaking up meat with spoon. Drain off any fat.

Stir in tomato sauce, basil, and salt and pepper to taste; simmer, uncovered, over medium-low heat for 15 minutes.

Meanwhile, in saucepan of boiling water, cook noodles until tender but firm; drain well.

Combine mozzarella cheese, green pepper, sour cream and remaining chopped onion; set aside.

In greased 12-cup (3 L) shallow casserole, spread half of the noodles. Top with mozzarella mixture, then half of the meat mixture. Cover with remaining noodles; top with remaining meat mixture. Sprinkle with Parmesan cheese. (Recipe can be covered and refrigerated for up to 6 hours. Remove from refrigerator 30 minutes before cooking.)

Bake, covered, in 350°F (180°C) oven for about 30 minutes or until hot and bubbly. Makes 8 servings.

ALMOST-CABBAGE-ROLLS CASSEROLE

With the flavor of cabbage rolls but a fraction of the work, this easy casserole is delicious served with sour cream on the side.

1 lb	lean ground beef	500 g
³/₄ cup	long-grain rice	175 mL
1	large onion, chopped	1
2	cloves garlic, minced	2
¹/₂ tsp	salt	2 mL
¹/₄ tsp	pepper	1 mL
1	can (28 oz/796 mL) tomato sauce	1
¹/₄ cup	cider vinegar	50 mL
2 tbsp	packed brown sugar	25 mL
1 tbsp	dry mustard	15 mL
8 cups	coarsely chopped cabbage (half a head)	2 L

In large bowl, mix together beef, rice, onion, garlic, salt and pepper. In small bowl, stir together tomato sauce, vinegar, brown sugar and mustard.

Layer one-third of the cabbage in 12-cup (3 L) deep casserole. Arrange half of the beef mixture on top. Cover with another one-third of the cabbage. Top with remaining beef mixture and remaining cabbage.

Pour tomato sauce mixture over top, but do not stir. (Casserole will be quite full.) Cover and let stand at room temperature for 20 minutes. Bake in 325°F (160°C) oven for 2 hours, without stirring. Makes 4 to 6 servings.

NEW-STYLE PEPPERY POT ROAST

Pour thin liquid mixture over a beef roast, add a few vegetables, and everything roasts to a comforting one-dish meal—with the added bonus of an intriguing sauce, no added fat and very little effort. Use homemade or canned stock, not powdered concentrate.

1	chuck or blade beef roast (4 lb/2 kg)	1
1	can (28 oz/796 mL) tomato sauce	1
2¹/₂ cups	beef stock	625 mL
1 cup	dry red wine	250 mL
¹/₄ cup	low-salt soy sauce	50 mL
2 tbsp	packed brown sugar	25 mL
2	bay leaves	2
¹/₂ tsp	*each* hot pepper flakes and pepper	2 mL
1	whole head garlic, separated into cloves and peeled	1
1	butternut squash, peeled and cut in large pieces	1
6 to 8	potatoes, peeled	6 to 8
6 to 8	wedges green cabbage	6 to 8

Place roast in very large roasting pan. In large bowl, stir together tomato sauce, beef stock, wine, soy sauce, sugar, bay leaves, hot pepper flakes and pepper; pour over roast. Add garlic. Cover and roast in 325°F (160°C) oven for 1½ hours.

Add squash, potatoes and cabbage; cover and roast for 1 to 1½ hours or until meat and vegetables are very tender. Remove meat and vegetables to heated platter; cover and set aside to keep warm.

Remove bay leaves. Boil liquid in pan until desired consistency for sauce, 5 to 10 minutes. Slice beef and pass sauce in heated sauceboat. Makes 6 to 8 servings.

GRILLED PARTY-STYLE FLANK STEAK WITH MUSTARD HORSERADISH

Extremely lean flank steak should not be overlooked for both family meals and entertaining. This easy marinade renders the meat fork-tender while adding a piquant flavor, due to the large amount of pepper. Accompany with rice and steamed broccoli.

1½ lb	flank steak	750 g
1	large clove garlic, halved	1
1 tsp	black pepper	5 mL
⅓ cup	dry sherry	75 mL
¼ cup	soy sauce	50 mL
2 tbsp	vegetable oil	25 mL
4 tsp	lemon juice	20 mL
1 tbsp	minced fresh ginger	15 mL

MUSTARD HORSERADISH:

¼ cup	Dijon mustard	50 mL
¼ cup	well-drained prepared horseradish	50 mL

MUSTARD HORSERADISH: In small bowl, stir together mustard and horseradish. Cover and refrigerate for up to 1 day.

Remove any membrane from meat surface. With sharp knife, score steak by cutting very shallow grooves on both sides. Rub cut side of garlic all over steak; reserve garlic. Sprinkle steak all over with pepper; lay flat in shallow dish.

In small bowl, combine sherry, soy sauce, oil, lemon juice and ginger. Mince reserved garlic and add to mixture; pour over meat. Cover and refrigerate for at least 3 hours or overnight. Remove from refrigerator about 30 minutes before cooking.

Remove meat from marinade, reserving marinade. Broil meat 3 inches (8 cm) from heat or barbecue 4 inches (10 cm) from hot coals or at high setting, basting occasionally with marinade and turning only once, for 3 to 5 minutes per side for rare meat. Don't overcook. Slice thinly across grain on diagonal. Serve with Mustard Horseradish. Makes 4 to 6 servings.

MYSTERY-MARINATED STEAK

No one will guess the interesting flavor strong coffee gives this marinade, but everyone will love the tender, delicious results.

1 ¹/₂ lb	flank steak	750 g
1	onion, chopped	1
2	cloves garlic, minced	2
¹/₂ cup	strong brewed coffee	125 mL
¹/₃ cup	low-salt soy sauce	75 mL
1 tbsp	*each* Worcestershire sauce, cider vinegar and vegetable oil	15 mL
¹/₂ tsp	pepper	2 mL

Score both sides of steak at 2-inch (5 cm) intervals; place in sturdy plastic bag. Add onion and garlic.

Stir together coffee, soy sauce, Worcestershire sauce, vinegar, oil and pepper; pour over steak. Close bag and refrigerate for at least 6 hours or overnight. Remove from refrigerator 30 minutes before grilling.

Remove steak from marinade, reserving marinade in small saucepan; bring to boil and boil for 1 minute. Keep warm on side of grill.

Meanwhile, place steak on greased grill 4 inches (10 cm) from medium-hot coals or on medium-high setting; grill, brushing often with marinade, for 4 to 6 minutes per side or until rare. Do not overcook.

Transfer steak to cutting board and pour marinade over top; tent with foil and let stand for 5 minutes. Thinly slice on diagonal. Makes 4 servings.

EVERYBODY'S FAVORITE CLASSIC CHILI

Everyone loves robust chili in which red kidney seems to be the classic bean.

1 tbsp	vegetable oil	15 mL
¹/₂ lb	small mushrooms	250 g
2 lb	lean ground beef	1 kg
2	stalks celery, sliced	2
1	large onion, chopped	1
1	sweet green pepper, diced	1
1	can (7¹/₂ oz/213 mL) tomato sauce	1
1	can (19 oz/540 mL) tomatoes (undrained)	1
1 tbsp	chili powder	15 mL
1 tsp	ground cumin	5 mL
¹/₂ tsp	*each* salt, pepper, dried oregano and hot pepper flakes	2 mL
¹/₄ tsp	cayenne pepper	1 mL
2	cloves garlic, minced	2
2	cans (19 oz/540 mL) red kidney beans (undrained)	2

In large saucepan, heat oil over medium heat; cook mushrooms for 5 minutes. Remove with slotted spoon and set aside.

Add beef, celery, onion and green pepper; cook over high heat, stirring to break up beef, until meat is no longer pink, about 7 minutes. Stir in tomato sauce and 1 tomato-sauce can of water; add tomatoes, chili powder, cumin, salt, pepper, oregano, hot pepper flakes, cayenne and garlic.

Return mushrooms and any accumulated liquid to pan; stir in beans. Bring to boil; reduce heat and simmer, covered, for 1 hour, stirring occasionally. Taste and adjust seasoning if necessary. (Chili can be refrigerated immediately and slowly reheated the next day. Or, cool in refrigerator and freeze for up to 3 months.) Makes 6 servings.

CHILI CHEESEBURGERS

Keep the cheese in the centre of these big juicy patties by sealing the meat around the edges and chilling well. Serve open-face style on top of crispy fried tortillas; sprinkle with additional grated cheese, slivers of hot pepper, chopped lettuce and a dollop of sour cream, guacamole or taco sauce. Or present them on toasted kaiser rolls with all the traditional trimmings.

1 ¹/₂ lb	ground beef	750 g
2 tbsp	*each* minced onion and ketchup	25 mL
1 tbsp	chili powder	15 mL
¹/₂ tsp	*each* salt and dried oregano	2 mL
1	egg	1
1 cup	shredded mild Cheddar cheese	250 mL
1 tbsp	diced jalapeño pepper (pickled or fresh)	15 mL

In large bowl, combine beef, onion, ketchup, chili powder, salt, oregano and egg; mix gently but well. Shape into 8 patties ¹/₄ inch (5 mm) thick and 5 inches (12 cm) wide.

Stir together cheese and pepper; mound in centre of 4 patties. Top with remaining patties, pressing meat around edges to seal well. With spatula, arrange in single layer on large plate; cover with plastic wrap and refrigerate until chilled or overnight.

Place patties on greased grill 4 inches (10 cm) from medium-hot coals or at medium-high setting; grill for 7 minutes. Turn and grill for 6 to 8 minutes longer or until no longer pink inside. Makes 4 servings.

MARINATED BEEF AND VEGETABLE SALAD

Turn leftover grilled steak or cold roast beef into a delicious main-course make-ahead salad that will leave your kitchen cool on hot nights. It will become one of your favorite summer suppers or company lunches just as it is at our house.

1/3 cup	tarragon vinegar	75 mL
1	clove garlic, minced	1
1 tsp	dry mustard	5 mL
1/2 tsp	Worcestershire sauce	2 mL
	Salt and pepper	
2/3 cup	vegetable oil	150 mL
1 lb	cold cooked roast beef or steak, cut in strips (about 4 cups/1 L)	500 g
1/2 lb	small mushrooms	250 g
2	large potatoes, cooked and cubed	2
1 cup	sliced celery	250 mL
8	cherry tomatoes	8
1	small red onion, thinly sliced	1
1	large dill pickle, sliced	1
1/2 cup	pitted black olives	125 mL
1 tbsp	chopped fresh parsley	15 mL
	Lettuce leaves	

In large bowl, whisk together vinegar, garlic, mustard, Worcestershire, and salt and pepper to taste. Gradually whisk in oil.

Add beef, mushrooms, potatoes, celery, tomatoes, onion, pickle, olives and parsley; toss gently to coat. Cover and chill for at least 6 hours or up to 24 hours, stirring occasionally.

To serve, line individual salad plates with lettuce. With slotted spoon, mound salad on top. Makes about 4 to 6 servings.

THREE-CHEESE MEAT LOAF

Bake potatoes and squash alongside this moist, flavorful meat loaf and accompany with a spinach salad.

	Dry bread crumbs	
2	slices Italian-style bread, cubed	2
1/3 cup	milk	75 mL
1 lb	ground beef	500 g
1	*each* small onion and sweet green pepper, chopped	1
1/4 cup	freshly grated Parmesan cheese	50 mL
2 tbsp	tomato paste or ketchup	25 mL
1 tbsp	chopped fresh parsley	15 mL
1	egg, lightly beaten	1
3/4 tsp	salt	4 mL

| ¼ tsp | *each* pepper and dried sage | 1 mL |
| ½ cup | *each* diced mozzarella and Swiss cheese (about 3 oz/90 g each) | 125 mL |

Grease 9- × 5-inch (2 L) loaf pan; sprinkle lightly with bread crumbs.

In large bowl, soak bread in milk for 5 minutes; with hands, squeeze out excess moisture. Break up beef with spoon and add to bowl; add onion, green pepper, Parmesan, tomato paste, parsley, egg, salt, pepper and sage; with moistened hands, mix together.

Press one-third of the meat mixture evenly into prepared pan; sprinkle mozzarella evenly on top. Press another one-third of the meat mixture on top; sprinkle with Swiss cheese. Cover with remaining meat mixture.

Bake in 350°F (180°C) oven for about 1 hour or until meat thermometer registers 170°F (75°C). Slice to serve. Makes 4 generous servings.

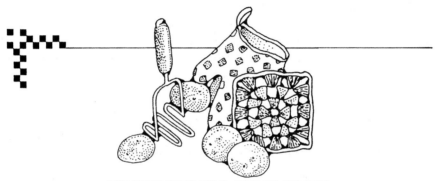

TIMELY TIPS FOR QUICK COOKS

•*If you have one, use your food processor to chop vegetables. For even results, place 1½-inch (4 cm) chunks in work bowl and pulse three times. Scrape down sides and pulse two or three more times.*

•*Grate or shred cheese in food processor and store in freezer.*

•*Chop parsley in quantity in food processor to have on hand for garnishing. Remove stems, wash and dry thoroughly; process until finely chopped. Store, covered, in refrigerator for up to one week.*

•*Wash greens ahead of time—as soon as you get home from shopping. Dry well and wrap loosely in paper towels in a plastic bag to store in crisper.*

•*Start water boiling for pasta before preparing other parts of a pasta supper.*

•*Speed up preparation with prepared vegetables from the produce section—more expensive but handy in a pinch and perhaps without as much wastage.*

•*Plan your cooking steps and move back and forth between recipes, working on one while part of another dish cooks.*

•*Cook enough potatoes, rice or pasta for two meals; serve hot the first night, and use the rest for salads, soups, desserts like Easy Rice Pudding (page 147) or creative reheating like stir-fried rice, home fries, potato patties, etc. the next night.*

SKILLET STEAK STROGANOFF

Serve with egg noodles and green peas for a fast and easy supper.

2 tbsp	vegetable oil	25 mL
1 lb	sirloin steak, slivered	500 g
2 cups	sliced or tiny whole mushrooms	500 mL
1	sweet red pepper, cut in small strips	1
2	cloves garlic, minced	2
4 tsp	Dijon mustard	20 mL
1 tbsp	Worcestershire sauce	15 mL
2/3 cup	light sour cream	150 mL
	Salt and pepper	

In large skillet, heat oil over medium-high heat; cook steak just until browned. Add mushrooms, red pepper and garlic; cook, stirring, for 4 minutes or until pepper is tender-crisp.

Reduce heat to low; stir in mustard, Worcestershire sauce and sour cream. Season with salt and pepper to taste; heat through. Makes 4 servings.

SANTA FE BRAISED SHORTRIBS

Serve these crisp, spicy ribs with barbecue-roasted potatoes and canned corn.

3 lb	lean beef shortribs, trimmed	1.5 kg
1	bottle (7 1/2 oz/213 mL) hot salsa	1
1/2 cup	lime juice	125 mL
1 tbsp	vegetable oil	15 mL
2	cloves garlic, minced	2
1	small onion, finely chopped	1

Place ribs in shallow glass dish just big enough to hold them in sturdy plastic bag. Stir together salsa, lime juice, oil, garlic and onion; pour over ribs. Cover and refrigerate for at least 2 hours or up to 4 hours. Remove from refrigerator 30 minutes before cooking.

Wrap ribs and marinade in heavy-duty foil; place on grill 6 inches (15 cm) from medium-hot coals or on medium-high setting. Cover barbecue and cook, turning often, for about 1 hour or until ribs are tender.

Remove ribs to greased grill, reserving marinade. Lower grill over hot coals or increase heat to high; grill, turning and basting occasionally with marinade, for 10 to 15 minutes or until crisp and brown on outside. Pass any remaining sauce with ribs. Makes 4 servings.

Veal

VEAL AND ONION RAGOUT
WITH GREMOLATA GARNISH

This delicious stew gains flavor when it's reheated. With buttered fettuccine, crusty bread and a salad of mixed greens, it's elegant enough for company. Gremolata is a mixture of lemon zest, garlic and parsley that is added to osso buco (braised veal shanks) for the last 5 minutes. Here, I've used it as a special garnish for an easy stew.

2 lb	boneless veal	1 kg
	Salt and pepper	
¼ cup	all-purpose flour	50 mL
¼ cup	(approx) olive oil	50 mL
1 tsp	sweet paprika	5 mL
1 cup	*each* dry vermouth and chicken stock	250 mL
1 tsp	crushed dried rosemary	5 mL
Pinch	dried thyme	Pinch
¾ lb	baby carrots, scrubbed	375 g
10 oz	small pearl onions, peeled	328 g
1	pkg (350 g) frozen green peas	1

GREMOLATA GARNISH:

1	clove garlic, minced	1
1 tbsp	chopped fresh parsley	15 mL
1 tsp	coarsely grated lemon rind	5 mL

Trim veal; cut into 2-inch (5 cm) cubes. Sprinkle with salt and pepper to taste; dredge with flour.

In large heavy saucepan (preferably nonstick), heat half of the oil over medium-high heat; brown meat, in batches and adding more oil as needed. Transfer meat to plate; sprinkle with paprika.

Drain fat from pan. Add vermouth and stock; bring to boil, stirring to scrape up any brown bits. Return meat and any accumulated juices to pan; stir in rosemary and thyme. Reduce heat and simmer, covered, for 45 minutes.

Add carrots and onions; simmer for about 15 minutes or until vegetables are tender. (Recipe can be prepared to this point, cooled, covered and refrigerated for up to 2 days or frozen. Reheat before continuing.) Stir in peas; heat through. Taste and adjust seasoning.

GREMOLATA GARNISH: Stir together garlic, parsley and lemon rind; sprinkle over stew. Makes 4 to 6 servings.

VEAL SCALLOPINI WITH CHEESE AND TOMATO

You can stretch this easy dish if extra people come along by just adding more veal. Try it also with chicken, turkey or pork cutlets or scallopini. A vegetarian version can be done with browned eggplant or zucchini. If you don't have homemade tomato sauce on hand, substitute a 14 oz/398 mL can. Serve with buttered noodles or garlic bread and a green salad.

1 1/2 lb	veal cutlets or scallopini (5 to 8)	750 g
2 tbsp	all-purpose flour	25 mL
	Salt and pepper	
3 tbsp	olive oil	50 mL
2 cups	tomato sauce (see page 182)	500 mL
1 1/2 cups	shredded mozzarella cheese (about 6 oz/175 g)	375 mL
1/2 cup	freshly grated Parmesan cheese	125 mL

Dust cutlets with flour, sprinkle with salt and pepper to taste.

In large skillet, heat 2 tbsp (25 mL) of the oil over medium heat; fry cutlets, in batches, for 1 minute on each side or until browned. Remove to plate and keep warm.

Pour off any excess oil in pan; pour in tomato sauce and bring to simmer. Arrange cutlets in one crowded layer on top of sauce, spooning sauce over each piece. Sprinkle with mozzarella and Parmesan; drizzle with remaining olive oil.

Cover tightly and cook over very low heat for 8 minutes or until cheese has melted and meat is tender. Makes 4 to 6 servings.

SPECIAL OCCASION GARLIC ROAST VEAL

This simple garlic-studded roast stays succulent and moist under its coating of butter and mustard. A round roast makes an elegant cut, but an excellent and less expensive substitute is a rolled, boned shoulder.

4 1/2 lb	boneless roast of veal	2 kg
4	cloves garlic, slivered	4
1/4 cup	Dijon mustard	50 mL
1/4 cup	butter, at room temperature	50 mL
1 tsp	crushed dried rosemary	5 mL
	Pepper	
3/4 cup	dry white wine	175 mL
1/2 cup	chicken stock	125 mL
1 tbsp	cornstarch	15 mL

Pierce meat in several places all around roast; insert garlic slivers. Set on rack in shallow roasting pan just large enough to hold it comfortably.
Stir together mustard and butter; spread all over roast. Sprinkle with rosemary and pepper to taste. Pour wine into pan.

Roast, uncovered and basting often in 350°F (180°C) oven for 2 hours and 15 minutes or until meat thermometer registers 150-155°F (65-68°C). Transfer to cutting board; cover loosely with foil and let stand for 20 minutes.

Meanwhile, pour stock into pan; bring to boil on stove top, stirring to scrape up any brown bits. Dissolve cornstarch in 2 tbsp (25 mL) cold water; add to pan and cook, stirring, until smooth and bubbly.

Carve roast into thin slices; arrange on warm platter. Pass sauce in warm sauceboat. Makes 8 servings.

STIR-FRIED LAMB WITH BABY CORN AND SNOW PEAS

If you don't have a can of baby corn on hand, this low-cal and quick supper is also good with crunchy strips of fennel or celery. You can substitute lean beef for the lamb. Serve on hot rice.

1 lb	lean lamb (loin, tenderloin or leg)	500 g
2 tbsp	low-salt soy sauce	25 mL
1 tbsp	*each* dry sherry, lemon juice and minced fresh ginger	15 mL
1	clove garlic, minced	1
½ tsp	pepper	2 mL
2 tbsp	peanut or vegetable oil	25 mL
¼ lb	snow peas, trimmed	125 g
1	sweet red pepper, cut in ¼-inch (5 mm) strips	1
½ tsp	granulated sugar	2 mL
2 tbsp	water	25 mL
1 tsp	cornstarch	5 mL
1	can (14 oz/398 mL) whole baby corn, drained	1

Cut lamb across the grain into ¼-inch (5 mm) thick strips; place in sturdy plastic bag or bowl.

Stir together soy sauce, sherry, lemon juice, ginger, garlic and pepper; pour over lamb. Close bag and squeeze to coat lamb, or stir to coat and cover bowl. Marinate at room temperature for 30 minutes or up to 4 hours in refrigerator.

In wok or large skillet, heat half of the oil over high heat; stir-fry meat for 2 minutes or until no longer pink. With slotted spoon, remove to warm platter and keep warm.

Heat remaining oil over high heat; stir-fry peas and red pepper for 1 minute. Stir in sugar and 1 tbsp (15 mL) of the water. Cover and reduce heat to medium; cook for 30 seconds or until vegetables are tender-crisp.

Stir cornstarch with remaining water. Increase heat to high and return lamb to wok; add corn. Pour cornstarch mixture into pan; cook, stirring constantly, for 1 minute or until liquid is clear and thickened. Serve immediately. Makes 4 servings.

LEMON-TARRAGON ROAST LEG OF LAMB

I have been developing hundreds of lamb recipes over a number of years and still consider it one of my favorite meats. A simple glaze gives a fresh flavor to this succulent roast of lamb. Serve with buttered fiddleheads or asparagus and mashed potatoes.

1	bone-in leg of lamb (about 4 lb/2 kg)	1
1 ¼ tsp	crumbled dried tarragon	6 mL
1 tsp	coarse salt	5 mL
¼ tsp	pepper	1 mL
½ cup	lemon marmalade	125 mL
2 tbsp	lemon juice	25 mL

Place lamb, flat side down, on rack in shallow roasting pan. In small bowl, rub together ¼ tsp (1 mL) of the tarragon, salt and pepper; rub all over leg.

Roast, uncovered, in 450°F (230°C) oven for 10 minutes. Reduce heat to 325°F (160°C); roast for 55 minutes.

Stir together marmalade, remaining tarragon and lemon juice; drizzle some over lamb. Roast, drizzling with marmalade mixture every few minutes until used, for 20 to 25 minutes for rare or until meat thermometer registers 140°F (60°C) and meat is dark brown. Cover loosely with foil and let stand for 15 to 20 minutes before carving. Makes about 8 servings.

WARM LAMB SALAD WITH RATATOUILLE VINAIGRETTE

When I served this warm salad at a dinner party I was giving for a number of my "food" friends, they all wanted the recipe. It's impressive, delicious and easy to make for company because its various components can be made ahead of time. Serve this with lots of crusty Italian or French bread.

1	boneless leg of lamb (about 3 lb/1.5 kg)	1
⅓ cup	olive oil	75 mL
¼ cup	dry red wine	50 mL
2 tbsp	chopped fresh thyme (or 2 tsp/10 mL dried)	25 mL
1 tbsp	anchovy paste	15 mL
3	cloves garlic, crushed	3
¼ tsp	pepper	1 mL
6	small eggplants, preferably Italian (1 lb/500 g total)	6
	Salt	
1 tbsp	chopped fresh parsley	15 mL
¼ cup	balsamic vinegar	50 mL
3 tbsp	tomato paste	50 mL
1	*each* tomato and sweet yellow pepper, finely diced	1
	Arugula or watercress	

Open out lamb and place in shallow glass dish. Combine 2 tbsp (15 mL) of the olive oil, the wine, half of the thyme, the anchovy paste, garlic and pepper; pour over lamb and turn to coat. Cover and refrigerate for at least 4 hours or up to 12 hours.

Meanwhile, trim and thinly slice eggplants. Place in colander and sprinkle lightly with salt; toss and let drain for 30 minutes. Rinse and pat dry; place in greased shallow roasting pan. Sprinkle with parsley and remaining thyme; drizzle with remaining oil. Roast in 450°F (230°C) oven for 25 minutes or until cooked through, stirring once. Transfer to bowl. Whisk together half of the balsamic vinegar and 2 tbsp (25 mL) of the tomato paste. Pour over eggplant and toss to coat. (Refrigerate, covered, if making several hours ahead. Bring to room temperature before serving.)

Reserving marinade, remove lamb and pat dry. Roast, meaty side up, on rack in shallow pan in 450°F (230°C) oven for 1 hour or until meat thermometer registers 140°F (60°C). Transfer to cutting board and tent with foil; let rest for 10 minutes before carving.

Pour marinade and remaining vinegar into roasting pan. Set pan on stove and bring liquid to boil, scraping up any brown bits. Stir in remaining tomato paste (and a tablespoon/15 mL or so of water if too dry), diced tomato and pepper. Remove from heat.

Arrange slices of lamb across centre of platter. Pile eggplant on either side. Place arugula alongside eggplant at ends of platter. Drizzle some of the tomato mixture down centre of meat, passing remainder in sauceboat. Makes 6 to 8 servings.

QUICK LAMB CHOP CURRY

Accompany this fast supper dish with bottled chutney, Carrot Pilaf (page 120), cherry tomatoes and a cucumber salad.

2 tbsp	olive oil	25 mL
1	onion, chopped	1
2	stalks celery, chopped	2
1	large apple, peeled and chopped	1
1	clove garlic, minced	1
½ cup	raisins	125 mL
2 tbsp	curry powder	25 mL
1 cup	beef stock	250 mL
½ cup	tomato sauce	125 mL
1	bay leaf	1
8	loin lamb chops (1 ½ lb/750 g total)	8

In heavy saucepan, heat 4 tsp (20 mL) of the oil over medium heat; cook onion, stirring, for 3 minutes or until softened. Add celery, apple, garlic, raisins and curry powder; cook for 3 minutes. Stir in stock and tomato sauce; add bay leaf. Bring to boil, reduce heat and simmer for 10 minutes. Discard bay leaf.

Meanwhile, slash edges of chops and brush with remaining oil. Grill or broil on greased grill over hot coals or on medium-high setting for 3 to 4 minutes per side for medium-rare or to desired doneness. Arrange on plates and pour sauce over lamb, or serve lamb on sauce. Makes 4 servings.

HONEY MUSTARD LAMB CHOPS

Lamb chops are incredibly delicious and fast to cook. This simple recipe, which includes many of my favorite seasonings with lamb, is best on the barbecue but fares very well under the broiler, too.

8	loin lamb chops	8
2 tbsp	*each* liquid honey and Dijon mustard	25 mL
1	large clove garlic, crushed	1
¹/₂ tsp	*each* dried thyme and rosemary	2 mL

Slash chops at edge. In small bowl, stir together honey, mustard, garlic, thyme and rosemary; spread over both sides of chops. Let stand at room temperature for at least 15 minutes and up to 30 minutes.

Place on greased grill 4 inches (10 cm) above medium-hot coals or on medium-high setting or on greased broiler rack; barbecue or broil for about 5 minutes on each side for rare, turning once and brushing with any marinade. For best flavor, do not overcook. Makes 3 or 4 servings.

EASY BISTRO-STYLE LAMB POT ROAST WITH BEANS

A classic French bistro dish, the combination of beans and lamb is a winner. I've used lima beans here, but white navy or great Northern beans are also good. The pot roast can be prepared ahead and reheated slowly at serving time.

1 lb	dried lima beans	500 g
1	boneless lamb shoulder (2 to 3 lb/1 to 1.5 kg)	1
1 tsp	dried thyme	5 mL
	Salt and pepper	
3	slices smoked side bacon, diced	3
4	carrots, thickly sliced	4
3	onions, coarsely chopped	3
2	stalks celery, sliced	2
1 cup	*each* dry white wine and chicken stock or 2 cups (500 mL) chicken stock	250 mL
2 tbsp	tomato paste	25 mL
¹/₄ cup	chopped fresh parsley	50 mL
2	cloves garlic, minced	2
2	bay leaves	2

Sort and rinse beans. Cover with three times their volume of cold water; let soak overnight in refrigerator. (Or cover with three times their volume of cold water and bring to boil; boil for 2 minutes. Cover and let stand for 1 hour.) Drain and set aside.

Sprinkle lamb with some of the thyme, and salt and pepper to taste. Roll up and tie at intervals with twine to make compact roast.

In large saucepan, cook bacon over medium-high heat until crisp. Remove with slotted spoon and set aside. Add lamb and brown on all sides in drippings. Remove to plate.

In same pan, cook carrots, onions and celery over medium heat for 10 minutes, stirring often. Stir in wine, stock, tomato paste, half of the parsley, garlic, bay leaves and beans; bring to boil.

Place lamb on top; cover and roast in 325°F (160°C) oven for 1½ to 2 hours or until lamb and beans are tender, stirring occasionally and adding more stock if necessary to keep beans covered.

Stir in remaining parsley, reserved bacon, and salt and pepper to taste. Discard bay leaves. Slice lamb. Makes 6 servings.

TARRAGON   SAGE   MINT   THYME   PARSLEY   BASIL

GRILLED LAMB SHANKS—RUNDLES' STYLE

I learned about the goodness of lamb shanks prepared this way from Neil Baxter, chef of Rundles Restaurant in Stratford, Ontario. Lamb shanks are braised ahead of time to a melting tenderness, cooled in their liquid, then grilled over a hot fire. The braising juice then becomes a wonderful sauce to serve with an accompanying pasta. Toss a crisp green salad to go alongside. The shanks are also delicious hot right after they are braised.

2 tbsp	olive oil	25 mL
4	lamb shanks (about 1¾ lb/875 g)	4
1	carrot, diced	1
1	onion, chopped	1
12	cloves garlic (unpeeled)	12
2 cups	beef stock	500 mL
¼ cup	chopped fresh parsley	50 mL
½ tsp	dried thyme	2 mL
1	bay leaf	1
	Salt and pepper	

In large saucepan, heat oil over medium-high heat; brown shanks on all sides. Remove lamb from pan and set aside.

Reduce heat to medium; cook carrot, onion and garlic for 5 minutes, stirring often. Stir in stock, parsley, thyme, bay leaf, and salt and pepper to taste; bring to boil.

Return lamb to pan; cover and cook in 325°F (160°C) oven for 2½ hours, turning meat occasionally. Let cool until steaming stops; cover and refrigerate overnight.

Remove lamb from braising mixture, reserving mixture. Place lamb on greased grill 4 inches (10 cm) from very hot coals or on high setting; grill for 15 minutes without turning. Turn lamb and grill until crust forms on other side and shanks are warmed through.

Meanwhile, heat braising liquid and vegetables; push through sieve and boil for 5 minutes until reduced and thickened. Serve with lamb. Makes 4 servings.

LEMON-HERB GRILLED LEG OF LAMB

One of the most delicious things you'll ever barbecue is lamb. This already-tender meat requires a relatively short time over the coals—just long enough to add a smokiness to its distinct flavor. A boneless leg needs little in the way of a marinade, but this simple one adds a certain interest. Accompany with minted new potatoes, grilled sweet peppers and a cucumber salad.

1	butterflied leg of lamb (about 3 lb/1.5 kg)	1
1/3 cup	lemon juice	75 mL
1/4 cup	vegetable oil	50 mL
1 tsp	dried rosemary	5 mL
1/4 tsp	dried thyme	1 mL
1/4 tsp	pepper	1 mL
2	large cloves garlic, minced	2

Make several slashes in thickest part of meat (on meaty side); place in shallow glass dish. In measuring cup, stir together lemon juice, oil, rosemary, thyme, pepper and garlic; pour over lamb. Cover and refrigerate at least 2 hours or up to 6 hours. Remove from refrigerator 30 minutes before cooking.

Reserving marinade, place lamb on greased grill 6 inches (15 cm) from medium-hot coals or on medium-high setting; grill for 15 to 20 minutes per side, brushing with marinade and turning once, or until meat thermometer registers 140°F (60°C) for rare. (Alternatively, broil 4 inches/ 10 cm from heat for 12 to 15 minutes per side.)

Transfer to cutting board; cover loosely with foil and let stand for 10 minutes before carving. Makes 6 to 8 servings.

HEARTY LOW-CAL LAMB STEW

When you brown mild, tender trimmed lamb cubes under the broiler, less fat is required and any accumulated fat is drained off, producing a stew high in flavor but low in calories. Serve with crusty country bread and a green salad.

1 1/2 lb	boneless lamb shoulder, trimmed	750 g
2 tbsp	all-purpose flour	25 mL
1/4 tsp	*each* salt and pepper	1 mL
2 cups	beef stock	500 mL
1 tbsp	tomato paste	15 mL
2	cloves garlic, minced	2
1	small sweet red pepper, diced	1
1/2 tsp	dried rosemary	2 mL
6	small potatoes, unpeeled and quartered	6
3	carrots, coarsely diced	3
1 1/2 cups	coarsely diced peeled rutabaga	375 mL
3/4 cup	*each* pearl onions and frozen peas	175 mL

Cut meat into 1 1/2-inch (4 cm) cubes. Broil on broiler rack in single layer for 10 to 15 minutes or until brown on all sides. Remove with slotted spoon to large stove-top and ovenproof casserole or large roasting pan.

Sprinkle meat with flour, salt and pepper; bake, uncovered, in 450°F (230°C) oven for 12 to 15 minutes or until flour browns.

Place over high heat on top of stove. Stir in stock, tomato paste, garlic, red pepper and rosemary; bring to boil, stirring to scrape up any brown bits on bottom of pan. Cover and return to 350°F (180°C) oven for 45 minutes. (Or, simmer on top of stove, stirring often.)

Stir in potatoes, carrots, rutabaga and onions; cover and bake for 1 hour or until vegetables and meat are tender. Stir in peas; bake for 10 minutes or until peas are cooked. Makes 6 servings.

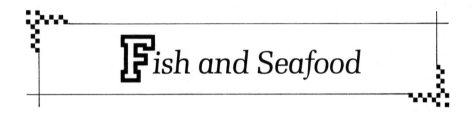

Fish and Seafood

GRILLED COD WITH LEMON-DILL MAYONNAISE

A simple mayonnaise mixture coats fish to keep it moist during barbecuing and then becomes a refreshing accompanying sauce. Use the same marinade for other types of fillets and for fish steaks. Serve with asparagus and oven-fried potatoes. If you can cook the fish right on the grill or in a hinged basket, the flavor is better than placing foil underneath to catch any pieces that might break off. Stand right over the grill and move the fish with two spatulas. Do not overcook.

1 lb	cod fillets	500 g
½ cup	light mayonnaise	125 mL
2 tbsp	plain yogurt	25 mL
1 tsp	grated lemon rind	5 mL
2 tbsp	fresh lemon juice	25 mL
1 tsp	dried dillweed	5 mL
¼ tsp	pepper	1 mL

Pat fish very dry and place in shallow dish. Stir together mayonnaise, yogurt, lemon rind, lemon juice, dillweed and pepper. Using about one-third of the mixture, generously brush on all sides of fish.

Place fish on clean greased grill 4 inches (10 cm) from hot coals or on high setting; grill for about 5 minutes or until fish flakes easily when tested with fork, turning thicker pieces. (Alternatively, broil 3½ inches/ 9 cm from heat.) Serve with remaining mayonnaise mixture. Makes 3 or 4 servings.

MARVELLOUS MUSSELS

Plain steamed mussels are a Friday night treat that's simple and cheap when you want something special for your family or an easy entertaining dish. Accompany with French bread and spoons so that everyone can enjoy the broth after the mussels are gone.

4 lb	mussels	2 kg
1 cup	dry white wine or chicken stock	250 mL
½ cup	chopped shallots, leeks or onions	125 mL
½ cup	*each* diced celery, carrots and chopped fresh parsley	125 mL
1	bay leaf	1
	Salt and pepper	
2 tbsp	butter	25 mL

With stiff brush, scrub mussels under cold running water. Remove any beards by pulling up toward rounded end of shell, or cutting it off. Discard any mussels that do not close after firmly tapping.

In large heavy saucepan, combine wine, shallots, celery, carrots, half of the parsley and bay leaf; bring to simmer. Add mussels; cover and simmer over medium heat for 4 to 7 minutes or until shells open and meat is loosened. Discard any mussels that do not open. Discard bay leaf.

Sprinkle with remaining parsley; season with salt and pepper to taste. Dot with butter. Serve in heated wide soup or pasta bowls. Makes 4 servings.

HOT SEAFOOD SALAD

Serve this quick and easy casserole with whole wheat rolls and a salad of orange slices and watercress. Since it makes a delicious company casserole, feel free to double it.

1½ cups	medium shell pasta	375 mL
2½ cups	cooked seafood (crabmeat, lobster, shrimp, scallops or a mixture)	625 mL
1 cup	diced celery	250 mL
¾ cup	*each* coarsely chopped sweet green pepper and finely chopped onion	175 mL
¼ cup	chopped fresh parsley	50 mL
¼ lb	fresh button mushrooms	125 g
¼ cup	toasted slivered almonds	50 mL
1½ cups	coarsely shredded Swiss cheese	375 mL
1 cup	light mayonnaise	250 mL
½ cup	low-fat plain yogurt	125 mL
¼ cup	*each* dry sherry and fresh lemon juice	50 mL
2 tsp	grated lemon rind	10 mL
½ tsp	dry mustard	2 mL
	Salt and pepper	
1 cup	fresh bread crumbs	250 mL
2 tbsp	butter, melted	25 mL

Cook pasta until barely tender; drain well. (There should be about 2 cups/ 500 mL.)

If using canned seafood, rinse thoroughly in cold water and drain well.

In large bowl, combine pasta, seafood, celery, green pepper, onion, parsley, mushrooms, almonds and cheese.

Stir together mayonnaise, yogurt, sherry, lemon juice and rind, mustard, and salt and pepper to taste; blend gently but thoroughly into seafood mixture. Pour into greased 8-cup (2 L) casserole.

Combine crumbs with melted butter; spread evenly over casserole. (Casserole can be prepared to this point, covered and refrigerated for up to 3 hours.) Bake, uncovered, in 350°F (180°C) oven for 30 to 35 minutes or until heated through. Makes 6 servings.

MEDITERRANEAN TOMATO AND FISH STEW

This bright, fresh stew is just right for inexpensive, casual entertaining as well as family meals. If you wish, add a dozen mussels to the stew for the last 3 to 5 minutes. Begin the meal with Mixed Spiced Olives (see page 14), accompany the stew with crusty Italian bread and beer, and follow it with a salad of leaf lettuce, red onion and goat cheese.

2 tbsp	olive oil	25 mL
1	large onion, chopped	1
4	cloves garlic, minced	4
1	sweet pepper (green, red or yellow), diced	1
1	can (28 oz/796 mL) tomatoes (undrained)	1
1	bottle (237 mL) clam juice	1
1/2 tsp	*each* dried thyme and fennel seeds	2 mL
1/4 tsp	*each* pepper and hot pepper flakes	1 mL
2	bay leaves	2
1 1/2 lb	haddock or cod fillets	750 g
1 tbsp	butter	15 mL
1/4 cup	chopped fresh parsley	50 mL
2 tbsp	chopped green onion	25 mL

In large heavy saucepan, heat oil over medium heat; cook onion, garlic and sweet pepper until softened, about 5 minutes.

Add tomatoes, crushing with potato masher. Stir in clam juice, thyme, fennel seeds, pepper, hot pepper flakes and bay leaves; bring to boil. Reduce heat and cook, uncovered and stirring occasionally, for 12 to 15 minutes or until thickened slightly. (Stew can be prepared to this point, cooled and refrigerated for up to 2 days. Bring to simmer before proceeding.)

Cut fish into 2-inch (5 cm) pieces; add to tomato mixture. Cover and cook over medium-low heat for about 5 minutes or until fish flakes easily when tested with fork. Do not stir, but baste with tomato mixture periodically. Discard bay leaves.

Dot with butter. Heat, uncovered, for 1 minute longer. Serve immediately sprinkled with parsley and green onion. Makes 4 to 6 servings.

TERRIFIC TERIYAKI SALMON

Salmon lends itself happily to these oriental flavors. Serve with fluffy rice and steamed spinach or broccoli.

¼ cup	*each* low-salt soy sauce and Japanese rice wine or dry sherry	50 mL
2 tbsp	granulated sugar	25 mL
2	cloves garlic, minced	2
1 tbsp	minced fresh ginger	15 mL
½ tsp	pepper	2 mL
4	salmon steaks	4
	Thin strips peeled cucumber	

Stir together soy sauce, rice wine, sugar, garlic, ginger and pepper until sugar is dissolved.

Place salmon in shallow glass dish; pour on marinade. Cover and let stand in refrigerator for at least 2 hours and no more than 4 hours, turning occasionally.

Remove fish from marinade, pouring marinade into small saucepan; bring to boil and boil for 3 minutes.

Meanwhile, place salmon on greased broiler rack or barbecue grill 4 inches (10 cm) from heat or above medium-hot coals or on medium-high setting; cook, turning once and brushing with hot marinade, until fish flakes easily when tested with fork, 3 to 5 minutes per side.

Serve hot garnished with cucumber strips and drizzled with any remaining marinade. Makes 4 servings.

LIME-GRILLED SALMON

An easy marinade and quick grilling produce juicy, flavorful fish without adding a great deal of fat. Try the same marinade for other fish steaks and fillets, but grill fillets for less time.

4	salmon steaks	4
1 tsp	grated lime rind	5 mL
¼ cup	fresh lime juice	50 mL
1 tbsp	vegetable oil	15 mL
1	clove garlic, minced	1
¼ tsp	hot pepper flakes	1 mL
Pinch	dried oregano	Pinch
	Fresh Tomato-Cucumber Salsa (see page 180)	

Pat steaks dry and place in shallow glass dish.

Stir together lime rind and juice, oil, garlic, hot pepper flakes and oregano; pour over salmon. Cover and refrigerate for 1 hour.

Reserving marinade, place steaks on greased grill 4 inches (10 cm) above medium-hot coals or on medium-high setting (or under broiler); cook for 5 to 6 minutes per side, turning once with spatula and basting with marinade or until fish flakes easily when tested with fork. Serve with Fresh Tomato Cucumber Salsa. Makes 4 servings.

OLD-FASHIONED SALMON LOAF

When you think there's nothing in the house for supper, remember that a couple of cans of salmon from the cupboard make a quick and nutritious loaf. If you wish, accompany with a sauce made with ¹/₂ cup (125 mL) plain yogurt or Remarkable Low-Fat Cream (see page 185) and 2 table-spoons (25 mL) chopped fresh dill. Round off the menu with baked potatoes, a crunchy cucumber salad and steamy glazed carrots. Slices of cold salmon loaf make a great salad with greens.

1¹/₂ cups	cracker crumbs (about 36 soda crackers)	375 mL
¹/₂ cup	milk	125 mL
2	cans (each 7.5 oz/213 g) salmon	2
¹/₄ cup	finely diced celery	50 mL
2	eggs, lightly beaten	2
2 tbsp	fresh lemon juice	25 mL
¹/₄ tsp	*each* salt, pepper and paprika	1 mL
Pinch	cayenne pepper	Pinch

In large bowl, soak crumbs in milk for 5 minutes. Stir in salmon with its juice, mashing to crush bones and flake salmon. Stir in celery, eggs, lemon juice, salt, pepper, paprika and cayenne.

Pack firmly into greased 9- × 5-inch (2 L) loaf pan; set pan in bigger pan of hot water. Bake in 350°F (180°C) oven for 40 minutes or until golden on top. Cover loosely with foil and let stand for 5 minutes before slicing. Makes 4 servings.

CRUNCHY OVEN-FRIED HADDOCK

Everyone loves crunchy deep-fried battered fish. This is an oven-baked low-fat version the kids are sure to enjoy. Bake a sheet of potato slices alongside and accompany with green peas and raw carrot sticks.

1 lb	haddock fillets (or other lean white fish)	500 g
	Salt, pepper and paprika	
	All-purpose flour	
2 cups	cornflakes	500 mL
1	egg, beaten	1
1 tbsp	vegetable oil	15 mL

Cut fillets into serving size pieces. Sprinkle lightly with salt, pepper and paprika. Dust lightly with flour.

Place cornflakes in sturdy plastic bag and roll gently with rolling pin to crush finely. In shallow bowl, beat egg with oil.

Dip each fish piece into egg mixture; coat evenly with cornflake crumbs, pressing firmly to make crumbs adhere. Place on well-greased baking sheet. (Recipe can be prepared to this point, covered and refriger-ated for up to 6 hours.)

Drizzle fish with oil; bake, uncovered, in 450°F (230°C) oven for 6 minutes. Turn and bake for 2 to 3 minutes longer or until crispy and fish flakes easily when tested with fork. Makes 3 or 4 servings.

SAUCY SPINACH AND TUNA CASSEROLE

This easy, low-cost family supper has lots of taste appeal. Enjoy it with crusty bread and a green salad.

2 tbsp	olive or vegetable oil	25 mL
1	onion, sliced	1
1	clove garlic, minced	1
1	can (19 oz/540 mL) tomatoes (undrained)	1
1 cup	water	250 mL
1	can (7 1/2 oz/213 mL) tomato sauce	1
1/2 tsp	*each* dried basil, granulated sugar and salt	2 mL
1/4 tsp	pepper	1 mL
1/4 lb	medium egg noodles	125 g
1	pkg (10 oz/284 g) fresh spinach, rinsed	1
2	cans (each 6 1/2 oz/184 g) tuna	2
1/2 cup	freshly grated Parmesan cheese	125 mL

In large saucepan, heat oil over medium heat; cook onion and garlic until softened, about 5 minutes.

Stir in tomatoes, breaking up with back of spoon; stir in water, tomato sauce, basil, sugar, salt and pepper; simmer, uncovered, for 15 minutes or until thickened. Taste and adjust seasoning.

Add noodles and wet spinach leaves; return to simmer. Cook, making sure noodles are immersed, for 15 to 20 minutes or until noodles are tender but firm.

Drain tuna and break into large chunks; add to tomato mixture. Transfer to shallow 6-cup (1.5 L) casserole; sprinkle with cheese. (Casserole can be prepared to this point, covered and refrigerated for up to 8 hours. Remove from refrigerator 30 minutes before cooking.) Bake in 375°F (190°C) oven for 20 to 25 minutes or until hot and bubbly. Makes 4 to 6 servings.

Egg Dishes, Beans and Pizzas

COLORFUL HARVEST FRITTATA

This quick meatless main course is lightened with a couple of extra egg whites. Serve with chili sauce and toast triangles for a quick lunch, brunch or light supper.

4	eggs	4
2	egg whites	2
1/2 tsp	salt	2 mL
Pinch	pepper	Pinch
1 tbsp	*each* butter and vegetable oil	15 mL
1	*each* onion and small zucchini, sliced	1
Half	sweet red pepper, diced	Half
1	clove garlic, minced	1
1 1/2 cups	cooked corn kernels, cut from cob (or 12 oz/341 mL can, well drained)	375 mL
1/2 tsp	dried basil	2 mL
1 1/2 cups	shredded Swiss cheese	375 mL

In bowl, whisk together eggs, egg whites, salt and pepper; set aside.

In large heavy ovenproof skillet, melt butter with oil over medium heat; cook onion and zucchini for 6 to 7 minutes or until light brown. Add red pepper and garlic; cook for 4 minutes or until softened. Stir in corn and basil. Remove from heat.

Spread mixture evenly over bottom of skillet; pour egg mixture over top. Cook over medium heat for 1 minute; sprinkle with cheese. Bake in 400°F (200°C) oven for 15 to 20 minutes or until golden brown and set. Cut into wedges to serve. Makes 3 or 4 servings.

LIGHT EGGS BENEDICT

Prosciutto and a butterless Hollandaise makes a lighter version of the classic brunch dish.

4	English muffins or slices French bread	4
2 tbsp	unsalted butter	25 mL
¼ lb	prosciutto ham slivered or sliced	125 g
8	poached eggs	8

LIGHT HOLLANDAISE SAUCE:

3	eggs	3
3 tbsp	fresh lemon juice	50 mL
¼ cup	hot water	50 mL
¼ tsp	white pepper	1 mL
Dash	hot pepper sauce	Dash

LIGHT HOLLANDAISE SAUCE: In large bowl, whisk together eggs, lemon juice and hot water. Place over pan of simmering, not boiling, water; whisk until fluffy and thickened, 3 to 4 minutes.

Whisk in pepper and hot pepper sauce; cover and keep warm over hot water for up to 30 minutes.

Meanwhile, split muffins; toast and place on hot plates. Keep warm.

In small skillet, melt butter; sauté prosciutto just until heated through. Place on top of muffins; top each with poached egg. Spoon sauce over. Makes 4 servings.

INCREDIBLY EASY HAM AND CHEESE STRATA

When I have houseguests, I always enjoy serving a one-dish breakfast that needs no last-minute attention.

8	slices firm white homemade-style bread	8
2 tsp	Dijon mustard	10 mL
¼ cup	butter, melted	50 mL
8	slices Black Forest ham, slivered	8
1 cup	shredded mild Cheddar or Swiss cheese	250 mL

¹/₄ cup	chopped fresh parsley	50 mL
3	eggs	3
¹/₂ tsp	salt	2 mL
1¹/₂ cups	milk	375 mL
¹/₂ cup	sour cream	125 mL
Dash	hot pepper sauce	Dash
2 tbsp	butter	25 mL

Remove crusts from bread; diagonally cut each slice in half. Spread each with mustard; dip one side in melted butter.

Arrange half of the slices, butter side down, in ungreased 13- x 9-inch (3.5 L) baking dish. Sprinkle evenly with half of the ham, cheese and parsley. Top with remaining bread, butter side up; repeat with remaining ham, cheese and parsley.

In bowl, beat together eggs, salt, milk, sour cream and hot pepper sauce; pour evenly over strata. Dot with butter. Cover with foil and refrigerate overnight.

Bake, covered, in 350°F (180°C) oven for 30 minutes; uncover and bake for about 10 minutes longer or until puffed and golden. Let stand for 5 minutes before cutting. Makes 8 servings.

EGGLESS BREAD AND CHEESE STRATA BAKE

Refrigerate this dish overnight for flavors to mingle and serve as a quick luncheon.

¹/₄ cup	butter	50 mL
1	clove garlic, minced	1
6	slices (1 inch/2.5 cm thick) French bread (or 12 slices baguette)	6
6	dill pickles, thinly sliced	6
6	thin slices cooked ham	6
2 cups	shredded Swiss cheese (¹/₂ lb/250 g)	500 mL
¹/₂ cup	chicken stock	125 mL
	Pepper	

In small bowl, cream together butter and garlic; spread on both sides of bread slices.

Line bottom of 13- x 9-inch (3.5 L) baking dish with single layer of bread slices. Arrange pickles on bread; top each with 1 slice of ham. Combine cheese and stock; spread evenly over top. Cover and refrigerate overnight. Remove from refrigerator 30 minutes before cooking.

Bake, uncovered, in 350°F (180°C) oven for 15 to 20 minutes or until cheese is melted and edges of bread start to brown. If desired, broil for a few minutes to brown bread more. Sprinkle with pepper to taste. Serve immediately. Makes 6 servings.

DRIED BEANS

Had it not been for dried beans and peas, many of our early settlers would have starved during the long Canadian winters. The Indians first introduced beans to French settlers, who quickly made them a staple part of their diet. They especially liked them as a convenience food for sailing and thus white dried beans got the nickname "navy."

Now beans and lentils are "chic" and appear in all the best restaurants. But they have a lot more going for them than fashion. Containing no preservatives or chemicals, they're real and nutritious food that's always available. They're also a cheap source of protein, which is a complete protein if combined with grains. And it's protein without the amount of fat that animal sources contain.

Dried beans are, of course, more economical than canned. But I did discover that canned beans of various varieties are handy to have in the cupboard for instant nutrition. Except for kidney beans, they're better drained and rinsed.

To rehydrate dried beans, pick them over and rinse in a sieve under cold, running water. Then, using 3 parts water to 1 part beans, either let them sit overnight in the refrigerator or bring them to a full boil for 2 minutes, removing them from the heat and letting them stand, covered, for 1 hour. Drain, add fresh water and cook for 40 to 60 minutes depending on type of bean and recipe. Whatever method of cooking you choose, be sure to bring beans to a full boil at some point in their cooking.

MAPLE BAKED BEANS

On a chilly day, I often get hungry for a big pot of old-fashioned baked beans. They make such a satisfying but easy supper with chili sauce. I stick some slices of side pork in a pan to bake alongside for an hour until it's crisp and brown; then I add a creamy cabbage salad to the meal.

2 cups	dried white navy (pea) beans (1 lb/500 g)	500 mL
1½ tsp	dry mustard	7 mL
1 tsp	*each* salt and pepper	5 mL
1	onion, minced	1
¼ lb	salt pork	125 mL
¾ cup	maple syrup (preferably dark cooking)	175 mL
2 tbsp	molasses	25 mL

Sort and rinse beans. In medium saucepan, cover beans with 6 cups

(1.5 L) cold water and let soak overnight in refrigerator. (Or, cover with water and bring to boil; boil for 2 minutes. Remove from heat; cover and let stand for 1 hour.)

Drain beans; cover again with cold water and bring to boil; reduce heat and simmer, covered, for 40 minutes.

Reserving liquid, drain and transfer beans to bean pot or heavy casserole. Stir in mustard, salt, pepper and onion. Rinse salt pork; dice and add to beans. Stir in enough reserved cooking liquid to reach top of beans.

Cover and bake in 350°F (180°C) oven for about 5 hours or until beans are very tender, stirring occasionally and adding more cooking liquid or water if necessary to ensure beans do not become too dry.

One hour before serving, uncover to let beans brown. Half an hour before serving, stir in maple syrup and molasses. Makes 6 servings.

BEAN BURRITOS

These easy burrito sandwiches make a terrific carry-away lunch. Enjoy them cold, or microwave at High for 35 seconds or until heated through and serve with sour cream if you wish. Look for refried beans in the grocery store with the other Mexican ingredients.

4 tsp	vegetable oil	20 mL
1/2 cup	chopped onion	125 mL
2	cloves garlic, minced	2
Half	sweet green or red pepper, diced	Half
1	can (455 mL) refried beans	1
1 tbsp	chopped pickled or fresh jalapeño pepper	15 mL
1/4 tsp	*each* ground cumin and dried oregano	1 mL
4	flour tortillas (9 or 10 inch/23 or 25 cm)	4
1 cup	shredded Cheddar or skim milk mozzarella cheese	250 mL
2	green onions, chopped	2

In large skillet, heat oil over medium heat; cook onion, garlic and green pepper until tender but not browned, about 5 minutes.

Stir in beans, jalapeño pepper, cumin and oregano; cook for about 2 minutes or until beans are heated through and flavors blended.

Spoon about 1/2 cup (125 mL) of the filling just below centre of each tortilla; sprinkle with one-quarter of the cheese and green onion. Fold lower edge over filling, then fold in sides and roll up. (Burritos can be wrapped in plastic and refrigerated for up to 3 days.) Makes 4 servings.

THE STAR'S QUICK CASSOULET

A few years ago, my husband and I spent a little time at a farm near Bergerac, France, an area famous for its preserved goose (confit) and the casserole that farm wives make with confit and dried beans, along with a number of other meats like lamb and pork. Of course, I came home from that visit inspired to make a true cassoulet, which I did for the following New Year's Eve. The dish was wonderful, but I had worked four days on it.

When Marion Kane, The Toronto Star Food Editor, asked me to develop a recipe for a cheap and cheerful casserole for an article on recession-proof recipes, I came up with the following updated easy cassoulet. Marion subsequently chose it as one of her favorite recipes of 1990, and referred to it as "a terrific version of the labour-intensive French bistro classic." Thanks Marion.

1 lb	garlic farmer's sausage	500 g
3	chicken thighs (³/₄ lb/375 g)	3
1 tbsp	vegetable oil	15 mL
3	cloves garlic, minced	3
2	onions, coarsely chopped	2
1	can (19 oz/540 mL) tomatoes (undrained), chopped	1
1¹/₄ cups	(approx) chicken stock	300 mL
¹/₂ tsp	dried thyme	2 mL
2	bay leaves	2
	Salt and pepper	
Pinch	*each* granulated sugar and dried savory	Pinch
2	cans (each 19 oz/540 mL) white navy (pea) beans	2
2 cups	fresh bread crumbs	500 mL
¹/₂ cup	finely chopped fresh parsley	125 mL
¹/₄ cup	butter, melted	50 mL

Cut sausage into ¹/₂-inch (1 cm) thick rounds. Remove chicken meat from bones; cut into large chunks.

In large flameproof casserole, brown sausage over medium-high heat for 5 to 7 minutes, adding oil if necessary. With slotted spoon, remove to drain on paper towels. Brown chicken for 5 minutes; remove to drain on towels.

Discard all but 1 tbsp (15 mL) of the drippings; cook garlic and onions, stirring, for 5 minutes. Stir in tomatoes, ¹/₂ cup (125 mL) of the stock, thyme, bay leaves, salt and pepper to taste, sugar and savory.

Return sausage and chicken to pot; bring to boil. Reduce heat and simmer, uncovered, for 30 minutes or until nearly all moisture has evaporated, stirring often. Discard bay leaves.

Drain and rinse beans; stir into tomato mixture. Add enough of the remaining chicken stock to make very moist, but not soupy mixture.

Toss together bread crumbs, parsley and melted butter; sprinkle over casserole. Bake, uncovered, in 350°F (180°C) oven for about 45 minutes or until golden-brown crust has formed and casserole is bubbly.

(Cassoulet can be cooled, covered and refrigerated up to 2 days. Let stand for 30 minutes at room temperature before reheating.) Makes 4 to 6 servings.

PIZZA DOUGH

You can make this ahead to have ready and waiting for when the urge to have pizza hits. The dough can be rolled out, wrapped and refrigerated on pan for up to 8 hours or frozen. Or wrap the risen dough in plastic wrap, then in plastic bag. Thaw before rolling out.

Pinch	granulated sugar	Pinch
2/3 cup	warm water	150 mL
2 tsp	active dry yeast	10 mL
2 tbsp	vegetable oil	25 mL
1 1/2 cups	(approx) all-purpose flour	375 mL
1/2 tsp	salt	2 mL

In small bowl, combine sugar and water; sprinkle with yeast and let stand in warm place until bubbly and doubled in volume, about 5 minutes. Stir in oil.

In large bowl, mix together flour and salt. Make well in centre of flour mixture; pour in yeast mixture. With fork, gradually blend together flour and yeast mixtures to form dough. With floured hands gather into a ball.

Turn out onto lightly floured surface; knead for about 5 minutes, adding just enough extra flour to make soft, slightly sticky dough. Place in greased bowl, turning once to grease all over. Cover bowl with greased waxed paper and tea towel. Let stand in warm draft-free place until tripled in size, 1 1/2 to 3 hours.

Punch down dough and form into ball. Turn out onto lightly floured surface and cover with bowl; let stand for 10 minutes. Roll out dough into 12-inch (30 cm) circle. Makes one 12-inch (30 cm) crust. Recipe can be doubled.

ASPARAGUS AND PROSCIUTTO PIZZA WITH GRUYERE

Celebrate asparagus season by teaming the fresh stalks with these two happy combinations.

1/2 lb	asparagus	250 g
2 tbsp	olive oil	25 mL
	Pizza Dough	
1/2 tsp	dried oregano	2 mL
1/4 tsp	pepper	1 mL
2 cups	shredded Gruyère cheese	500 mL
6 oz	thinly sliced prosciutto ham, cut into 1-inch (2.5 cm) strips	175 g

Trim asparagus; arrange in single layer on 12-inch (30 cm) pizza pan. Drizzle with 2 tsp (10 mL) of the oil; roast in 500°F (260°C) oven for 4 minutes. Cut each stalk into 3 diagonal pieces; set aside.

Place dough on same pan; brush lightly with some of the remaining oil. Sprinkle with oregano, pepper and two-thirds of the cheese.

Arrange asparagus and prosciutto on top; sprinkle with remaining cheese. Drizzle with remaining oil. Bake in 500°F (260°C) oven for 12 to 15 minutes or until crust is golden brown. Makes 2 or 3 servings.

FRIDAY NIGHT FAMILY PIZZA

This quick and easy pizza is a fun way to celebrate the week's end. For extra convenience, you can pick up a good prepared pizza shell and use a can of pizza sauce.

¾ lb	Italian sausage	375 g
3 tbsp	olive oil	50 mL
½ lb	mushrooms, sliced	250 g
Half	sweet green pepper, cut in chunks	Half
1	12-inch (30 cm) round pizza dough (see page 99)	1
½ lb	mozzarella cheese, shredded	250 g
½ tsp	dried Italian herb seasoning	2 mL
Pinch	hot pepper flakes	Pinch
1	can (7½ oz/213 mL) pizza sauce	1

Cut sausage into ½-inch (1 cm) thick rounds. In large skillet, brown sausage over medium heat, stirring often and adding some oil if needed, until no longer pink, about 8 minutes. Add mushrooms for the last 5 minutes. Stir in green pepper; cook for 1 minute.

Meanwhile, grease 12-inch (30 cm) pizza pan with oil; top with pizza dough. Brush with some of the oil; sprinkle with half of the cheese. Stir Italian herb seasoning and hot pepper flakes into pizza sauce; spread over dough.

Drain off fat from sausage mixture; arrange on sauce. Sprinkle with remaining cheese; drizzle with remaining oil. Bake near bottom of 500°F (260°C) oven for about 15 minutes or until crust is golden brown. Makes 4 servings.

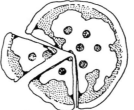

PROSCIUTTO, ROASTED GARLIC AND RED PEPPER PIZZA

This flavorful pizza is well worth a trip to your local Italian grocery store for the prosciutto, cheese and roasted peppers. The garlic can be roasted ahead of time when you happen to have the oven on for something else.

2	heads garlic	2
¼ cup	olive oil	50 mL
1 tsp	dried thyme	5 mL
	Pizza Dough (see page 99)	
3 cups	shredded mozzarella or fontina cheese or combination	750 mL
1	jar (125 mL) roasted red peppers, drained and sliced	1
2 oz	thinly sliced prosciutto ham, cut into 1-inch (2.5 cm) strips	50 g

Cut top from garlic just to expose top of cloves; place on greased foil. Drizzle with dash of the olive oil; sprinkle with pinch of the thyme. Fold up foil to enclose garlic; bake in 350°F (180°C) oven for 1½ hours. Let cool and press garlic out of skins.

Place dough on greased 12-inch (30 cm) pizza pan. Brush lightly with some of the oil; sprinkle with two-thirds of the cheese. Dot with garlic; sprinkle with remaining thyme.

Arrange peppers and prosciutto on top; sprinkle with remaining mozzarella. Drizzle with remaining oil. Bake in 500°F (260°C) oven for 12 to 15 minutes or until crust is golden brown. Makes 2 or 3 main-course servings.

PEAR AND BRIE PIZZA WITH CARAMELIZED RED ONIONS ON WALNUT CRUST

Pears and brie complement each other so well that I couldn't resist combining them with tart caramelized onions in a pizza. The dough gets a new toasted walnut flavor by kneading in a few of the nuts just after you punch it down to let stand for 10 minutes.

1	pear (unpeeled)	1
2 tsp	butter	10 mL
½ tsp	dried thyme	2 mL
	Pepper	
1 tbsp	(approx) olive oil	15 mL
1	small red onion, thinly sliced in rings	1
1½ tsp	red wine vinegar	7 mL
½ tsp	salt	2 mL
Pinch	granulated sugar	Pinch
	Pizza Dough (see page 99)	
¼ cup	finely chopped toasted walnuts	50 mL
6 oz	Brie cheese (unpeeled)	175 g

Core and slice pear. In skillet, melt butter over medium heat; cook pear for 5 minutes. Sprinkle with thyme and generously with pepper; remove to bowl with slotted spoon.

In same skillet, heat oil over low heat; cook onion, covered, for 5 minutes. Stir in vinegar, salt and sugar; cover and cook for 5 minutes.

Meanwhile, punch down dough; knead in walnuts and form into ball. Turn out onto lightly floured surface and cover with bowl; let stand for 10 minutes. Press into 12-inch (30 cm) pizza pan; brush lightly with more of the oil. Scatter evenly with onion and pear mixtures.

Cut cheese (including rind) into ½-inch (1 cm) cubes. Scatter over pizza. Drizzle with any juice from skillet. Bake in 500°F (260°C) oven for 12 to 15 minutes or until crust is golden brown. Makes 2 or 3 main-course servings.

SAGE-ONION FOCACCIA

This wonderful Italian flatbread is a tribute to my father, who loved Spanish onion sandwiches. Serve as an appetizer to a light dinner or an accompaniment to a main-course soup. Prepare the pizza dough just to the point where you punch down dough, then use in this recipe.

1	very small Spanish onion, thinly sliced	1
1/4 cup	white vinegar	50 mL
2 tbsp	liquid honey	25 mL
	Pizza Dough (see page 99)	
3/4 cup	freshly grated Parmesan cheese	175 mL
	Cornmeal	
1 tsp	crumbled dried sage	5 mL
2 tbsp	vegetable oil	25 mL

In small bowl, combine onion, vinegar and honey; let stand for at least 30 minutes and no longer than 1 hour, stirring occasionally.

Punch down dough; blend in 1/4 cup (50 mL) of the cheese and form into ball. Turn out onto lightly floured surface and cover with bowl; let stand for 10 minutes. Roll out into 10-inch (25 cm) circle. Transfer to baking sheet lightly sprinkled with cornmeal.

Make indentations all over top with fingertips. Drain onion and scatter over dough. Sprinkle with remaining cheese, then sage and oil.

Sprinkle all over with 1 tsp (5 mL) cold water; bake in 425°F (220°C) oven for 20 to 25 minutes or until golden. Cut into wedges to serve warm. Makes 4 servings.

TUNA AND FRESH TOMATO PIZZAS

These little pizzas are made with ingredients you probably already have on hand. You can make your own pizza dough rounds or buy them; they are often available at bakeries and supermarkets.

	Cornmeal	
4	7-inch (18 cm) pizza dough rounds	4
1/4 cup	olive oil	50 mL
3/4 lb	mozzarella cheese, thinly sliced	375 g
1 tsp	dried thyme	5 mL
2	cloves garlic, minced	2
2	cans (each 6 1/2 oz/184 g) tuna, drained and flaked	2
2	tomatoes, thinly sliced	2
1/4 cup	freshly grated Parmesan cheese	50 mL

Sprinkle 2 baking sheets with cornmeal; place pizza rounds on top. Brush rounds with half of the oil.

Divide mozzarella among pizza rounds, leaving small border all around; sprinkle thyme and garlic over cheese.

Arrange tuna and tomato on pizzas; sprinkle with Parmesan. Drizzle with remaining oil. Bake in lower third of 500°F (260°C) oven for 10 to 15 minutes or until bottoms are golden brown. Makes 4 servings.

Pasta Presto

PASTA

Fresh will take as little as 2 minutes to cook; dried will take 7 to 10 minutes or more. Use a large pot with about 16 cups (4 L) of cold, salted water for every pound (500 g) pasta, but fill pot no more than two-thirds full of water.

Bring to full boil before adding pasta a bit at a time. Cover to bring back to boil, but remove lid as soon as you hear rolling boil again. Start timing and stir often, preferably with a wooden fork. Pasta is cooked when it's al dente, tender but still firm to the bite and not mushy.

Save energy and cut back on clean-up time, too, by trying to use the same bowl or pot for more than one purpose: for example, cook a vegetable with the pasta.

SPICY PENNE WITH CLAMS AND FRESH TOMATOES

Canned fish or seafood is always handy to have in the cupboard for quick and easy pasta sauces like this one. Perfect for tomato season.

4	tomatoes, seeded and diced (1 ½ lb/750 g)	4
1	clove garlic, minced	1
2 tbsp	chopped fresh parsley	25 mL
1 tbsp	anchovy paste	15 mL
1 tbsp	chopped fresh oregano (or 1 tsp/5 mL) dried	15 mL
½ tsp	salt	2 mL
¼ tsp	*each* pepper and hot pepper flakes	1 mL
¼ cup	olive oil	50 mL
1	can (5 oz/142g) baby clams, drained and rinsed	1
¾ lb	penne or linguine	375 g
	Freshly grated Parmesan cheese	

In large bowl, stir together tomatoes, garlic, parsley, anchovy paste, oregano, salt, pepper, hot pepper flakes and oil; stir in clams.

In large pot of boiling salted water, cook pasta until *al dente* (tender but firm). Drain well and toss with tomato-clam mixture. Serve immediately with Parmesan cheese. Makes 4 servings.

JIFFY MAC AND CHEESE

This easy version of old-fashioned macaroni and cheese will be ready in a matter of minutes. Serve with warm stewed tomatoes and toast for instant comfort at lunch or dinner.

4 cups	corkscrew pasta (³/₄ lb/375 g)	1 L
2 tbsp	butter	25 mL
1 tbsp	Dijon mustard	15 mL
¹/₂ tsp	*each* pepper and Worcestershire sauce	2 mL
¹/₄ tsp	salt	1 mL
2 cups	shredded old Cheddar cheese	500 mL
¹/₄ cup	light sour cream	50 mL

In large pot of boiling salted water, cook pasta until tender but firm. Drain in colander.

In pasta pot, melt butter over low heat; stir in mustard, pepper, Worcestershire sauce and salt. Return pasta to pot and toss to coat.

Remove from heat. Add cheese and sour cream; toss to combine. Let cheese melt and serve. Makes 3 or 4 servings.

OLD-FASHIONED BAKED MACARONI AND CHEESE WITH TOMATOES

Occasionally, I get a real craving for a big dish of macaroni and cheese just like my mother used to bake. You can divide this recipe between two 6-cup (1.5 L) casserole dishes and reduce the baking time to 35 minutes. Freeze the second one to have on hand when the craving strikes again.

¹/₂ lb	elbow macaroni (2 cups/500 mL)	250 g
¹/₂ lb	Cheddar cheese, preferably old	250 g
1	can (28 oz/796 mL) tomatoes	1
1 tsp	*each* granulated sugar and Worcestershire sauce	5 mL
¹/₂ tsp	*each* dried summer savory and salt	2 mL
¹/₄ tsp	pepper	1 mL
2	eggs, beaten	2
1 cup	milk	250 mL

In large pot of boiling salted water, cook macaroni until just tender, about 8 minutes; do not overcook. Drain well and transfer to well-buttered 12-cup (3 L) casserole.

Meanwhile, shred half of the cheese; set aside. Thinly slice remainder; set aside.

Drain ³/₄ cup (175 mL) of the juice from tomatoes and reserve for another use. Pour tomatoes and remaining juice into bowl; chop tomatoes. Stir in shredded cheese, sugar, Worcestershire sauce, savory, salt and pepper; pour over macaroni and mix well. Top with cheese slices.

In small bowl, blend eggs with milk; pour over cheese-covered macaroni but do not stir. Bake in 350°F (180°C) oven for 40 to 50 minutes or until top is golden brown. Makes 6 to 8 servings.

FETTUCCINE WITH CREAMY ROSEMARY SHRIMP

Serve this quick, delicious main course as a celebration meal with hot crusty rolls and a green salad.

1 lb	fettuccine	500 g
2 tbsp	butter	25 mL
2 tbsp	chopped green onion	25 mL
1 lb	shrimp, peeled and deveined	500 g
1/2 cup	whipping cream	125 mL
2 tsp	minced fresh parsley	10 mL
2 tsp	minced fresh rosemary (or 1/2 tsp/2 mL dried)	10 mL
1/4 cup	dry vermouth	50 mL

In large pot of boiling salted water, cook pasta until tender but firm; drain well.

Meanwhile, in skillet, melt butter over low heat; cook green onion until softened, about 3 minutes. Add shrimp and increase heat to medium-low; cook for 5 minutes, turning until just pink all over.

Reduce heat to low; stir in cream, parsley and rosemary. Increase heat to medium and bring to boil, stirring often. Add vermouth and mix gently. Serve immediately on hot pasta. Makes 4 servings.

QUICK HOT OR COLD PASTA WITH FRESH TOMATO SAUCE

The uncooked tomato sauce has to be made ahead for flavors to mingle. Serve on hot pasta or as a cold pasta salad with tossed greens and crusty rolls.

4	large ripe tomatoes (about 2 lb/1 kg)	4
2 cups	julienned cooked smoked ham, turkey or chicken (about 1/2 lb/250 g)	500 mL
2	cloves garlic, minced	2
1/3 cup	chopped fresh basil (or 1 tbsp/15 mL dried)	75 mL
1/3 cup	chopped fresh parsley	75 mL
2 tbsp	chopped fresh oregano (or 1 tsp/5 mL dried)	25 mL
1 tsp	red wine vinegar	5 mL
1/2 tsp	*each* salt and granulated sugar	2 mL
1/4 tsp	pepper	1 mL
6 cups	corkscrew pasta	1.5 L
2 tbsp	olive oil	25 mL
2	small zucchini, shredded	2
	Freshly grated Parmesan cheese	

Peel, seed and chop tomatoes. In bowl, combine tomatoes, ham, garlic, basil, parsley, oregano, vinegar, salt, sugar and pepper. Cover and refrigerate for at least 1 hour or overnight.

In large pot of boiling salted water, cook pasta until tender but firm. Drain well and toss with olive oil, tomato sauce and zucchini. Pass cheese separately. Makes 4 servings.

MONDA ROSENBERG'S EASY SPICY LASAGNA

Monda Rosenberg, my long-time good friend and food editor of Chatelaine *magazine, knows her readers want lots of great taste in food without spending hours in the kitchen. Monda's spicy lasagna is an excellent example of this theory. Accompany with crusty bread and a green salad.*

2 tbsp	vegetable oil	25 mL
2 lb	hot or sweet Italian sausage, casings removed	1 kg
1	can (28 oz/796 mL) meatless spaghetti sauce	1
2	cloves garlic, crushed	2
12	lasagna noodles	12
1 lb	ricotta, drained if necessary	500 g
2	eggs	2
1/2 lb	mozzarella cheese, grated	250 g

In large heavy-bottomed saucepan, heat oil over medium heat; cook sausage, breaking up with fork, until no longer pink. Drain off fat.

Stir in spaghetti sauce and garlic; bring to boil. Cover and reduce heat; simmer for 15 minutes, stirring occasionally.

Meanwhile, cook lasagna noodles according to package directions until tender but firm. Drain and lay flat on clean tea towels.

If not using smooth tub ricotta, whirl with eggs in food processor or blender until fairly smooth. If ricotta is already smooth, just beat eggs and stir in ricotta in bowl.

To assemble, spread 1 cup (250 mL) meat sauce in 13- x 9-inch (3 L) baking dish. Cover with layer of noodles, half of the ricotta mixture, one-third of the remaining meat sauce and one-third of the mozzarella. Repeat layers, ending with noodles, meat sauce and mozzarella. (Recipe can be prepared to this point, covered and refrigerated or frozen. Thaw in refrigerator before proceeding. Remove from refrigerator 30 minutes before cooking.)

Bake, uncovered, in 350°F (180°C) oven for 30 to 45 minutes or until bubbly around edges. Makes 8 servings.

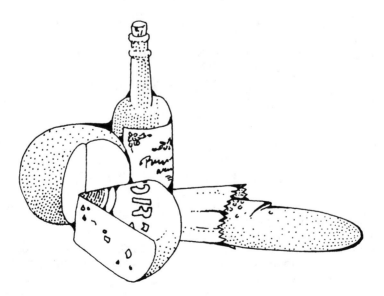

PASTA WITH FLAVORFUL SPINACH PESTO

One of my favorite no-cook sauces is pesto made with fresh basil leaves. However, if your basil crop is not as plentiful as you would like, try this version of pesto, which is especially good with fresh-market bunch spinach. Enjoy with a fresh tomato salad and crusty bread.

4 cups	loosely packed stemmed spinach	1 L
1/2 cup	loosely packed stemmed fresh parsley	125 mL
1/2 cup	(approx) freshly grated Parmesan cheese	125 mL
1/3 cup	coarsley chopped walnuts	75 mL
1/4 cup	olive oil	50 mL
2	cloves garlic	2
	Salt and pepper	
1 lb	pasta	500 g

In food processor or blender, chop spinach and parsley; add cheese, walnuts and oil. With motor running, drop in garlic through feed tube. Season with salt and pepper to taste. (Recipe can be prepared to this point, covered and refrigerated for up to 2 days.)

In large pot of boiling salted water, cook pasta until *al dente* (tender but firm). Reserving 1/4 cup (50 mL) of the cooking water, drain pasta well. Blend hot liquid into purée; toss with hot pasta. Serve immediately with additional cheese. Makes 4 servings.

SHORT-CUT ROTINI WITH BROCCOLI AND CLAMS

Fresh broccoli cooks in less time than it will take the frozen variety to thaw. You can usually buy pre-cut broccoli florets in produce departments for this quick and pretty dish. The recipe is easily divided in half for one person. Freeze the other half can of clams for another night.

1/4 lb	rotini or other pasta (1 1/3 cups/325 mL)	125 g
2 cups	small broccoli florets (1/4 lb/125 g)	500 mL
1 tbsp	*each* butter and olive oil	15 mL
2	cloves garlic, minced	2
Pinch	hot pepper flakes	Pinch
1	can (3.1 oz/87 g) clams (preferably pink)	1
	Pepper	
	Freshly grated Parmesan cheese	

In large pot of boiling salted water, cook rotini for 4 minutes. Add broccoli and cook for 2 minutes or until rotini is tender but firm.

Meanwhile, in large skillet, melt butter with oil over low heat; cook garlic and hot pepper flakes for 3 minutes. Reserving liquid, add clams to skillet and heat through; stir in liquid.

Drain broccoli and pasta well; stir into skillet. Increase heat to high; cook until pasta has absorbed most of the liquid, stirring often, about 4 minutes. Sprinkle generously with pepper. Serve on warmed plates. Sprinkle with lots of cheese and serve immediately. Makes 2 servings.

CHEVRE AND FRESH TOMATO PASTA

The heat of the pasta will bring out the sunny flavor of garden-fresh tomatoes and the creamy goodness of fresh goat cheese. The flavor is still delightful if you substitute a good-quality feta and dried basil to taste. To seed tomatoes, cut them in half crosswise, squeeze gently and help out seeds with end of sharp knife. There's no need to peel them.

2 lb	ripe plum or regular tomatoes, seeded and diced (about 20 plum)	1 kg
¾ cup	coarsely chopped pitted black olives	175 mL
¼ cup	loosely packed slivered fresh basil	50 mL
¼ cup	olive oil	50 mL
1 tbsp	slivered lemon zest (outer rind)	15 mL
1	clove garlic, minced	1
¼ tsp	pepper	1 mL
¾ lb	fresh goat cheese (chèvre) crumbled (about 1½ cups/375 mL)	375 g
½ cup	freshly grated Parmesan cheese	125 mL
4 cups	corkscrew pasta or penne (¾ lb/375 g)	1 L

In large bowl, stir together tomatoes, olives, basil, oil, lemon zest, garlic and pepper; gently stir in goat cheese and Parmesan.

In large pot of boiling salted water, cook pasta until *al dente* (tender but firm). Drain well and add to sauce. Toss and serve immediately. Makes 4 to 6 servings.

TORTELLINI TOSS WITH BROCCOLI AND ROASTED RED PEPPERS

Broccoli florets cook in a colander as you drain the hot pasta over them for an easy and colorful pasta supper. Bottled roasted red peppers are available in most supermarkets.

½ cup	drained bottled roasted red peppers, cut in strips	125 mL
¼ cup	*each* olive oil and chopped fresh parsley	50 mL
¼ cup	(approx) freshly grated Parmesan cheese	50 mL
2	cloves garlic, minced	2
½ tsp	pepper	2 mL
1 lb	tortellini with meat	500 g
4 cups	small broccoli florets	1 L

In large bowl, stir together red peppers, oil, parsley, cheese, garlic and pepper.

In large pot of boiling salted water, cook pasta until *al dente* (tender but firm).

Place broccoli in colander; drain pasta over broccoli. Add to bowl and toss to combine. Serve immediately with more Parmesan cheese. Makes 4 servings.

$\mathbb{S}$imple Sides

When locally-grown produce is fresh and in season, a simple treatment is best. Little needs to be done to dewy-fresh corn or sun-ripe tomatoes right off the vine. Even storage vegetables, like carrots or rutabaga, have such wonderful real flavor that a straightforward preparation is all that's necessary. The important thing to remember is not to overcook any of these good things.

The recipes in this chapter are therefore short, simple and delicious little twists on the accompaniments to main courses with many make-ahead ideas for festive meals with the potato, one of my all-time favorite foods, taking the spotlight.

POTATOES

I find almost no other food as satisfying as a potato. It's such a simple vegetable, but brings great comfort—whether it's baked to steamy softness inside crunchy skin and slathered with yogurt; perfectly mashed with milk and butter; deep-fried to a golden crispness; dressed in a tangy salad; or made into a soothing, creamy soup.

There must be other Canadians who share my love of potatoes, since it is the country's most important vegetable crop, with the Maritimes leading the way in production since potatoes were first cultivated in Port Royal, Nova Scotia, in 1623.

My one big complaint about potatoes is that when we buy them here, we can't tell what kind they are—not like apples that are either Empires, McIntoshes and so on. Some companies are now labeling some potatoes as baking, which at least gives you an idea of what to do with them. As a general rule, without knowing any names for potatoes, you can discover their best use by looking at them. Round, smooth potatoes are best for boiling, scalloped potatoes or salads. Oblong potatoes with a faint criss-cross kind of pattern on the skin usually have the floury texture that's best for baking, deep-frying and mashing.

DO-AHEAD MASHED POTATO CASSEROLE WITH PARSLEY CRUMB TOPPING

I always prepare potatoes in a make-ahead casserole like this for special holiday dinners. It eliminates peeling and mashing potatoes when visiting is more important.

8	potatoes, peeled	8
¼ cup	butter	50 mL
½ lb	cream cheese, in bits	250 g
¾ cup	light sour cream	175 mL
	Salt and pepper	
¼ cup	*each* fine fresh bread crumbs and chopped fresh parsley	50 mL

In saucepan of boiling salted water, cover and cook potatoes for about 30 minutes or until tender. Drain well and return to heat briefly to dry.

Mash potatoes with half of the butter. Add cream cheese, sour cream, and salt and pepper to taste. With electric hand mixer, beat potato mixture until creamy. Spoon into greased 8-cup (2 L) casserole.

Melt remaining butter; stir together with bread crumbs and parsley. Sprinkle evenly over potato mixture. Let cool, cover and refrigerate overnight.

Bake, covered, in 350°F (180°C) oven for 20 minutes. Uncover and bake for 10 minutes longer or until heated through. Makes 8 servings.

LEAN BUT COMFORTABLE COLCANNON

One of the most comforting vegetable dishes ever whipped up, colcannon is a favorite Irish recipe that is topped off with a little pool of melted butter. I've updated an old favorite by removing most of the butter and beating in yogurt, but you'll be glad to know it's still as comfortable as ever.

5	potatoes, peeled	5
Half	small cabbage, coarsely shredded	Half
1	small onion, chopped	1
1 tbsp	butter	15 mL
4	green onions, finely sliced	4
1/2 cup	low-fat yogurt (at room temperature)	125 mL
1/4 tsp	nutmeg	1 mL
	Salt and pepper	

Quarter potatoes. In saucepan of small amount of boiling salted water, cook potatoes for 20 minutes. Add cabbage and onion; cook for about 10 minutes or until potatoes are tender. Drain well in colander.

Meanwhile, in same saucepan, melt butter over medium heat; cook green onions until softened, about 3 minutes. Add potato mixture; mash well.

Whisk in yogurt, nutmeg, and salt and pepper to taste until light and fluffy. Serve immediately. Makes 4 servings.

DILLED NEW-POTATO KABOBS

Tiny new waxy potatoes are on the market before you know it in the spring. One of my favorite ways of enjoying them is to boil them until just tender, then grill them for a few minutes just to reheat and give them a barbecued taste. These are particularly good with grilled fish.

16	small new potatoes (unpeeled)	16
3 tbsp	vegetable oil	50 mL
2 tbsp	finely chopped fresh dill (or 2 tsp/10 mL dried dillweed)	25 mL
1	green onion, minced	1
1/2 tsp	salt	2 mL
Pinch	hot pepper flakes	Pinch

Scrub potatoes. In saucepan of boiling salted water, cook potatoes until barely tender, about 10 minutes; drain well.

In small bowl, stir together oil, dill, onion, salt and hot pepper flakes; add potatoes and toss well. (Potatoes can be prepared to this point and left at room temperature for up to 4 hours.)

Thread 4 skewers with 4 potatoes each. Pour remaining oil over potatoes and lay skewers on greased grill 4 inches (10 cm) above medium-hot coals or on medium-high setting. Barbecue, turning often, for 3 to 4 minutes or until skins are crisp and potatoes are heated through. Makes 4 servings.

NEW POTATOES ROASTED
WITH OLIVE OIL AND GARLIC

When you can buy waxy little new potatoes at the farmers' markets, I love to toss them with olive oil, garlic and herbs and roast them until they're tender but crusty on the outside.

12	small new potatoes (about 2 lb/1 kg), unpeeled	12
4	cloves garlic, crushed	4
2 tbsp	olive oil	25 mL
2 tsp	finely chopped fresh rosemary or thyme (or ½ tsp/2 mL dried)	10 mL
1 tsp	paprika	5 mL
	Salt and pepper	

Scrub potatoes and dry. In small roasting pan, toss together potatoes, garlic, oil, rosemary and paprika.

Cover and roast in 375°F (190°C) oven until tender, 30 to 40 minutes, stirring occasionally. Season with salt and pepper to taste. Makes about 4 servings.

OLD-FASHIONED SCALLOPED POTATOES

When I make scalloped potatoes, I make a thin layer of potatoes and onions; then sprinkle with flour, salt and pepper, repeating until the dish is full. I pour in milk until I can see it from the top, then I dot with butter and bake. The following method is just as easy (although it does dirty a bowl and a wooden spoon), and gives a novice cook some idea of quantity.

2 lb	potatoes (about 8), peeled	1 kg
2 tbsp	all-purpose flour	25 mL
1 tsp	salt	5 mL
¼ tsp	pepper	1 mL
1	small onion, thinly sliced	1
2 tbsp	butter	25 mL
2 cups	milk	500 mL

Dry potatoes well; thinly slice. In bowl, toss together potatoes, flour, salt and pepper; layer half in greased 8-cup (2 L) casserole. Sprinkle with half of the onion; dot with half of the butter. Repeat layers. Pour in milk.

Cover and bake in 350°F (180°C) oven for 30 minutes. Uncover and bake until golden and bubbly, 30 to 35 minutes longer. Makes 4 servings.

PARMESAN OVEN-FRIED POTATO SLICES

Crisp and delicious, these oven-baked slices rival potato chips because they are cooked with little fat and much less bother than deep-frying. If you wish, omit the lemon juice and Parmesan; sprinkle with salt instead.

4	large potatoes (unpeeled)	4
2 tbsp	*each* vegetable oil and butter	25 mL
	Pepper	
1 tbsp	fresh lemon juice	15 mL
2 tbsp	freshly grated Parmesan cheese	25 mL

Scrub potatoes well; slice no thicker than ¼ inch (5 mm), dropping slices into bowl of cold water as you work. (Leave for at least 15 minutes or up to 3 hours.)

Line 15- × 10-inch (2 L) jelly-roll pan with foil for easier cleanup. Put oil and butter in pan; place in 450°F (230°C) oven until butter melts.

Drain potatoes and pat dry. Add to pan and toss to coat, spreading out as much as possible. Sprinkle with pepper to taste. Bake for 15 minutes.

With spatula, turn potatoes; sprinkle with lemon juice and Parmesan cheese. Bake for 10 to 15 minutes or until golden brown and crusty. Makes 4 servings.

CHEESE MUSHROOM POTATOES

Joan Doyle of Kitchener serves this yummy mixture as a dip for crackers, but it's fantastic on baked potatoes, too, for a fun supper with the happy quality of something you can prepare ahead. Accompany with a green salad.

8	slices bacon, cut in ½-inch (1 cm) pieces	8
2 tbsp	butter	25 mL
1	small onion, finely chopped	1
1 lb	mushrooms, sliced (about 2 cups/500 mL)	500 g
2 tbsp	all-purpose flour	25 mL
1 cup	light sour cream	250 mL
1 tsp	fresh lemon juice	5 mL
Pinch	cayenne pepper	Pinch
2 cups	shredded old Cheddar cheese (about ½ lb/ 250 g)	500 mL
4	hot large baked potatoes	4

In large skillet, cook bacon until almost crisp; with slotted spoon, transfer to 9-inch (23 cm) pie plate. Discard drippings from skillet.

In same skillet, melt butter over medium heat; cook onion until softened but not browned, about 3 minutes. Add mushrooms and cook, stirring often, until golden brown, about 3 minutes longer. Stir in flour; cook, stirring constantly, over low heat for 3 minutes.

Stir in sour cream, lemon juice and cayenne. Spoon into pie plate; sprinkle evenly with cheese. (Mixture can be prepared to this point, covered and refrigerated for up to 4 hours.)

Bake, uncovered, in 350°F (180°C) oven for 20 to 30 minutes or until bubbly and heated through. Cut "X" in each potato, gently squeeze potatoes to loosen pulp slightly and spoon on topping. Makes 4 servings.

SWEET POTATO PARTY FLAN

A smooth, flavorful purée is garnished with slices of the vegetable itself to resemble a crust on a flan.

3½ lb	sweet potatoes (unpeeled)	1.75 kg
¼ cup	whipping cream	50 mL
2 tbsp	*each* butter and liquid honey	25 mL
½ tsp	nutmeg	2 mL
	Salt and pepper	

Scrub potatoes. In large saucepan of boiling salted water, cover and cook sweet potatoes for about 25 minutes or until tender but not mushy. Drain, peel and thinly slice. Set aside enough slices to overlap in ring around rim of deep 9-inch (23 cm) pie plate or baking dish.

In food processor or blender, purée remaining sweet potatoes, cream, half of the butter, the honey, nutmeg, and salt and pepper to taste until smooth and fluffy. Taste and adjust seasoning.

Spoon into greased dish; and arrange slices overlapping slightly around inside rim. Dot with remaining butter. (Recipe can be prepared to this point, covered with foil and refrigerated for up to 2 days.)

Bake, covered, in 325°F (160°C) oven for about 30 minutes or until heated through. Makes 8 to 10 servings.

FAST OVEN-ROASTED ASPARAGUS

One year, when I was doing a lot of work with asparagus, I discovered that oven-roasting at a high temperature was not only fast, but also easy and provided a new dimension to asparagus. It becomes nuttier and of a more substantial texture. I do it often for guests, and it never fails to impress them. The recipe can be doubled easily.

1 lb	asparagus spears	500 g
1 tbsp	vegetable oil	15 mL
	Salt and pepper	

Spread asparagus in single layer in large baking dish. Drizzle with oil; sprinkle with salt and pepper to taste.

Roast, uncovered, in 500°F (260°C) oven for about 8 minutes stirring once, or until tender but still slightly firm. Makes 4 servings.

SAUTEED ROSEMARY PARSNIPS

Although parsnips are especially sweet if allowed to stay in the garden over the winter, I can never wait that long to enjoy this beautiful vegetable. This version is especially good with roast lamb.

1 lb	parsnips (about 4)	500 g
¼ cup	all-purpose flour	50 mL
½ tsp	*each* crushed dried rosemary and salt	2 mL
¼ tsp	pepper	1 mL
2 tbsp	(approx) butter	25 mL

Peel parsnips; cut into pieces about 2 inches (5 cm) long and 1 inch (2.5 cm) wide. In saucepan of boiling salted water, cover and cook parsnips for about 5 minutes or until almost tender. Drain well.

In small shallow bowl, stir together flour, rosemary, salt and pepper; add parsnips and roll to coat each piece.

In large heavy skillet, melt butter over medium heat; cook parsnips until golden brown on all sides, about 3 minutes, adding a bit more butter if necessary and turning often. Makes 4 servings.

MAPLE-GLAZED ONIONS

Maple syrup adds a wonderful depth of flavor to little pearl onions in this simple side dish, which would make a delicious accompaniment to roast pork or poultry.

2	pkg (each 10 oz/283 g) pearl onions	2
1/3 cup	maple syrup	75 mL
1/4 cup	butter	50 mL
	Salt and pepper	

In pot of boiling water, blanch onions for 3 minutes; drain and refresh under cold running water. Drain well and peel; cut "X" in bottom of each. Place in greased shallow baking dish just big enough to hold in single layer.

In small saucepan, boil maple syrup until reduced by one-quarter; stir in butter until melted. Pour over onions; sprinkle with salt and pepper to taste and stir to coat. Bake, uncovered and basting occasionally, in 350°F (180°C) oven for about 45 minutes or until tender and browned. Makes 6 to 8 servings.

BRUSSELS SPROUTS TOSSED IN ORANGE BUTTER

These tiny, elegant members of the cabbage family will remain mild and retain their color if not overcooked and served immediately. I serve them often for company and holiday meals.

1 1/2 lb	Brussels sprouts	750 g
2 tbsp	butter	25 mL
1/4 cup	fresh orange juice	50 mL
1 1/2 tsp	grated orange rind	7 mL
	Salt and pepper	

Trim sprouts and if large, cut "X" in each bottom. Steam for 6 to 10 minutes or until barely tender when pierced with knife. (Or, boil, uncovered, in large pot of salted water for 4 to 8 minutes. Or, microwave with a small amount of water for 8 to 10 minutes.) Drain and halve lengthwise.

In large skillet, melt butter; toss in sprouts and heat through. Toss with orange juice and rind; season with salt and pepper to taste. Makes about 6 servings.

GINGERED SQUASH AND PEAR PUREE

Take advantage of the wonderful array of sweet winter squash in fall markets for this smooth purée with its intriguing ginger-pear flavor.

2¼ lb	winter squash	1.125 kg
¼ cup	butter	50 mL
2	pears, peeled and cut into 1-inch (2.5 cm) chunks	2
2 tbsp	chopped candied ginger	25 mL
1 tbsp	fresh lemon juice	15 mL
½ tsp	salt	2 mL
¼ tsp	*each* pepper and ground ginger	1 mL
Pinch	ground cardamom	Pinch

Cut squash in half and remove seeds; cover and bake in 350°F (180°C) oven for 40 to 60 minutes or until tender. (Or, cover with vented plastic wrap and microwave at High for 8 to 10 minutes or until tender. Drain off any excess moisture.)

Meanwhile, in skillet melt 2 tbsp (25 mL) of the butter over medium-low heat; cook pears for about 15 minutes or until tender, stirring occasionally. Transfer to food processor or blender.

Scoop out pulp from squash; add to food processor with remaining butter, candied ginger, lemon juice, salt, pepper, ground ginger and cardamom; process until very smooth. (Purée can be cooled, covered and refrigerated for up to 8 hours. Reheat for about 20 minutes in top of double boiler over boiling water.) Taste and adjust seasoning. Makes 8 servings.

BRAISED RED CABBAGE WITH CRANBERRIES

Both red cabbage and cranberries add a beautiful splash of color to any plate. Here, they team up in a delicious side dish that goes well with goose or duck.

1	red cabbage (1½ lb/750 g)	1
¼ cup	red wine vinegar	50 mL
2 tbsp	vegetable oil	25 mL
2	small onions	2
2	apples, peeled and chopped	2
1¼ cups	granulated sugar	300 mL
¼ cup	fresh orange juice	50 mL
4	whole cloves	4
1	3-inch (7 cm) cinnamon stick, broken	1
4 cups	cranberries	1 L
	Strips orange rind	

Core cabbage and thinly shred into large glass bowl; toss with vinegar and set aside.

In large stainless steel saucepan, heat oil over medium heat; chop 1 of the onions and cook until softened. Stir in apples, sugar and orange juice.

Push cloves into remaining onion; add to pan along with cinnamon stick.

Stir in cabbage mixture; bring to boil. Reduce heat to low; simmer, partially covered and stirring occasionally until cabbage is tender, about 15 minutes.

Increase heat to medium-high and add cranberries; cook, uncovered and stirring often, until berries begin to pop, about 5 minutes. Discard whole onion and cinnamon stick.

(Cabbage can be served warm or cooled, spooned into serving bowl, covered and refrigerated for up to 1 day. Bring to room temperature to serve.) Garnish with orange rind. Makes 8 servings.

MAKE-AHEAD BAKED RUTABAGA CARROT PUREE

No traditional Christmas table would be complete without rutabaga (a vegetable we used to call yellow turnip), but don't wait for a holiday to make this creamy do-ahead casserole. The sweetness of carrots adds a certain mellowness to the rutabaga in an ideal accompaniment to turkey, roast capon, pork or beef.

1	small rutabaga	1
4	carrots	4
Half	onion, coarsely chopped	Half
1 ½ cups	chicken stock	375 mL
¼ cup	butter	50 mL
1 tsp	packed brown sugar	5 mL
Pinch	nutmeg	Pinch
¼ cup	whipping cream or light sour cream	50 mL
	Salt and pepper	
2 tbsp	finely chopped pecans or walnuts	25 mL

Peel rutabaga and carrots; cut into ½-inch (1 cm) chunks.

In saucepan, combine rutabaga, carrots, onion, stock, three-quarters of the butter, sugar and nutmeg; bring to boil. Reduce heat and cook, partially covered, for about 45 minutes or until vegetables are very tender, stirring occasionally.

With slotted spoon, transfer vegetables to food processor or blender. Set pan over high heat and boil remaining liquid for 2 to 3 minutes or until reduced to about 1 tbsp (15 mL). Add to vegetable mixture along with cream; purée until smooth. Taste and season with salt and pepper. Transfer to greased 6-cup (1.5 L) casserole or soufflé dish.

Melt remaining butter; stir together with nuts. Sprinkle evenly around edge of casserole to make border. Let cool, cover and refrigerate for up to 24 hours. Remove from refrigerator 30 minutes before reheating.

Bake, covered, in 350°F (180°C) oven for about 30 minutes or until heated through, removing lid for last 10 minutes. Makes 8 to 10 servings.

SIMPLE GARLIC-SAUTEED GREEN BEANS

This is my favorite treatment of green beans when I have a dinner party. The beans can be cooked early in the day, wrapped in a tea towel and just sautéed briefly at the last minute.

2 lb	green beans, trimmed	1 kg
3 tbsp	olive oil	50 mL
2	cloves garlic, cut in half	2
	Salt and pepper	
2 tsp	fresh lemon juice	10 mL

In large saucepan, bring large quantity of salted water to boil; gradually add beans and cook over medium-high heat, uncovered, for about 5 minutes or until cooked but still firm. Drain in colander and refresh under cold running water. (Beans can be prepared to this point, wrapped in tea towel and refrigerated for up to 8 hours.)

In large skillet, heat oil over medium heat; cook garlic until browned. Discard garlic. Add beans and shake pan to coat. Season with salt and pepper to taste. Cover and cook over low heat for about 2 minutes or until heated through. Toss with lemon juice. Makes 8 servings.

SPECIAL OCCASION CARROTS
GLAZED WITH HONEY AND MINT

This quick and easy side dish goes particularly well with grilled or roast lamb. If you want a wonderful accompaniment to roast chicken, substitute sage for the mint, cutting the amount in half.

15	thin carrots (about 1 1/4 lb/625 g)	15
2 tbsp	butter	25 mL
1/2 tsp	granulated sugar	2 mL
1/4 tsp	*each* salt and pepper	1 mL
1/3 cup	water	75 mL
2 tbsp	liquid honey	25 mL
1/4 cup	whipping cream	50 mL
1 tbsp	finely chopped fresh mint	15 mL

Cut carrots into 1-inch (2.5 cm) pieces; set aside.

In large skillet, melt butter over medium heat; cook carrots, sugar, salt and pepper for 3 minutes, stirring occasionally. Add water and reduce heat; cover and simmer for 5 minutes or just until tender-crisp.

Uncover and increase heat to medium-high; cook for 2 to 4 minutes or until liquid has evaporated. Add honey and stir for 1 minute to coat carrots. Pour in cream; boil until thick enough to coat spoon, about 2 minutes. Taste and adjust seasoning if necessary. Sprinkle with mint. Makes about 4 servings.

CREAMED SKILLET CORN

When corn is in season, this easy side dish has all the good flavor of corn on the cob and is elegant enough for company.

3 tbsp	butter	50 mL
2 cups	uncooked corn kernels (about 2 ears)	500 mL
1/4 cup	minced shallots or mild onion	50 mL
Pinch	granulated sugar	Pinch
2 tbsp	water	25 mL
1/2 cup	whipping cream	125 mL
Pinch	*each* salt, pepper and nutmeg	Pinch

In large skillet, melt butter over medium-high heat; cook corn, shallots and sugar, stirring, for 3 minutes.

Add water and cover; reduce heat to low and cook for 5 to 7 minutes or until corn is tender.

Gradually stir in cream; increase heat to medium and cook, uncovered, for 3 to 5 minutes or until cream is reduced and coats kernels. Season with salt, pepper and nutmeg. Makes 4 servings.

ANNE LINDSAY'S COUSCOUS WITH LEMON AND FRESH BASIL

My good friend Anne Lindsay shares with me one of her favorite recipes for couscous from her latest cookbook, Lighthearted Everyday Cooking. Couscous is made from semolina wheat and looks like a grain. Because it's so fast and easy to prepare, having a package on hand is a good idea for "instant" side dishes for things like chicken or fish. Almost all couscous sold in this country is the quick-cooking type, but follow the package directions in terms of the amount of liquid needed because it might vary.

2 cups	chicken stock	500 mL
1 tbsp	olive oil	15 mL
1 1/2 cups	couscous	375 mL
2 tbsp	fresh lemon juice	25 mL
1/2 cup	lightly packed chopped fresh basil	125 mL
	Pepper	

In saucepan, bring chicken stock to boil; add oil and couscous. Remove from heat; cover and let stand for 5 minutes or until grains are tender and liquid is absorbed.

Fluff couscous with fork; add lemon juice and basil. Season with pepper to taste. Makes 8 servings.

WILD RICE LEMON PILAF

Wild rice is special to serve at dinner parties and celebrations. Here, I've extended this treat by combining it with some white rice in a wonderful full-flavored accompaniment to roast poultry or pork.

4 cups	chicken stock	1 L
1 cup	wild rice, rinsed (6 oz/175 g)	250 mL
1/4 cup	butter	50 mL
2 tbsp	fresh lemon juice	25 mL
1 tbsp	grated lemon rind	15 mL
2	onions, chopped	2
1 1/2 cups	long-grain white rice	375 mL
1 cup	chopped pecans, lightly toasted	250 mL
1/2 cup	chopped fresh parsley	125 mL

In large saucepan, combine stock, wild rice, 1 tablespoon (15 mL) of the butter, lemon juice and half of the rind; bring to boil. Cover and reduce heat to medium-low; simmer for 35 minutes.

Meanwhile, in skillet, melt remaining butter over medium heat; cook onions until softened, about 8 minutes. Add white rice and stir to coat; stir into wild rice mixture after rice has cooked for 35 minutes. Cover and cook over medium-low heat until liquid is absorbed, 15 to 20 minutes. Remove from heat; let stand, covered, for 5 minutes.

Stir in remaining rind, pecans and parsley. (Pilaf may be cooled, covered and refrigerated in casserole dish for up to 2 days. Microwave, covered, at High for 6 to 8 minutes or bake covered in 350°F/180°C oven, stirring occasionally, for about 20 minutes or until heated through.) Makes 8 servings.

CARROT PILAF

Your food processor can make short work of chopping the carrots and parsley for this pretty rice dish that makes a perfect accompaniment to Quick Lamb Chop Curry (page 83).

2 tbsp	butter	25 mL
3	carrots, chopped	3
1 cup	long-grain rice	250 mL
1 tsp	cumin	5 mL
2 1/2 cups	chicken stock	625 mL
1/4 cup	chopped fresh parsley	50 mL
	Salt and pepper	

In large saucepan, melt butter over medium heat; cook carrots for 2 minutes. Stir in rice and cumin; cook for 1 minute.

Stir in stock and bring to boil; reduce heat, cover and simmer for about 15 minutes or until rice is tender and stock absorbed.

Stir in parsley; season with salt and pepper to taste. Makes 4 servings.

FIDDLEHEADS SAUTEED WITH MORELS

When some people move to a new area, they seek out a new dentist, doctor or hairdresser. We try to find the local fern patch. The summer show of majestic big fronds of the ostrich fern (no other should be eaten) signals where in mid-April we start looking for the tight, furled fronds or fiddleheads just peeking up from the midst of last year's old dead ferns.

I'm not telling you where our patch is, but if you find your own (they can be anywhere in Canada.), leave about half the fiddleheads in each clump to ensure a continued crop.

To clean, pull out each curl and shake off the husk, then wash in several changes of water and trim any dark ends.

They're wonderful cooked simply—uncovered, in a large amount of boiling, salted water for 5 to 7 minutes, then seasoned with butter, lemon juice and salt and pepper. Or, try this quick sauté. If morels (wild honeycombed mushrooms) are unavailable, substitute regular mushrooms.

¹/₂ lb	fresh fiddleheads, cleaned (or 10 oz/300 g pkg frozen)	250 g
¹/₄ cup	butter	50 mL
1 lb	morels or small mushrooms	500 g
2 tbsp	fresh lemon juice	25 mL
1 tsp	finely chopped fresh tarragon (or ¹/₄ tsp/1 mL dried)	5 mL
	Salt and pepper	

In saucepan of boiling salted water, blanch fiddleheads for 1 minute. (If using frozen, thaw just to separate.)

In large heavy skillet, melt butter over medium heat; cook fiddleheads and morels, stirring often, for about 8 minutes or until tender.

Stir in lemon juice, tarragon, and salt and pepper to taste. Makes 6 servings.

GLISTENING MAPLE RUTABAGA SLICES

Mashed rutabaga (also called yellow turnip or Swede) is a popular side dish to serve with roast poultry, beef or pork. Sometimes, however, I like to serve slices glazed with butter and honey or maple syrup so that I can enjoy the somewhat substantial texture of the vegetable.

2 lb	rutabaga (1 small)	1 kg
1 tbsp	butter	15 mL
¹/₄ cup	maple syrup	50 mL
¹/₄ tsp	dried thyme	1 mL
Pinch	ginger	Pinch
	Salt and pepper	

Peel rutabaga and cut into ¹/₂-inch (1 cm) thick slices; quarter slices. In saucepan of boiling, salted water, cook rutabaga for 15 minutes or just until tender; drain.

Immediately stir in butter and toss to coat. Stir in maple syrup, thyme and ginger; cook, stirring, for 1 minute. Season with salt and pepper to taste. Makes about 4 servings.

RUM-GLAZED SQUASH SLICES

Rum gives winter squash a very interesting flavor, but if you wish, substitute maple syrup for the rum and sugar. Although the long striped sweet potato squash yields uniform slices, you can use any winter squash available.

2	large sweet potato squash	2
¼ cup	dark rum	50 mL
2 tbsp	butter	25 mL
1 tbsp	*each* diced candied ginger and granulated sugar	15 mL
¼ tsp	pepper	1 mL
1 tbsp	chopped fresh parsley	15 mL

Halve squash lengthwise and scoop out seeds and stringy membrane; cut into ½-inch (1 cm) thick slices without peeling. (Slices will stay together better if not peeled.)

In large skillet with small amount of boiling salted water, cook squash for 7 to 10 minutes or until almost tender; drain off water. Add rum, butter, ginger, sugar and pepper. (Recipe can be prepared to this point and set aside at room temperature for up to 2 hours.)

Cook squash over medium heat, uncovered, basting often and turning slices, for 5 to 10 minutes or until tender and richly glazed. Sprinkle with parsley to serve. Makes 8 servings.

Special Salads

There's great variety in salads. They can be as simple as a bowl of lettuce tossed with a light vinaigrette. Or, when used as a main course, they can be a composed arrangement of any number of vegetables, meats, fish, grains or pastas. The dressings are limitless, and the end result can be served chilled, at room temperature or even warm.

The great choice of greens available now will add interesting shapes, colors and tastes. Look for peppery arugula, delicate oakleaf, purplish red and crisp radicchio, lemony sorrel, Belgian endive and chewy mâche (corn salad or lamb's lettuce) along with the more regularly found romaine, escarole, watercress and cabbage.

And don't be shy about combining fruit and vegetables or adding cheese or grains. They'll vary not only the flavor but also the texture and appearance of a salad.

In this chapter, you'll find updated favorites and some new combinations, all with lighter and fresher dressings.

SPARKLING BEET AND ORANGE SALAD

There's something homey about the distinctive aroma that pervades your kitchen when beets are cooking. And I love their earthy flavor so much that I often serve beets to guests. The cooking time given is for small garden-fresh beets; larger storage beets available later in the year will take longer, maybe even an hour.

7	small beets (about 1 lb/500 g)	7
1/3 cup	olive oil	75 mL
2 tbsp	fresh lemon juice	25 mL
1 tsp	Dijon mustard	5 mL
Pinch	cayenne pepper	Pinch
	Salt and pepper	
2	oranges	2
2	heads Belgian endive	2

In saucepan of boiling salted water, cook beets, covered, for 10 to 20 minutes or until tender. Drain and cool under cold running water. Peel and slice thinly; place in bowl.

In small bowl, whisk together olive oil, lemon juice, mustard, cayenne, and salt and pepper to taste; pour over beets and toss to coat.

Peel oranges. Using knife, remove outer membrane; cut into slices 1/4 inch (5 mm) thick. (Recipe can be prepared to this point, covered and refrigerated for up to 8 hours.)

Separate endive leaves; arrange around edge of large round platter. With slotted spoon, remove beets and arrange overlapping slices in circle inside endive. Mound orange slices in centre of plate, sprinkling with any remaining dressing. Makes about 4 servings.

INTRIGUING GRILLED ASPARAGUS, MANGO AND RED PEPPER SALAD

Barbecued asparagus has great flavor. Here it's combined with fruit and bits of red pepper for an interesting and colorful salad that everyone will love.

3/4 lb	asparagus	375 g
2 tbsp	white wine vinegar	25 mL
1 tbsp	Dijon mustard	15 mL
2 tsp	chopped fresh tarragon (or 1/2 tsp/2 mL dried)	10 mL
1/2 tsp	salt	2 mL
1/4 tsp	pepper	1 mL
1/3 cup	olive oil	75 mL
1	ripe mango, peeled and sliced	1
Half	sweet red pepper, diced	Half

Trim asparagus and place in sturdy plastic bag. In small bowl, whisk together vinegar, mustard, tarragon, salt and pepper; whisk in oil. Pour over asparagus, turning to coat and let stand for 30 minutes at room temperature.

Reserving marinade in bag, place asparagus on greased grill 4 inches (10 cm) from medium-hot coals or on medium-high setting; grill for about 4 minutes or until still bright green and tender-crisp, turning often with tongs.

Meanwhile, add mango and red pepper to marinade, squeezing bag gently to coat.

Let asparagus cool slightly; cut each stalk into 3 diagonal pieces. Add to mango mixture to coat with dressing. (Recipe can be refrigerated for up to 2 hours.) Transfer to serving bowl. Makes 4 servings.

BAKED GERMAN POTATO SALAD

Set this robust hot salad down beside Homey Apple-Baked Sausage (page 60), Quick Pickled Beets (page 131) and perhaps even a casserole of Maple Baked Beans (page 96) for a hearty but easy supper—perfect for an après-ski meal.

16	small red potatoes (unpeeled)	16
1/4 lb	side bacon, diced (about 1 cup/250 mL)	125 g
2	stalks celery, sliced	2
1	onion, chopped	1
2 tbsp	all-purpose flour	25 mL
1/2 tsp	*each* dry mustard and salt	2 mL
1/4 tsp	pepper	1 mL
1/2 cup	cider vinegar	125 mL
1/3 cup	granulated sugar	75 mL
1 cup	water	250 mL
1/4 cup	chopped fresh parsley	50 mL

Scrub potatoes. In saucepan of boiling salted water, cook potatoes until barely tender when pierced with tip of knife. Do not overcook. Drain and peel; cut into 1/4-inch (5 mm) thick slices and arrange in greased shallow 8-cup (2 L) casserole.

In skillet, fry bacon until crisp. Remove with slotted spoon and set aside to drain on paper towels.

Add celery and onion to pan; cook over medium heat for 3 minutes. Stir in flour, mustard, salt and pepper; cook for 2 minutes, stirring.

Stir in vinegar, sugar, then water all at once, stirring constantly; bring to boil and cook for 1 minute. Stir in parsley and cooked bacon; pour over potatoes and toss gently to coat. (Potatoes can be prepared to this point, covered and refrigerated for up to 6 hours. Remove from refrigerator 30 minutes before baking.

Bake, uncovered, in 375°F (190°C) oven for 45 minutes or until bubbly. Serve hot or warm. Makes 6 servings.

CRANBERRIES

The bouncy little cranberry has a lot going for it. People fall in love with its beautiful rich color—the "ruby of the bogs" at harvesttime. Early settlers used strings of cranberries to add a bright red sparkle to their Christmas trees.

Indians used cranberries (which they called assamanesh, or bitter fruit) extensively as food, of course, especially in pemmican—ground venison, fat and pounded, dried cranberries. A kind of medicine to Indians, too, they found the fruit's acidity made it a good poultice for wounds.

Actually, the medicinal properties of the cranberry have been greatly acclaimed over the years. Because of their high vitamin C content, barrels of cranberries were carried on long voyages in wooden ships to be eaten by early sailors to fend off scurvy, much as British seafarers drank lime juice. For years, cranberries have been considered a remedy for kidney or bladder maladies. Some even think the fruit helpful in relieving asthma, while others believe a glass of cranberry juice a day is a sure preventative for colds.

This native berry, long considered a valuable crop to Indians in its wild form in peat and bog areas across the country, was commercially cultivated for the first time around 1870 in Nova Scotia.

Commercial cultivation, known only in North America, is carried on in British Columbia, Ontario, the Maritimes and Quebec. Although the methods of harvest vary from producer to producer, the time is usually October for most of the country.

Such timing provides fresh cranberries long enough to enjoy not only with Thanksgiving dinner, but at Christmas as well. Their hard, outer skin allows cranberries to adapt well to baking and storing, and if the dry method of harvesting is used, they will keep for weeks without freezing. This long storage will not deplete their high nutritive content since they contain benzoic acid, a natural preservative.

It's this acid that also allows cranberries to stay fresh, whole and separate when frozen. When you want to use them, they come rolling out of the bag without sticking together. This unique characteristic, discovered by native Indians in a cold climate, allows you to treat the frozen fruit exactly as you would fresh berries. When cranberries are in season, therefore, remember to stock up since they will keep in your freezer for ten months—just before the annual harvest across the country. To freeze, just pop them into the freezer in the bag in which you buy them; don't thaw to use.

With a good supply on hand, you don't have to restrict cranberries to their excellent role as an accompanying sauce to cut the richness of poultry. Try them wherever you would use other berries (especially blueberries) in a whole range of sweet or savory dishes.

CRANBERRY WALDORF

This unusual salad is absolutely delicious with roast chicken or turkey. The juice drained from the cranberries would make a good basis for a punch or a refreshing cranberry spritzer with soda water. If you use frozen cranberries, do not thaw first.

4 cups	raw cranberries	1 L
1 1/2 cups	packed brown sugar	375 mL
4	large pears, peeled and sliced	4
2 tbsp	fresh lemon juice	25 mL
2	stalks celery, sliced	2
1 cup	toasted walnut halves	250 mL
1/3 cup	*each* light mayonnaise and light sour cream	75 mL
	Watercress or celery leaves	

In food processor or by hand, coarsely chop cranberries. In large bowl, gently stir together cranberries, brown sugar, pears and lemon juice; cover and let stand in refrigerator overnight.

About 30 minutes before serving, drain cranberry mixture in large sieve set over large bowl. Set aside juice for another use.

Just before serving, return drained cranberry mixture to bowl; gently fold in celery and walnuts.

Stir together mayonnaise and sour cream; blend into cranberry mixture. Serve in large shallow glass bowl lined with watercress or celery leaves. Makes 8 to 10 servings.

CARROT FRUIT SALAD

When you think there's nothing in the house for an interesting salad, you probably do have the ingredients for this delicious combination—sure to become a favorite with all age groups. Rachel Van Nostrand, a wonderful cook in Ontario's Niagara Peninsula, gave me the idea for this salad.

1 cup	raisins	250 mL
2 tbsp	fresh lemon juice	25 mL
4	carrots, finely grated	4
2	bananas, sliced	2
2 tbsp	grated shallots or onion	25 mL
1/2 cup	light sour cream or plain yogurt	125 mL
2 tbsp	light mayonnaise	25 mL
1/2 tsp	salt	2 mL
	White or black pepper	
1/4 cup	chopped fresh parsley	50 mL

In large bowl, soak raisins in lemon juice for 30 minutes. Stir in carrots, bananas and shallots.

Stir together sour cream, mayonnaise, salt, and pepper to taste; stir into carrot mixture until well mixed. Sprinkle with parsley. Makes 4 to 6 servings.

NEW-WAY OLD-FASHIONED POTATO SALAD

Nothing is more appealing with tangy-sweet ribs like Barbecued Spareribs with Apple-Sage Glaze (page 61) than old-fashioned creamy potato salad. I've cut down on the fat in this one without sacrificing any of the traditional flavor by substituting plain yogurt for most of the salad dressing.

4 lb	potatoes (about 12), unpeeled	2 kg
1/3 cup	vegetable oil	75 mL
2	onions, chopped	2
3/4 cup	chopped dill pickles	175 mL
2 tbsp	cider vinegar	25 mL
1 tsp	*each* dry mustard and granulated sugar	5 mL
	Salt and pepper	
3/4 cup	plain yogurt	175 mL
1/4 cup	Microwave Old-Fashioned Salad Dressing (see page 183)	50 mL
1/4 cup	chopped fresh parsley	50 mL
2 tsp	Dijon mustard	10 mL
4	hard-cooked eggs, peeled and chopped	4
	Paprika	

Scrub potatoes. In saucepan of boiling salted water, cook potatoes until just tender. Peel and dice.

Meanwhile, in small skillet, heat 2 tbsp (25 mL) of the oil over medium heat; cook onions for 3 minutes. Transfer to large bowl; add warm potatoes and pickles.

Whisk together remaining oil, vinegar, dry mustard, sugar, and salt and pepper to taste; pour over potato mixture and toss to coat well. Cover and refrigerate for several hours or overnight.

Stir together yogurt, Salad Dressing, parsley, Dijon mustard and eggs; toss with potato mixture. Taste and adjust seasoning. Refrigerate at least 1 hour or up to 3 hours. Sprinkle with paprika to serve. Makes 8 servings.

BROWN RICE AND GREEN BEAN SALAD WITH LEMON-MUSTARD DRESSING

The nutty flavor of brown rice and toasted pine nuts perfectly complements the good taste of fresh green beans. Little else is needed if you serve this salad for a family supper. It also makes a great salad for a party buffet. Just double the recipe for a company crowd.

1 cup	whole grain or brown rice	250 mL
1 tsp	salt	5 mL
1/4 cup	fresh lemon juice	50 mL
2 tsp	Dijon mustard	10 mL
1/4 tsp	pepper	1 mL
1/2 cup	olive oil	125 mL
1/4 cup	diced sweet red pepper	50 mL

1 lb	**green beans, trimmed**	**500 g**
¹/₂ cup	**toasted pine nuts**	**125 mL**

In large saucepan, combine rice, half of the salt and 2¹/₂ cups (625 mL) boiling water for whole grain or 3 cups (750 mL) for brown rice; cover and reduce heat to low; cook for 25 minutes for whole grain, 45 minutes for brown rice, or until tender and water has been absorbed. Let stand for 5 minutes; fluff with fork.

In large bowl, whisk together lemon juice, mustard, pepper and remaining salt; gradually whisk in oil. Add warm rice and red pepper; toss. (Salad can be prepared to this point, covered and refrigerated for up to 12 hours.)

In large saucepan of boiling water, cook green beans for 4 to 5 minutes or just until tender; drain and refresh under cold running water. Drain well; cut crosswise into ³/₄-inch (2 cm) pieces. Stir into rice mixture along with pine nuts. Taste and adjust seasoning if necessary. Makes about 4 servings.

BLACK BEAN AND RED PEPPER SALAD

Perfect for a buffet or potluck supper, this easy salad will keep for several days in the refrigerator. If you wish to make it even easier, you could use a can of rinsed and drained black beans. I discovered that although cooking the dried beans in a microwave oven isn't faster than on top of the stove, the beans do have a better texture.

1 cup	**dried black beans**	**250 mL**
¹/₄ cup	**olive oil**	**50 mL**
2 tbsp	**red wine vinegar**	**25 mL**
1 tsp	**salt**	**5 mL**
¹/₂ tsp	***each* pepper, granulated sugar and ground cumin**	**2 mL**
1	**clove garlic, crushed**	**1**
1	**sweet red pepper, diced**	**1**
1 cup	**diced Spanish onion**	**250 mL**
3	**stalks celery, sliced**	**3**
1	**jalapeño pepper, diced**	**1**
¹/₃ cup	**coarsely chopped fresh coriander**	**75 mL**

Sort and rinse beans. In saucepan, cover beans with 3 times their volume of cold water; let soak overnight in refrigerator.

Drain beans and place in 16-cup (4 L) microwaveable casserole; cover with 3¹/₂ cups (875 mL) cold water. Cover and microwave at High for 45 minutes or until tender. (Or, in large saucepan, cover beans with 3 times their volume of cold water; bring to boil on stove. Reduce heat and cook, uncovered, for 45 to 60 minutes or until tender.) Drain well.

Whisk together oil, vinegar, salt, pepper, sugar, cumin and garlic; pour over beans and toss to coat.

In large bowl, toss together red pepper, onion, celery and jalapeño pepper; add beans and toss to mix. Gently stir in coriander. Cover and refrigerate for at least 2 hours for flavors to mingle and up to 3 days. Makes about 6 servings.

FRESH CORIANDER

There are certain ingredients that I really love, and you'll see them appearing often in these pages. Coriander is one. This lovely, refreshing green herb has a very intriguing flavor.

Used extensively in various corners of the world under other names like cilantro and Chinese parsley (not to be confused with flat-leaf Italian parsley to which it bears a remarkable resemblance), fresh coriander is becoming very popular in this country with our growing admiration for ethnic cooking.

Just a few years ago, I would have to go on pilgrimages to stores selling Chinese, East Indian, Mexican or Thai ingredients to find fresh coriander. Now it is turning up in many supermarkets across the country.

Its seed, either as a seed or powder, is often used in dishes like curries, but it cannot be substituted for fresh coriander.

CUCUMBERS IN SWEET-AND-SOUR CREAM DRESSING

My friend and assistant, Mary Lou Ruby Jonas generously shares with me one of her best-loved family recipes. This sweet and tangy old-fashioned salad will soon become one of your favorites, too. If the cucumber skins are tender, leave them on.

2	cucumbers	2
1/2 cup	whipping cream	125 mL
3 tbsp	*each* white vinegar and granulated sugar	50 mL
1/4 tsp	salt	1 mL
	Tomato wedges	

Thinly slice cucumbers. Transfer to bowl of ice water; let stand for 30 minutes. Drain and pat dry. Transfer to shallow baking dish.

Meanwhile, in blender or food processor, blend cream, vinegar, sugar and salt until very thick. Cover and refrigerate if making ahead. Pour over cucumbers and mix. Garnish with tomato. Makes about 4 servings.

QUICK PICKLED BEETS

When I used to line my cold cellar with preserves, pickled beets were always there—ready to round out lots of winter menus. Now I no longer have time to do much preserving, but when I get hungry for the old-fashioned pickle, I throw some beets in the oven and finish them off this way.

12	small beets	12
¹⁄₄ cup	red wine vinegar	50 mL
1 tsp	Dijon mustard	5 mL
Pinch	*each* salt, granulated sugar, cinnamon, allspice and pepper	Pinch
¹⁄₄ cup	olive oil	50 mL

Wash beets and remove all but 1 inch (2.5 cm) of stems and tails. Place in shallow pan with ¹⁄₄ inch (5 mm) water. Cover with foil and bake in 375°F (190°C) oven for about 35 minutes or until tender when pierced with knife. (Time depends very much on age and size of beets.) Drain and let cool; slip off skins and slice into ¹⁄₄-inch (5 mm) thick rounds. Place in bowl.

In measuring cup, whisk together vinegar, mustard, salt, sugar, cinnamon, allspice and pepper; gradually whisk in oil. Pour over beets and toss gently to coat. (Beets can be covered and refrigerated for up to 5 days.) Makes 6 to 8 servings.

HOT TRICOLOR SALAD OF GRILLED PEPPERS

Grilled peppers are one of the delights of the harvest season. Often I grill them until they're charred all over and peel them before dressing with a vinaigrette. This time, I grill them a short time so that the salad is crispy.

4 tsp	white wine vinegar	20 mL
1 tbsp	chopped fresh parsley	15 mL
2	cloves garlic, minced	2
1 tsp	finely chopped fresh oregano (or ¹⁄₄ tsp/1 mL dried)	5 mL
¹⁄₂ tsp	ground cumin	2 mL
¹⁄₄ tsp	*each* salt and pepper	1 mL
Dash	hot pepper sauce	Dash
¹⁄₄ cup	(approx) olive oil	50 mL
2	*each* sweet yellow, red and green peppers	2

In small bowl, whisk together vinegar, parsley, garlic, oregano, cumin, salt, pepper and hot pepper sauce; gradually whisk in ¹⁄₄ cup (50 mL) olive oil. Set aside.

Cut peppers into 2-inch (5 cm) squares; brush all over with more olive oil. Place on grill 4 inches (10 cm) from medium-hot coals or on medium-high setting; grill for 3 minutes. Turn carefully so pieces do not slip through grill; cook for 3 minutes longer or just until lightly browned and still crisp. Place in heatproof bowl; toss with dressing. Serve immediately. Makes 6 to 8 servings.

HOT BROCCOLI AND RED PEPPER SALAD

This easy, colorful salad is a nice contrast to a smooth vegetable purée on the same menu. If the broccoli is all ready to steam and the dressing made ahead, the salad takes only seconds to finish.

2 tbsp	fresh lemon juice	25 mL
1/4 cup	minced shallots	50 mL
1/2 tsp	*each* dry mustard and salt	2 mL
1/4 tsp	*each* pepper and hot pepper sauce	1 mL
1/4 cup	olive oil	50 mL
2	bunches broccoli (1 1/2 lb/750 g total)	2
1	sweet red pepper, slivered	1

In small bowl, whisk together lemon juice, shallots, mustard, salt, pepper and hot pepper sauce; gradually whisk in oil. Let stand at room temperature for at least 1 hour or up to 6 hours. Whisk again to re-combine.

Cut florets from broccoli; peel stalks and cut into 1/4-inch (5 mm) thick slices. Steam for 4 to 5 minutes or until just tender but still bright green. Do not overcook.

In salad bowl, toss hot broccoli with shallot dressing and red pepper; serve immediately. Makes 8 servings.

WATERCRESS AND PEAR SALAD
WITH STILTON VINAIGRETTE

This is one of my favorite simple green salads. If you wish, use two bunches of watercress and omit the radicchio. If walnut oil is unavailable, use all vegetable oil.

2 tbsp	red wine vinegar	25 mL
2 tsp	Dijon mustard	10 mL
1/2 tsp	(approx) coarsely ground pepper	2 mL
Pinch	salt	Pinch
1/4 cup	walnut oil	50 mL

2 tbsp	vegetable oil	25 mL
1	large bunch watercress	1
1	small head radicchio	1
2	large pears, peeled and sliced	2
1/2 cup	crumbled Stilton or other blue cheese	125 mL
1/2 cup	toasted walnut halves or pieces	125 mL

In medium bowl, whisk together vinegar, mustard, pepper and salt; gradually whisk in walnut and vegetable oils. (Dressing can be refrigerated for up to 3 hours.)

Remove large stems from watercress; tear radicchio into bite-size pieces. Arrange in shallow salad bowl or on individual plates. Arrange pear slices on top.

Whisk dressing and stir in cheese; pour over salad. Sprinkle with walnut halves, and more pepper if desired. Makes 4 to 6 servings.

ROMAINE, RADICCHIO AND WALNUT SALAD

Make this simple salad with the freshest greens you can find. (Greens, dressing and walnuts can be prepared ahead.) Anchovy paste is available in tubes from most supermarkets.

1 cup	coarsely chopped walnuts	250 mL
Half	head romaine lettuce	Half
Half	head radicchio	Half
Half	head Boston lettuce	Half
2 tbsp	red wine vinegar	25 mL
1/2 tsp	anchovy paste	2 mL
1/4 tsp	*each* salt, pepper and dry mustard	1 mL
1/3 cup	olive oil (preferably extra-virgin)	75 mL

On baking sheet, toast walnuts in 350°F (180°C) oven for 5 minutes; let cool. Tear romaine, radicchio and Boston lettuce into bite-size pieces. In large salad bowl, combine lettuces and walnuts.

In small bowl, whisk together vinegar, anchovy paste, salt, pepper and mustard; gradually whisk in oil. Pour over salad and toss to coat well. Makes 8 servings.

VARIATION: WARM CHEVRE SALAD ON MIXED GREENS

This tangy hot salad makes an inviting opening to a special meal, or a refreshing course between the main course and dessert. Increase olive oil to 1/2 cup (125 mL). Cut 1 lb (500 g) unripened cream-style goat cheese into 8 rounds and marinate overnight in oil, anchovy paste and mustard. Cut 8 circles of whole wheat bread just slightly bigger than rounds of cheese.

Drain oil mixture from cheese, stir in vinegar, salt and pepper; use as dressing, proceeding with salad as above. Just before serving, arrange salad on 8 individual plates. Set bread rounds on baking sheet and toast lightly under broiler. Set cheese on toast rounds and broil until cheese is bubbling and brown, 5 to 6 minutes. Transfer each round to centre of salad and serve immediately. Makes 8 servings.

THREE-INGREDIENT CREAMY COLESLAW

This easy, pretty salad would be perfect to carry out to a potluck supper or to serve with Maple Baked Beans (Page 96) at home.

6 cups	finely shredded green cabbage	1.5 L
1/2 cup	*each* diced red onion and (unpeeled) English cucumber	125 mL

DRESSING:

2/3 cup	light mayonnaise	150 mL
2 tbsp	cider vinegar	25 mL
4 tsp	granulated sugar	20 mL
1/2 tsp	salt	2 mL
Pinch	paprika	Pinch

In large bowl, toss together cabbage, red onion and cucumber.

DRESSING: In small bowl, whisk together mayonnaise, vinegar, sugar, salt and paprika until smooth. Pour over cabbage mixture and toss to coat; cover and refrigerate for at least 1 hour or up to 4 hours. Makes 6 servings.

NEW LIGHT CAESAR SALAD

The dressing and croutons for this ever-popular salad can be made and refrigerated for up to 2 weeks. That way you can make the salad for one or more whenever the craving hits. The dressing is a little lighter than usual with less oil and no eggs.

2	slices Italian bread	2
	Olive oil	
	Dried oregano	
1	large head romaine lettuce	1
	Freshly grated Parmesan cheese	

DRESSING:

2 tsp	anchovy paste	10 mL
1	clove garlic, minced	1
2 tbsp	*each* fresh lemon juice and white wine vinegar	25 mL
1 tbsp	Dijon mustard	15 mL
1/3 cup	olive oil	75 mL

Cut bread into 1/2-inch (1 cm) cubes to make about 2 1/4 cups (550 mL). On baking sheet, drizzle bread cubes lightly with olive oil; sprinkle with oregano. Bake in 375°F (190°C) oven for 10 minutes.

DRESSING: In small bowl, mash anchovy paste with garlic; whisk in lemon juice, vinegar and mustard. Gradually whisk in oil.

Just before serving, tear lettuce into bite-size pieces; place in salad bowl. Toss with dressing; sprinkle with croutons and cheese. Makes 6 to 8 servings.

WARM DANDELION SALAD
WITH BACON AND POACHED EGGS

When we first moved to Cambridge, Ontario, I remember our dear friend Edna Staebler arriving at our house one spring with two huge shopping bags full of dandelions. She proceeded to show my son, Allen, how to make her delicious dandelion salad that appears in her best-selling cookbook, Food That Really Schmecks. "In Waterloo County," she explained, "we say that dandelion greens purify the blood, grown sluggish and thick through the winter."

Where did Edna get these voluminous leaves? "From my lawn, of course," she said. "If you have enough of them, you don't have to go anywhere. You just sit on the lawn and pick!"

If you have no source for wild unsprayed dandelion leaves, you can still make this delightful salad with those grown especially under sawdust or straw for markets. This isn't Edna's salad, but I'm sure she'd enjoy it. Serve as a special spring brunch for two with slices of crusty French bread.

³/₄ lb	dandelion leaves (about 4 cups/1 L, packed)	375 g
4	slices side bacon, diced	4
¹/₄ cup	olive oil	50 mL
2 tbsp	minced shallots	25 mL
	Salt and pepper	
3 tbsp	white wine vinegar	50 mL
2	eggs	2
¹/₄ cup	white vinegar	50 mL

Remove white base from dandelion stalks; thoroughly wash leaves and dry well. Break each stalk into 2-inch (5 cm) pieces; place in large heatproof bowl.

In large skillet, cook bacon over medium-low heat until crisp and golden brown. Transfer to drain on paper towels.

Discard fat and wipe out skillet. Heat 2 tbsp (25 mL) of the oil over medium heat; cook shallots, stirring often, for 5 minutes. Sprinkle with salt and pepper to taste. With slotted spoon, add to dandelion greens. Add wine vinegar to pan and bring to boil; pour over greens. Toss with remaining oil and bacon; set aside.

In large amount of water and white vinegar, poach eggs, uncovered, for about 2½ minutes, bringing whites up over yolks with spoon. With slotted spoon, lift out eggs and drain on paper towels; trim uneven edges.

Meanwhile, return dandelion mixture to skillet; toss over medium heat for 1 minute or until greens are wilted. Divide between 2 small plates. Carefully set egg in centre of each salad and serve immediately. Makes 2 servings.

SPINACH AND MUSHROOM SALAD WITH CREAMY BUTTERMILK DRESSING

Low on calories but high on flavor, this crunchy salad is delicious with grilled beef or Oven-Fried Golden Crisp Chicken Legs (page 55). If possible, use nice fresh loose spinach instead of the cellophane-packaged kind.

1 cup	buttermilk	250 mL
1/2 cup	light mayonnaise	125 mL
2	cloves garlic, crushed	2
2 tsp	Dijon mustard	10 mL
	Salt and pepper	
10 oz	spinach	284 g
1/2 lb	mushrooms, sliced	250 g
1/4 lb	bean sprouts (about 2 cups/500 mL)	125 g
5	slices crisply cooked bacon, crumbled	5

Whisk together buttermilk, mayonnaise, garlic, mustard, and salt and pepper to taste until frothy. (Dressing can be covered and refrigerated for up to 8 hours.)

Wash and dry spinach well; remove any thick stems and tear into bite-sized pieces. Toss in large salad bowl with mushrooms and bean sprouts. (Salad can be covered and refrigerated without dressing for up to 3 hours.)

Just before serving, toss spinach mixture gently with dressing to coat. Sprinkle with bacon. Makes 6 to 8 servings.

FRESH PEACH AND ROQUEFORT SALAD WITH WALNUT DRESSING

An assertive blue cheese, tangy greens and a nut dressing are happy companions to juicy bright peach slices in this quick salad.

1/3 cup	fresh lime juice	75 mL
1/4 cup	walnut or olive oil	50 mL
2 tsp	white wine vinegar	10 mL
1/2 tsp	Dijon mustard	2 mL
	Salt and pepper	
3	peaches	3
	Bunch watercress or arugula	
3 oz	Roquefort cheese (or other blue cheese)	75 g
1/4 cup	toasted coarsely chopped walnuts	50 mL

In bowl, whisk together lime juice, oil, vinegar, mustard, and salt and pepper to taste. Peel, pit and slice peaches 1/4 inch (5 mm) thick; add to dressing and toss to coat. Let stand to marinate for 30 minutes.

Arrange watercress on large platter or individual plates. Arrange peach slices on top, drizzling with any dressing. Crumble cheese over peaches; sprinkle with walnuts. Serve immediately. Makes 4 servings.

GRILLED VEGETABLE SALAD
WITH GARLIC-HERB DRESSING

I've been appearing on CBC's "Radio Noon" (Ontario) for over ten years now, and for the last two years, I've done a summer open-line program out on a street in Toronto while I've barbecued. This full-flavored and attractive salad caught everyone's eye and taste buds. In addition, it's easy enough to make while you talk on the radio!

Use whatever vegetables you have on hand, and if you like the peppers crunchy, seed them, cut in big pieces and grill only 5 to 6 minutes without charring or peeling.

DRESSING:

3	cloves garlic, minced	3
2 tbsp	*each* red wine vinegar and olive oil	25 mL
1 tbsp	chopped fresh parsley	15 mL
2 tsp	*each* chopped fresh thyme and oregano (or ¹/₂ tsp/2 mL dried)	10 mL
	Salt and pepper	
2	small eggplants	2
3	sweet peppers (red, orange, yellow)	3
1	red onion	1
¹/₄ cup	vegetable oil	50 mL
8	fat spears asparagus or 2 small zucchini, cut in half lengthwise	8
4	large mushrooms	4
	Leaf lettuce	

DRESSING: Whisk together garlic, vinegar, olive oil, parsley, thyme, oregano, and salt and pepper to taste; set aside for at least 30 minutes or cover and refrigerate for up to 24 hours.

Cut eggplants in half lengthwise; place in sieve and sprinkle cut side with salt. Set aside to drain for 30 minutes.

Place peppers on greased grill 4 inches (10 cm) from medium-hot coals or on medium-high setting and grill, turning often, until charred all over, about 20 minutes. Pop into paper bag for 10 minutes. Then peel, seed and cut lengthwise into 8 strips. Transfer to large bowl.

Meanwhile remove outer skin from onion, leaving root and stem ends intact; cut in half crosswise. Brush with some of the vegetable oil and grill for 15 to 20 minutes or until lightly charred, turning once. Remove charred skin and cut each half into quarters. Add to bowl.

Rinse eggplant under cold running water; dry well and brush with vegetable oil. Grill for about 5 minutes or until golden brown but not charred, turning once. Add to bowl.

Brush asparagus or zucchini and mushrooms with vegetable oil; grill for 5 minutes, turning asparagus and mushrooms often and zucchini once. Add to bowl, quartering mushrooms.

Whisk any remaining vegetable oil into dressing; pour over vegetables and very gently toss to coat. Line platter with lettuce; arrange grilled vegetables on top. Makes 4 servings.

THAI PICKLED CUCUMBER SLICES

Everyone will find this salad very refreshing even though it is hot and spicy. It would be great with Hoisin-Orange Chicken Legs (page 48).

3	medium cucumbers	3
1	hot red pepper	1
1/4 cup	*each* rice vinegar and fresh lime juice	50 mL
1 tbsp	granulated sugar	15 mL
1/4 tsp	salt	1 mL
1/4 cup	diced red onion	50 mL
	Lettuce	

Score cucumber by running tines of fork down sides. Cut crosswise into very thin slices; place in heatproof bowl. Stem and remove seeds by working from end of hot pepper; thinly slice crosswise into rounds.

In small saucepan, stir together vinegar, lime juice, sugar and salt; add hot pepper and bring to boil, stirring. Simmer for 2 minutes; pour over cucumber and toss to coat.

Cover and refrigerate for up to 6 hours. Just before serving, stir in onion. With slotted spoon, transfer to lettuce-lined bowl. Makes 12 servings.

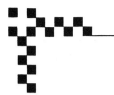

Exquisite Endings

The final course of a meal should be like the punch line of a joke—simple and to the point but with a lasting impact so that your audience will leave remembering your wit or good taste.

Since I think most families tend not to have dessert at every meal, or if they do, it might be something like fresh fruit, ice cream or sherbet, I've included only a handful of family desserts in this chapter.

The majority of the recipes here are for entertaining—all simple, but with the lasting impression that you have served your guests something special indeed.

When you have a dinner party, these desserts are great fun because they are all make-ahead, look spectacular, taste great, but they are almost all made in a flash . . . the kind of thing your guests will think you've slaved over for hours, but on which, in fact, you have spent very little time.

MAPLE CREME BRULEE

Easy elegance personified, this creamy dessert gains a whole new dimension of flavor when finely grated maple sugar is caramelized on top. Serve the little custards with crisp cookies like the Pecan Lace Cookies (page 168). If you can't find maple sugar, grate or finely chop the sugar candy maple leaf moulds found in gift shops and farmers' markets.

1 1/2 cups	whipping cream	375 mL
1/4 cup	maple syrup	50 mL
4	egg yolks	4
1/3 cup	finely grated maple sugar	75 mL

In small heavy saucepan, heat cream and maple syrup together until bubbles just start to form around outside. Remove from heat. In bowl, whisk egg yolks slightly without allowing them to foam. Very gradually pour hot cream into yolks, stirring constantly.

Strain custard through fine sieve into pitcher or measuring cup. Pour into six 1/2-cup (125 mL) heatproof ramekins. Place in baking pan just big enough to hold them; pour hot water into pan to come two-thirds up sides of ramekins.

Cover with foil; bake in 325°F (160°C) oven for about 25 minutes or until custards are just set but still slightly jiggly in centres. Remove ramekins to cool on rack; refrigerate until very cold. (Custards can be prepared a day ahead.)

Just before serving, sprinkle custards with maple sugar; broil on rack nearest heat for about 3 1/2 minutes, watching carefully, or until sugar caramelizes to golden brown. Serve immediately. Makes 6 servings.

PAVLOVA WITH FRESH SEASONAL FRUIT

Although it takes a while sitting in the oven, pavlova is one of the easiest desserts you'll ever make. This recipe comes from a good friend Catherine Betts, a New Brunswick caterer who lived for a while in Tasmania and New Zealand, close to where the recipe originated in Australia. Top with whatever fresh fruit is in season—sliced strawberries and kiwifruit, raspberries or peaches.

8	egg whites (1 cup/250 mL)	8
1 1/2 cups	granulated sugar	375 mL
4 tsp	*each* white vinegar, cornstarch and vanilla	20 mL
	Sweetened whipped cream or Remarkable Low-Fat Cream (page 185)	
	Fresh seasonal fruit	

Line baking sheet with parchment paper; draw 11-inch (28 cm) circle on it. (Or grease 11-inch/28 cm quiche dish.)

In bowl, beat egg whites until soft peaks form; gradually beat in sugar until stiff shiny peaks form. Stir together vinegar, cornstarch and vanilla; carefully fold into whites.

Spread onto circle in prepared pan, swirling and building up sides to form well in middle. Bake in 300°F (150°C) oven for 30 minutes. Reduce heat to 200°F (93°C); bake for 1½ hours longer. Turn off oven and leave pavlova in oven until cooled.

Just before serving, pile whipped cream into well of cooled meringue; arrange fruit attractively on top. Makes 8 to 12 servings.

CHOCOLATE-MARZIPAN TORTE

When I'm pressed for time but want to make an elegant dessert, I always turn to this easy but absolutely delicious torte. The better the chocolate, the better the taste.

²/₃ cup	granulated sugar	150 mL
4	eggs, separated	4
³/₄ cup	unsalted butter	175 mL
6 oz	bittersweet chocolate	175 g
¹/₄ cup	all-purpose flour	50 mL
2 tbsp	ground blanched almonds	25 mL
Pinch	*each* cream of tartar and salt	Pinch
2 tbsp	granulated sugar	25 mL
¹/₂ lb	marzipan	250 g
GLAZE:		
¹/₃ cup	whipping cream	75 mL
6 oz	sweet chocolate, coarsely chopped	175 g
¹/₃ cup	sliced blanched almonds, lightly toasted	75 mL

In large bowl, beat together ²/₃ cup (150 mL) sugar and egg yolks until pale yellow. In top of double boiler, melt butter with chocolate over simmering water, stirring until smooth. Remove from heat. Add yolk mixture and blend well. Thoroughly stir in flour and almonds.

In medium bowl, beat egg whites until foamy. Add cream of tartar and salt; beat until soft peaks form. Gradually beat in 2 tbsp (25 mL) sugar until stiff peaks form. Stir one-quarter of the beaten whites into chocolate mixture; fold in remaining whites.

Turn batter into well-greased and floured 9-inch (2.5 L) springform pan, tapping pan on counter to smooth top. Bake in 375°F (190°C) oven until edge is dry but centre still moist, about 30 minutes. Do not over-bake. Let cool completely on rack before removing pan.

Transfer to large plate. Between 2 pieces of waxed paper, roll out marzipan into circle almost as big as top of cake. Place on cake.

GLAZE: In small saucepan, bring cream to boil over medium-low heat; add chocolate and stir until melted and smooth. Let cool for a few minutes until it is spreadable.

Place strips of waxed paper under edge of cake; spread cake with glaze. Sprinkle almonds around top of cake to form border about 1 inch (2.5 cm) from edge. Refrigerate until chilled or for up to 2 days. Let stand at room temperature for about 20 minutes before serving. Makes 8 servings.

DECADENT CHOCOLATE FRUITCAKE

For something quick, easy and delicious, this moist fruitcake gets a new twist with chocolate. Wrap it with brandy-moistened cheesecloth for a week or two to quickly ripen it. The strips I've suggested facilitate slicing and make convenient gifts if you wish to share this good cake with friends.

2 lb	mixed candied pineapple and cherries (about 4½ cups/1.125 L)	1 kg
2 cups	coarsely chopped toasted pecans	500 mL
4 oz	unsweetened chocolate, finely chopped	125 g
3 oz	semisweet chocolate, finely chopped	90 g
1 cup	golden raisins	250 mL
2 cups	all-purpose flour	500 mL
2 tsp	baking powder	10 mL
½ tsp	salt	2 mL
¾ cup	unsalted butter (at room temperature)	175 mL
1 cup	granulated sugar	250 mL
6	eggs	6
¾ cup	brandy	175 mL
1 tsp	vanilla	5 mL

In large bowl, toss together pineapple, cherries, pecans, unsweetened and semisweet chocolate, raisins and half of the flour. Stir together remaining flour, baking powder and salt; set aside.

In large bowl, cream butter; beat in sugar until light and fluffy. Add eggs, one at a time, beating thoroughly. Beat in ¼ cup (50 mL) of the brandy and vanilla. Gradually stir in dry ingredients until well blended. Stir in fruit mixture.

Turn into greased 13- × 9-inch (3.5 L) metal baking pan. Tap on counter several times to fill all corners and prevent holes in batter. Bake in 300°F (150°C) oven for about 1½ hours or until cake tester inserted in centre comes out clean. Let cool on wire rack.

Cut cake crosswise into 6 strips. Heat remaining brandy but do not boil. Make several holes through cake with skewer; pour in brandy.

Moisten cheesecloth with additional brandy; wrap around individual strips. Wrap in waxed paper, then foil; store in airtight tin in cool place for at least 1 week or up to 2 months. Occasionally check that cake is not too dry and add more brandy, if necessary. Each strip can be cut into 14 pieces, making 84 pieces in total.

LEMON-ALMOND POUND CAKE

This moist lemon pound cake was created by my good friend, Elizabeth Baird, Food Director of Canadian Living magazine. Elizabeth says that it freezes well for a head start on weekend company or a casual party.

1 cup	butter, softened	250 mL
1 cup	granulated sugar	250 mL
4	eggs	4

2¹/4 cups	sifted cake-and-pastry flour	550 mL
1 tsp	baking powder	5 mL
¹/2 tsp	salt	2 mL
1¹/4 cups	sliced almonds	300 mL
1 tbsp	coarsely grated lemon rind	15 mL
3 tbsp	lemon juice	50 mL

GLAZE:

¹/2 cup	icing sugar	125 mL
2 tbsp	lemon juice	25 mL

In bowl, cream butter with sugar until fluffy. Beat in eggs, one at a time.

In separate bowl, stir together flour, baking powder and salt; mix in 1 cup (250 mL) of the almonds. Stir half of the flour mixture, lemon rind and juice into butter mixture; stir in remaining flour mixture. Spoon into parchment- or waxed paper-lined 9- x 5-inch (2 L) loaf pan, smoothing top. Sprinkle with remaining almonds.

Bake in 350°F (180°C) oven for 40 to 45 minutes or until tester inserted into centre comes out clean.

GLAZE: Pierce cake all over with cake tester. Combine icing sugar with lemon juice; spoon evenly over top of hot cake. Let cool on rack before removing from pan. Wrap and store at room temperature for 1 day before slicing. Makes 12 slices.

STRAWBERRIES WITH ALMOND CREAM SAUCE

When I was growing up on a farm at Duntroon, near Collingwood, Ontario, there was always fruit to pick—from the first pink stalks of rhubarb in the spring to the last crisp apple in late fall. But there was something special about getting out in the warm June sun to find perfectly ripe red strawberries hidden under protective green leaves. Today, no matter how busy I am, I still feel a compulsion to go picking at least once during the season, usually with my daughter.

I like to present good fresh berries simply—mounded in a dish to enjoy with cream and sugar, or to eat out-of-hand with some sour cream and a bit of brown sugar for dipping.

This recipe is also a simple celebration of the rich flavor of ripe fruit, yet the cream sauce adds a touch of elegance that makes it suitable for the finale of a special dinner party.

5 cups	ripe strawberries	1.25 L
¹/4 cup	instant dissolving (fruit/berry) sugar (or granulated sugar processed in blender)	50 mL
1 cup	sour cream	250 mL
2 tbsp	almond liqueur	25 mL

Hull strawberries; slice if large. In sieve set in large bowl, sprinkle strawberries with sugar; refrigerate, covered, for 1 hour.

Divide berries among 6 serving dishes. Whisk sour cream and liqueur into berry juice until smooth; pour over berries and serve immediately. Makes 6 servings.

APPLE CUSTARD TORTE

This make-ahead company dessert is much like a baked cheesecake but creamier, with a lovely syrup layer at the bottom. If you can, use an apple that doesn't break up when cooked, perhaps something like a Golden Delicious.

1 cup	all-purpose flour	250 mL
1/4 cup	granulated sugar	50 mL
2 tsp	grated lemon rind	10 mL
1	egg yolk	1
1/2 tsp	vanilla	2 mL
1/4 cup	butter, softened	50 mL

FILLING:

5	large apples	5
1/4 cup	butter	50 mL
3/4 cup	granulated sugar	175 mL
6	eggs	6
2 cups	sour cream or plain yogurt	500 mL
1/2 cup	packed brown sugar	125 mL
1 tsp	grated lemon rind	5 mL
1 tsp	vanilla	5 mL
	Icing sugar	

In small bowl, combine flour, sugar and lemon rind. Make a well in centre; put in egg yolk, vanilla and butter. With fork, stir to make fairly crumbly dough that starts to hold together. Pat onto bottom and partway up side of greased 9-inch (2.5 L) springform pan. Bake in 325°F (160°C) oven for 12 minutes.

FILLING: Meanwhile, peel and core apples; slice into rings 1/3 inch (3 mm) thick. In large heavy skillet, melt butter and granulated sugar; gently cook apple rings, in batches until tender but not mushy. (Don't worry if some rings break up.)

Reserving syrup, arrange apple rings on baked crust, reserving 5 of the best rings. Boil syrup to reduce to glaze if necessary; spoon over apples.

In bowl, beat eggs until light; stir in sour cream, brown sugar, lemon rind and vanilla. Pour over apples; top with reserved apple rings. Bake in 350°F (180°C) oven for about 1 hour or until custard is set. Let cool to room temperature; dust with icing sugar. Makes 6 to 8 servings.

ALMOND TORTE WITH RASPBERRY SAUCE

This close-textured cake is so delicious that you will never believe how easy it is to make.

2/3 cup	granulated sugar	150 mL
1/2 cup	unsalted butter (at room temperature)	125 mL
1/2 lb	almond paste, softened	250 g
3	eggs	3

1 tbsp	almond liqueur	15 mL
1/4 tsp	almond extract	1 mL
1/4 cup	all-purpose flour	50 mL
1/2 tsp	baking powder	2 mL
	Icing sugar	
	Raspberry sauce (recipe follows)	

In bowl, beat together granulated sugar, butter and almond paste; beat in eggs, one at a time. Stir in liqueur and almond extract. Add flour and baking powder, stirring only until mixed; do not overbeat. (This can be done in food processor, but be sure not to overprocess after adding flour.)

Pour into well-greased and floured 9-inch (2.5 L) springform pan; bake in 350°F (180°C) oven for about 40 minutes or until tester inserted in centre comes out clean. Let cool in pan on rack.

To serve, remove from pan and place on serving plate; dust with icing sugar and accompany with Raspberry Sauce. Makes 12 servings.

RASPBERRY SAUCE

1	pkg (12 oz/325 g) frozen raspberries, thawed	1
2 tbsp	granulated sugar	25 mL
1 tbsp	kirsch	15 mL

In food processor or blender, process raspberries and sugar until puréed. Press through sieve to remove seeds; stir in kirsch. Makes about 1 1/2 cups (375 mL).

TROPICAL MANGO ICE WITH KIWI COULIS

Tasty mangoes are better known than apples in more than half the world, but to us they're still exotic and wonderful. Let the ice stand for a few minutes at room temperature to soften slightly before serving.

1 cup	water	250 mL
1/2 cup	granulated sugar	125 mL
2 cups	cubed peeled ripe mangoes	500 mL
3/4 cup	fresh orange juice	175 mL
1/4 cup	fresh lime juice	50 mL

KIWI COULIS:

3	kiwifruit, peeled and coarsely chopped	3
2 tbsp	Cointreau	25 mL
2 tsp	granulated sugar	10 mL

In saucepan, bring water and sugar to boil over high heat; boil rapidly, uncovered, for about 5 minutes or until reduced to 2/3 cup (150 mL). Let cool and chill.

In food processor or blender, purée mangoes, orange juice, lime juice and chilled syrup. Transfer to an ice-cream maker and freeze according to manufacturer's directions.

KIWI COULIS: In food processor or blender, purée kiwifruit; blend in liqueur and sugar, spread on 4 dessert plates; top with scoops of mango ice. Makes 4 servings.

FRESH STRAWBERRY TORTE

This is one of those desserts I love to serve—impressive, but easy to make. Guests will also find it quite light.

5	eggs, separated	5
3/4 cup	granulated sugar	175 mL
1/3 cup	unsweetened cocoa powder	75 mL
1/2 cup	ground almonds	125 mL
1 tsp	baking powder	5 mL
	Icing sugar	
1 1/2 cups	whipping cream	375 mL
1/3 cup	icing sugar	75 mL
3 tbsp	amaretto	50 mL
4 cups	strawberries, hulled	1 L
1/4 cup	red currant jelly	50 mL

Line greased 15- × 11-inch (40 × 26 cm) jelly roll pan with waxed paper; set aside.

In large bowl, beat egg yolks, 1/2 cup (125 mL) of the granulated sugar and cocoa for 5 minutes or until thickened. In separate bowl and using clean beaters, beat egg whites until soft peaks form; gradually beat in remaining granulated sugar until stiff peaks form. Fold into egg yolk mixture along with almonds and baking powder.

Spread batter evenly in prepared pan. Bake in 350°F (180°C) oven for 15 to 20 minutes or until cake comes away from edges of pan. Place clean tea towel on wire rack; dust with icing sugar. Turn out cake onto towel and carefully remove waxed paper. Let cool for 20 minutes with another tea towel draped over top.

Whip cream with icing sugar. Drizzle cake with 2 tbsp (25 mL) of the amaretto; spread with cream. Cut crosswise into 6 strips. Roll up one strip, starting from short end; place cut side up in centre of serving plate. Wrap remaining strips, cream side in, around centre roll. (Cake can be prepared to this point and refrigerated for up to 2 hours.)

Slice enough of the strawberries to cover top attractively; use any remaining berries to garnish plate.

Melt jelly with remaining liqueur; brush over strawberries. (Torte can be refrigerated up to 1 hour.) Makes 6 to 8 servings.

CHOCOLATE MERINGUE TORTE
WITH GRAND MARNIER CREAM

This easy make-ahead dessert has such a delightful flavor and texture that it's bound to be a real hit at any dinner party.

8	egg whites	8
1/4 tsp	cream of tartar	1 mL
Pinch	salt	Pinch
1 tsp	vanilla	5 mL
1 1/2 cups	instant dissolving (fruit/berry) sugar (or granulated sugar processed in blender)	375 mL

1 cup	semisweet chocolate chips (6 oz/175 g)	250 mL
2 cups	whipping cream	500 mL
1/4 cup	Grand Marnier or other orange liqueur	50 mL
	Chocolate curls	

Cover 2 baking sheets with parchment or brown paper. On paper, draw three 9-inch (23 cm) circles.

In large bowl, beat egg whites until frothy. Beat in cream of tartar, salt and vanilla until soft peaks form. Very gradually beat in sugar until stiff peaks form.

Spoon mixture onto circles, smoothing tops with spatula. Bake in 250°F (120°C) oven for 1 hour; turn off oven and let meringues cool in oven for at least 6 hours or overnight. Using metal spatula, carefully remove meringues from paper.

Melt chocolate chips; using metal spatula, spread over 2 meringue layers. Whip cream; beat in liqueur.

Place one chocolate-covered meringue on serving plate; spread with one-third of the cream. Top with plain meringue, then half of the remaining cream. Place second chocolate-covered layer on top; spread with remaining cream.

Garnish with chocolate curls. Cover loosely and chill for 24 hours before serving. (If there's any moisture on plate at serving time, blot with paper towel.) Makes 8 servings.

EASY RICE PUDDING

Leftover rice takes on a total disguise in this old-fashioned favorite, a baked rice custard. Make family dessert in a flash; stir it together right in the baking dish.

1 cup	cooked rice	250 mL
1/2 cup	packed brown sugar	125 mL
2	eggs, beaten	2
2 cups	milk	500 mL
1/2 cup	raisins	125 mL
1 tsp	grated lemon rind	5 mL
1/2 tsp	vanilla	2 mL
1/4 tsp	salt	1 mL
	Grated nutmeg	
	Milk (optional)	

In 8-inch (2 L) baking dish, combine rice, sugar and eggs; stir well to blend. Stir in milk, raisins, lemon rind, vanilla and salt; sprinkle with nutmeg to taste.

Place in pan of hot water; bake in 325°F (160°C) oven for about 1 hour or until almost set. Serve warm or cold with milk (if using). Makes 4 to 6 servings.

GLAZED CRANBERRY CHEESECAKE

Lighter and less sweet than most, this delicious cheesecake would make an attractive finale to any company meal.

CRUST:

1 cup	all-purpose flour	250 mL
1/4 cup	finely chopped almonds	50 mL
1/4 cup	granulated sugar	50 mL
1/3 cup	butter, softened	75 mL
1	egg yolk	1
1/2 tsp	vanilla	2 mL

FILLING:

1 1/2 cups	cranberries	375 mL
1 lb	cream cheese	500 g
1 cup	*each* granulated sugar and sour cream	250 mL
5	eggs	5
2 tbsp	all-purpose flour	25 mL
1 tsp	vanilla	5 mL
1/2 tsp	almond extract	2 mL

GLAZE:

1 cup	cranberry juice	250 mL
1 tbsp	cornstarch	15 mL

CRUST: In bowl, stir together flour, almonds and sugar; make well in middle. Place butter, egg yolk and vanilla in well; blend with fork, then mix with fingers just until dough holds together yet is still fairly crumbly. Press evenly onto bottom and sides of lightly greased 9-inch (2.5 L) springform pan; bake in 325°F (160°C) oven for 10 minutes.

FILLING: In food processor or by hand, coarsely chop cranberries; set aside.

In food processor or bowl with electric mixer, break up cream cheese slightly. Add sugar, sour cream, eggs, flour, vanilla and almond extract; process just until smooth and blended, being careful not to let mixture liquefy. Stir in cranberries.

Pour into partially baked crust; bake for 1 hour and 15 minutes or until almost set and starting to crack around outside while still wobbly in centre. Remove from oven and immediately run sharp knife around inside of pan. Let cool to room temperature on wire rack.

GLAZE: In small saucepan, stir together cranberry juice and cornstarch; cook over medium heat, stirring constantly, until clear and thickened, about 4 minutes. Let cool for 10 minutes. Spoon thin layer over top of cheesecake; let stand for 5 to 10 minutes or until set. Spoon remaining glaze over top. Cover and refrigerate for at least 6 hours. Remove sides of pan and cut into wedges to serve. Makes about 12 servings.

OLD-FASHIONED FRESH STRAWBERRY SHORTCAKE

Throughout the decades, strawberry shortcake has been the focus of many festivals and summer suppers—a dessert everyone must have at least once in strawberry season. Use this old-fashioned shortcake base (which is best served slightly warm) for peach, blueberry or raspberry shortcakes throughout the summer. Just sweeten the fruit to taste. If you'd like a lighter version, use the sweet version of Remarkable Low-Fat Cream (page 185) instead of whipped cream.

2 cups	all-purpose flour	500 mL
3 tbsp	granulated sugar	50 mL
1 tbsp	baking powder	15 mL
1/2 tsp	salt	2 mL
1/2 cup	butter	125 mL
2/3 cup	light cream	150 mL
1	egg	1
1 cup	whipping cream	250 mL
4 cups	strawberries, hulled	1 L
1/3 cup	icing sugar	75 mL
1 tsp	vanilla	5 mL
	Butter, softened	

In large bowl, sift or stir together flour, 2 tbsp (25 mL) of the granulated sugar, baking powder and salt; cut in butter until it resembles fine crumbs. In measuring cup, beat together light cream and egg; quickly stir all at once into dry ingredients to moisten.

Form into ball; pat into ungreased 8-inch (2 L) square cake pan. Brush with 2 tsp (10 mL) of the whipping cream; sprinkle with remaining granulated sugar. Bake in 450°F (230°C) oven for 12 to 15 minutes or until golden brown on top. Place on rack and let cool for about 30 minutes.

Meanwhile, set aside 6 whole strawberries for garnish. Slice or chop remaining berries and place in bowl; sprinkle with all but 1 tbsp (15 mL) of the icing sugar. Set aside for at least 30 minutes.

In chilled bowl, beat remaining whipping cream with remaining icing sugar and vanilla. Cut shortcake into 6 pieces; slice each horizontally in half. Set bottom halves on individual serving plates, cut side up. Butter both cut sides. Spoon on sliced berries and their juices; top with remaining shortcake. Spread whipped cream over top; garnish with whole berry. Makes 6 servings.

RESPLENDENT RASPBERRY SUMMER PUDDING

On our farm, as I grew up, the fruit season began with a few strawberries, and there were currants of two colors, gooseberries, a line of sour cherry trees, a couple of peach trees, with pears, plums and apples later on. But it was raspberries on which we really concentrated. The patch was huge, and the berries bigger than I've ever seen since.

I do often think of all the wonderful fruit that used to grow on our farm and haunt the local market to find as much as I can of summer's bounty. Then I make the following glorious pudding. Pass a pitcher of pouring custard with it, but you can accompany it with sweetened whipped cream or vanilla ice cream if you wish.

6 to 8	slices homemade-style bread, crusts removed	6 to 8
4 cups	red raspberries	1 L
2 cups	pitted black sweet cherries	500 mL
1 1/2 cups	stemmed red currants	375 mL
1 1/2 cups	black raspberries*	375 mL
3/4 cup	(approx) granulated sugar	175 mL
4 tsp	cornstarch	20 mL
2 tbsp	cold water	25 mL
4 tsp	quick-cooking tapioca	20 mL
1 tbsp	amaretto liqueur or kirsch	15 mL

Line bottom and sides of 6-cup (1.5 L) bowl or mould with as much bread as needed to cover completely, trimming where necessary. Reserve remaining pieces for top.

In large heavy saucepan, sprinkle red raspberries, cherries, currants and black raspberries with sugar. Bring to boil over medium-low heat; cook, stirring, for about 3 minutes or until sugar has melted. Remove from heat; transfer 2 tbsp (25 mL) of the juice to small container and refrigerate.

Stir cornstarch into water; stir in tapioca and immediately mix into fruit mixture. Cook over low heat, stirring frequently, until slightly thickened, about 3 minutes. Remove from heat; stir in amaretto. Taste and add more sugar if too tart.

Spoon fruit mixture into bread-lined mould; cover surface completely with layer of remaining bread. Place plate that fits just inside dish on top of pudding; weigh down with heavy object. Refrigerate overnight.

To serve, remove weight and plate. Invert onto serving plate; brush with reserved juice. Makes 6 to 8 servings.

*Although black raspberries make the dessert extra-special, you can increase amount of red raspberries to 5 1/2 cups (1.4 L) if black ones are not available. I have also used thimbleberries instead of black raspberries.

APPLE BREAD PUDDING

Bread puddings were the invention of thrifty cooks to make good use of stale bread. This pudding is packed with sautéed apple slices to give a memorable reminder of the past. Serve on its own or accompanied by cream, custard sauce or yogurt.

2 tbsp	dry bread crumbs	25 mL
6	large slices firm white stale bread (preferably home-made style)	6
1/4 cup	butter	50 mL
3 cups	cored peeled sliced apples	750 mL
2/3 cup	granulated sugar	150 mL
2	eggs	2
2 cups	hot milk	500 mL
1 tsp	vanilla	5 mL
1/2 tsp	cinnamon	2 mL
Pinch	salt	Pinch
2 tbsp	red currant jelly	25 mL

Sprinkle crumbs in well-greased 8-inch (2 L) square baking dish. Cut crusts from bread; spread bread with half of the butter and cut into quarters. Line dish with half of the bread, buttered side up.

In large skillet, melt remaining butter over medium-high heat; sauté apples for 5 minutes. Add 3 tbsp (50 mL) of the sugar; sauté for 3 to 5 minutes or until apples start to turn golden but don't become mushy.

In bowl, beat eggs well; beat in remaining sugar. Gradually whisk in hot milk, vanilla, cinnamon and salt; pour half of the mixture over bread in dish. Evenly spread apple mixture over top. Cover with remaining bread; pour remaining egg mixture over top.

Place baking dish in larger shallow pan. Pour in enough boiling water into larger pan to come 1 inch (2.5 cm) up sides; bake, uncovered, in 325°F (160°C) oven for about 45 minutes or until custard is almost set. Remove baking dish to wire rack.

In small saucepan, melt currant jelly over medium heat; brush over pudding. Serve hot or warm. Makes 6 servings.

PEACHES CATHERINE

Catherine Betts, a good friend who has a catering business in St. John, New Brunswick, brought this delightful recipe home with her from New Zealand. It's one of those recipes that takes very little work to put together and everyone loves. Since it can be made only in peach season, I always plan a big party just around this dessert. Invariably I find a guest out in the kitchen after dinner scraping the empty dish clean with a spoon.

15	ripe peaches	15
2 tbsp	fresh lemon juice	25 mL
2 cups	whipping cream	500 mL
3/4 cup	packed brown sugar	175 mL

Peel, slice and arrange peaches in 12-cup (3 L) shallow gratin dish or other attractive baking dish, sprinkling with lemon juice as you work.

Whip cream; spread all over peaches. Sprinkle with brown sugar by putting it through fine sieve. Cover with plastic wrap and refrigerate overnight. (This is necessary.)

Just before serving, broil peaches about 4 inches from heat for about 2 minutes or until crispy golden on top. Makes 12 servings.

QUICK COBBLER

This luscious fruit dessert was served to me at a bed and breakfast in New Brunswick many years ago. My hostess' name was Eunice, but this well-used recipe had "Mary's Dessert" at the top. It's kind of a cobbler but a lot quicker to make and has a shiny, sugary crust.

3 cups	blueberries or raspberries (fresh or frozen)	750 mL
2 tsp	fresh lemon juice	10 mL
½ tsp	cinnamon	2 mL
1 cup	granulated sugar	250 mL
2 tsp	butter	10 mL
1½ cups	all-purpose flour	375 mL
1½ tsp	baking powder	7 mL
Pinch	salt	Pinch
¾ cup	milk	175 mL
2 tsp	cornstarch	10 mL
1 cup	boiling water	250 mL

In greased 6- or 8-cup (1.5 or 2 L) soufflé dish or casserole, combine berries, lemon juice and cinnamon.

In large bowl, cream half of the sugar with butter; stir in flour, baking powder and salt. Stir in milk just to blend; spread over fruit.

Combine remaining sugar with cornstarch; sprinkle over top and pour boiling water over everything. Bake in 350°F (180°C) oven for about 1 hour or until tester inserted in topping comes out clean. Makes about 6 servings.

WONDERFULLY SATISFYING APPLE CRISP

I remember occasionally relishing a cold dish of my mother's apple crisp when I returned home from public school at the end of the day. But this family favorite is best served warm with Cheddar cheese, vanilla ice cream or Remarkable Low-Fat Cream (page 185).

8	tart apples (about 2 lb/1 kg)	8
½ cup	water	125 mL
¼ cup	granulated sugar	50 mL
1 tsp	cinnamon	5 mL
½ tsp	vanilla	2 mL
Pinch	salt	Pinch
¾ cup	packed brown sugar	175 mL
¾ cup	all-purpose flour	175 mL
¼ tsp	nutmeg	1 mL
⅓ cup	butter	75 mL

Peel, core and thinly slice apples. Place in greased 8-inch (2 L) square baking dish. Stir in water, granulated sugar, ½ tsp (2 mL) of the cinnamon, vanilla and salt.

In small bowl, stir together brown sugar, flour, remaining cinnamon and nutmeg. With pastry blender or two knives, cut in butter until mixture is crumbly.

Sprinkle over apple mixture; bake, uncovered, in 375°F (190°C) oven for 30 minutes or until apples are very tender. Makes 4 to 6 servings.

FROZEN STRAWBERRY YOGURT

When you crave a rich, creamy ice cream, try this smooth low-cal cousin with its fresh, intense strawberry flavor. It's quick to make and superior to commercial frozen yogurts, which often contain enough sweeteners and artificial flavors to equal ice cream in calories.

For best results, use plain low-fat yogurt (with about 1% milk fat) and have it at room temperature to prevent lumping. The frozen yogurt is best when first made, but it can be stored in a covered container in the freezer for up to 1 week. You will have to leave it out of the freezer for a few minutes to soften enough to scoop.

2 cups	strawberries, hulled	500 mL
¹/₂ cup	instant dissolving (fruit/berry) sugar (or granulated sugar processed in blender)	125 mL
1 tbsp	fresh lemon juice	15 mL
¹/₂ tsp	grated orange rind	2 mL
1	envelope unflavored gelatin	1
1 ¹/₂ cups	plain low-fat yogurt (at room temperature)	375 mL

In food processor or blender, purée strawberries, sugar, lemon juice and orange rind.

In small saucepan, sprinkle gelatin over 3 tbsp (50 mL) cold water; let stand to soften for 5 minutes. Stir over medium-low heat until gelatin is dissolved, about 5 minutes. (Or, in microwaveable bowl soften gelatin in water, then microwave at High for 30 seconds; stir.) Stir into fruit purée.

Stir in yogurt; transfer to ice cream maker and freeze according to manufacturer's instructions. Makes about 3 cups (750 mL).

CARDAMOM PEAR YOGURT

Since some fruit yogurts are quite high in sugar, you might prefer to toss together your own economic, low-cal version, like this easy pear combination. Try it with a peach or a few cubes of melon, too.

1	pear	1
1 tbsp	fresh lemon juice	15 mL
¹/₂ cup	plain yogurt	125 mL
1 tsp	packed brown sugar	5 mL
Pinch	ground cardamom	Pinch

Core pear and coarsely cube. In small bowl, toss pear with lemon juice.

Stir together yogurt, sugar and cardamom; stir into pear mixture just to mix. Makes 1 serving.

BLACK FOREST CUPCAKES

Even as a young child, my daughter, Anne, did the bulk of the family baking. These dense chocolate cakes with their cherry-cheese topping baked right on was one of her favorite recipes. They were certainly much easier to make than the traditional Black Forest cake my son, Allen, sometimes requested for his birthday.

½ cup	butter, softened	125 mL
1½ cups	packed brown sugar	375 mL
1	egg	1
1½ cups	all-purpose flour	375 mL
½ cup	unsweetened cocoa powder	125 mL
½ tsp	baking powder	2 mL
Pinch	salt	Pinch
1 tsp	baking soda	5 mL
1 cup	sour cream	250 mL

TOPPING:

1	can (14 oz/398 mL) pitted sour red cherries	1
¼ lb	light cream cheese	125 g
1	egg	1
½ cup	chocolate chips	125 mL

TOPPING: Drain cherries; coarsely chop and set aside. In bowl, cream cheese; beat in egg until fluffy. Stir in chocolate chips and cherries. Set aside.

Line twenty-four 2½-inch (6 cm) muffin cups with paper liners.

In large bowl, cream butter; beat in sugar. Beat in egg. Sift or stir together flour, cocoa, baking powder and salt. Stir baking soda into sour cream. Stir dry ingredients into creamed mixture alternately with sour cream just until mixed.

Spoon into prepared cups, filling three-quarters full. Place heaping spoonful of topping on each; bake in 350°F (180°C) oven for about 20 minutes or until tester inserted in cake part comes out clean. Makes 24 cupcakes.

FRESH FRUIT SALAD WITH HONEY-GINGER DRESSING

A touch of ginger makes fresh fruit sing as in this colorful make-ahead combination—perfect for a brunch. Omit the strawberries if you can't get any fresh ones.

5	grapefruit	5
½ cup	water	125 mL
¼ cup	liquid honey	50 mL
3 tbsp	finely slivered fresh ginger	50 mL
1	small cantaloupe, peeled and cubed	1
Half	fresh pineapple, peeled and cubed	Half
2 cups	fresh strawberries	500 mL
2	kiwifruit	2

Peel grapefruit and cut away white pith. Holding over large bowl to catch juice, cut grapefruit sections away from membranes, placing sections in another bowl as you work. Squeeze all juice from membranes into large bowl; discard membranes. Measure out ⅔ cup (150 mL) juice, adding water if necessary.

In small stainless steel saucepan, combine grapefruit juice, water, honey and ginger; bring to boil. Reduce heat to low; cover and simmer until ginger is tender, 20 to 25 minutes. Let cool; pour over grapefruit. Add cantaloupe and pineapple; toss to mix. Cover and refrigerate for at least 4 hours or overnight.

One hour before serving, hull strawberries; slice lengthwise. Peel kiwifruit; slice crosswise. Add strawberry and kiwi slices to grapefruit mixture, tossing gently. Let stand at room temperature until serving. Makes 8 to 10 servings.

OVEN-CARAMELIZED PEARS

This wonderful fruit dessert takes only a few minutes to prepare and can cook while you enjoy your main course. It's best served warm with a crisp cookie on the side. Use pears that are ripe but firm.

6	pears	6
⅓ cup	granulated sugar	75 mL
¼ cup	butter, in bits	50 mL
½ cup	whipping cream	125 mL
Pinch	*each* nutmeg and ginger	Pinch

Peel, core and slice pears; arrange in well-greased 9-inch (2.5 L) square baking dish. Sprinkle with sugar; dot with butter.

Bake, uncovered, in 500°F (260°C) oven for 30 minutes or until sugar is golden, gently stirring once.

Stir together cream, nutmeg and ginger; pour over pears. Bake for about 5 minutes or until light brown syrup has formed. Makes 4 servings.

CIDER-BAKED APPLESAUCE

I often make this simple, apple-intense sauce when I have a pork roast or chicken in the oven to serve alongside. It's also good as dessert or with yogurt and granola for breakfast. Use Empire or McIntosh apples or, if you're lucky enough to find them in an August farmers' market, Yellow Transparents.

5	apples	5
1 tbsp	fresh lemon juice	15 mL
¼ cup	packed brown sugar	50 mL
Pinch	*each* cinnamon and nutmeg	Pinch
¼ cup	apple cider or apple juice	50 mL

Peel, core and cut apples into eighths; place in 8-inch (2 L) square baking dish. Toss with lemon juice; sprinkle with brown sugar, cinnamon and nutmeg. Drizzle with cider; stir gently until sugar dissolves.

Cover and bake in 350°F (180°C) oven for 35 to 45 minutes or until apples are soft. Mash with potato masher. Makes about 2 cups (500 mL).

SPICY RAISIN-FILLED BAKED APPLES

When I was growing up on the farm, fragrant baked apples were a standard fall and winter dessert. Like many good-tasting ideas, this one comes from the farm kitchen of Mary Lou Ruby Jonas. Cutting the apples in half enables more of their surface to be cloaked in the spicy syrup. Choose an apple that holds its shape when cooked—something like Northern Spy. Serve warm with unsweetened lightly whipped cream or Remarkable Low-Fat Cream (page 185).

1 cup	water	250 mL
1/3 cup	*each* granulated sugar and packed brown sugar	75 mL
1 tbsp	*each* butter and lemon juice	15 mL
1/2 tsp	cinnamon	2 mL
1/4 tsp	ground cloves	1 mL
3	large apples	3
2/3 cup	raisins	150 mL

In small saucepan, combine water, granulated and brown sugars, butter, lemon juice, cinnamon and cloves; bring to boil. Reduce heat to brisk simmer and cook, uncovered, for 10 minutes.

Meanwhile, cut apples in half crosswise and remove cores; arrange cut side up in shallow baking dish just large enough to hold them. Fill hollow centres with raisins. Pour sugar mixture over top. Bake, uncovered and basting often with syrup in 375°F (190°C) oven for 30 to 45 minutes or until apples are tender. Makes 6 servings.

FRESH PINEAPPLE WITH HOT RUM SAUCE

Here's a quick, light dessert for a taste of the tropics.

1/4 cup	light rum	50 mL
4	slices fresh pineapple (at least 1/2 inch/1 cm thick)	4
1 tsp	granulated sugar	5 mL
1/4 cup	*each* unsalted butter and granulated sugar	50 mL
3	egg yolks, beaten	3
1/4 cup	coarsely grated coconut (preferably fresh)	50 mL

In bowl, pour rum over pineapple slices; sprinkle with 1 tsp (5 mL) sugar. Cover and marinate at room temperature for several hours or overnight, stirring occasionally.

Drain pineapple slices completely, reserving marinade; place slices on 4 dessert plates.

In top of double boiler over simmering water, combine butter and 1/4 cup (50 mL) sugar until melted but not cooked. Stir in 1/4 cup (50 mL) of the marinade and egg yolks; whisk over simmering water until thickened, about 4 minutes.

Pour over pineapple; sprinkle with coconut. Serve immediately. Makes 4 servings.

SILKY GINGER ICE CREAM
WITH DARK CHOCOLATE SAUCE

This creamy golden ice cream with its quick and easy chocolate sauce reminds me of the spicy-sweet candied ginger enveloped in bitter-cool chocolate at our favorite candy shop.

1/2 cup	water	125 mL
1/3 cup	mild-flavored liquid honey	75 mL
1/3 cup	minced peeled fresh ginger	75 mL
3/4 cup	light cream	175 mL
1 tbsp	finely chopped crystallized ginger	15 mL
6	egg yolks	6
1/4 cup	granulated sugar	50 mL
1/4 tsp	grated lemon rind	1 mL
1 1/2 cups	whipping cream	375 mL
	Dark Chocolate Sauce (recipe follows)	

In small saucepan, stir together water, honey and fresh ginger; bring to boil. Reduce heat and simmer, uncovered and stirring occasionally, for 5 minutes.

Scald light cream with crystallized ginger; add fresh ginger syrup. Cover and steep for 20 minutes.

In large bowl, beat yolks with granulated sugar and rind until pale yellow; transfer to heavy saucepan. Gradually whisk in light cream mixture, then whipping cream. Cook, stirring constantly, over medium-low heat until slightly thickened, about 8 minutes. Do not boil.

Strain through fine sieve into cool large clean bowl. When mixture stops steaming, press plastic wrap onto surface; refrigerate until very cold, several hours or overnight.

Freeze in ice cream maker according to manufacturer's directions. Serve topped with warm Dark Chocolate Sauce. Makes 4 cups (1 L).

DARK CHOCOLATE SAUCE

3/4 cup	whipping cream	175 mL
5 oz	bittersweet or semisweet chocolate, broken up	150 g
1 tbsp	butter	15 mL

In small heavy saucepan, bring cream to boil; remove from heat. Add chocolate and stir until melted. Stir in butter; let cool slightly before using. (Sauce can be cooled, covered and refrigerated for up to 1 week. Reheat over low heat until warm to serve.) Makes 1 cup (250 mL) sauce.

DESSERT CREPES

³/4 cup	milk	175 mL
3 tbsp	pear or apple liqueur	50 mL
3	eggs	3
Pinch	salt	Pinch
2 tbsp	granulated sugar	25 mL
1 cup	all-purpose flour	250 mL
	Unsalted butter, melted	
³/4 cup	soda water	175 mL

In blender or food processor, place milk, liqueur, eggs, salt, sugar and flour in that order. Cover and blend at top speed for 1 minute in blender or 20 seconds in food processor, scraping down sides once. Cover and refrigerate for at least 2 hours or overnight.

Place 8-inch (20 cm) crêpe or omelette pan over medium-high heat and brush with melted butter; heat until drops of water bounce and sputter when sprinkled on pan.

Stir soda water into batter. Lift pan and pour in about 3 tbsp (50 mL) batter; swirl to coat pan and quickly pour any excess batter back into blender.

With spatula, lift up edge of crêpe when set; cook just until bottom is lightly browned. Turn crêpe over and cook for 2 to 3 seconds longer or until edge is lightly browned. Remove to plate and let cool. Repeat with remaining batter, brushing pan with butter when necessary. Don't stack crêpes until cool. (Crepes can be covered and refrigerated overnight or frozen in airtight container for up to 3 weeks.) Makes 18 to 24 crêpes.

FRESH WINTER FRUIT CREPES WITH HOT MAPLE SYRUP

The mellow sweetness of maple syrup complements tart apples and pears in this easy, but elegant dessert. Serve with pitcher of additional maple syrup and more whipped cream if desired. If you wish, serve with maple whipped cream made by adding ¹/4 cup (50 mL) maple syrup to 1 cup (250 mL) whipping cream just as you finish beating it.

1 tsp	grated lemon rind	5 mL
¹/4 cup	fresh lemon juice	50 mL
2	apples (Ida Red or Spy)	2
2	pears	2

¹/₄ cup	unsalted butter	50 mL
¹/₂ cup	packed brown sugar or maple sugar	125 mL
¹/₄ tsp	nutmeg	1 mL
1 tbsp	pear or apple liqueur	15 mL
12	dessert crêpes	12
	Whipped cream	
	Mint sprigs	
	Maple syrup	

Divide lemon rind and juice between 2 small bowls. Peel and thinly slice apples and pears, placing apples in 1 bowl and pear slices in other as you work. Toss slices to coat well.

In large skillet, melt butter with sugar over medium heat. Add apple mixture and nutmeg; cook, stirring often, for 4 minutes. Add pear mixture; cook for 3 or 4 minutes or until fruit is tender but not mushy. Stir in liqueur.

Spread each crêpe with about 2 tbsp (25 mL) filling; fold in quarters and arrange on platter. Garnish with rosettes of whipped cream and mint sprigs. In small saucepan, warm maple syrup over low heat or in pitcher in microwave. Drizzle over crêpes. Makes 6 servings.

BRANDIED PEACH CLAFOUTI

A cakelike custard or thick fruit pancake from Limousin, France, clafouti was originally made with black cherries, but I think it's more wonderful with peaches. It's one of those quick, simple, not-too-sweet desserts just right for either family or company and great for brunch. If you wish, serve with a dollop of whipped cream or sweetened Remarkable Low-Fat Cream (page 185).

3¹/₂ cups	sliced peeled peaches (6 to 8)	875 mL
2 tbsp	brandy or cognac	25 mL
¹/₃ cup	granulated sugar	75 mL
2 cups	light cream	500 mL
3	eggs	3
¹/₄ cup	all-purpose flour	50 mL
Pinch	salt	Pinch
1 tsp	vanilla	5 mL
	Icing sugar	

In bowl, toss peaches with brandy; set aside.

Grease 8-cup (2 L) shallow baking dish; sprinkle with 2 tbsp (25 mL) of the sugar.

In blender or food processor, blend cream, eggs, flour and salt for 2 minutes in blender or 1 minute in processor. Add remaining sugar and vanilla; blend for a few seconds.

Arrange peaches and any juice in prepared dish; pour cream mixture over top.

Bake in 375°F (190°C) oven for 45 to 50 minutes or until puffed and golden. Let cool until barely warm. (Clafouti will naturally fall as it cools.) Sprinkle with icing sugar and serve. Makes 8 servings.

HARVEST PIES

There would be a choice of apple, squash, plum and maybe even an old-fashioned butterscotch pie with meringue topping. I can remember those noon meals when a crowd of men would come in from the fields to gather around our big, round kitchen table. Before my family bought a modern combine, harvesttime meant a threshing machine travelled from farm to farm and everyone helped his neighbor. Each farmer's wife would take her turn at providing meals for the hungry threshers.

There was always pie for dessert—with I'm sure much expert assessment among the men as to who made the best elderberry or peach.

The variety was infinite—raisin, pear, lemon meringue, grape, custard, maple syrup, even green tomato—but it always depended on what was in season and what was at hand, abundant choices, indeed, at harvesttime. Although it may seem extraordinary to many young cooks, a pie was just about the easiest thing a busy farm wife could make. It was also an economical method of making a few ingredients go a long way around a table of hungry diners. Early cooks had already discovered that round pans could help them literally cut corners and stretch ingredients. The other advantage was that a pie didn't have to be eaten immediately. Farm men came in for dinner when they were ready, not when dinner was ready.

Appetites have changed, and my own family hasn't seen as many pies as I remember from my own well-fed childhood, but no matter what other sophisticated desserts I serve, a good old-fashioned pie is still a treat—especially during harvest season.

PIE POINTERS:
—Measure ingredients exactly—dry ingredients in dry measures and liquids in liquid.
—Work quickly and do not overwork the dough.
—Keep work surface, equipment and hands cool and use chilled shortening, lard or butter and ice water.
—If the dough has a chance to rest in the refrigerator before baking, it will be more tender and will not shrink as much.
—Use as little flour as possible when rolling out dough. A stockinette covering for your rolling pin will help.
—Invest in a good pie plate or two. Avoid foil plates or plates that are too shallow.
—Bake pies in the bottom third of your oven following the exact temperatures given.

FOOD PROCESSOR PASTRY

Mary Lou Ruby Jonas, who sometimes assists me, is of Mennonite back-ground and one of the most accomplished pie-makers I know. This is her pastry and along with it goes the advice to work quickly and not to overwork the pastry.

1 1/2 cups	all-purpose flour	375 mL
Pinch	salt	Pinch
1/2 cup	cold lard or shortening, in bits	125 mL
1/4 cup	ice water	50 mL
1 tsp	vinegar or fresh lemon juice	5 mL

In food processor, blend flour and salt; cut in lard with on/off pulse until crumbly.

In measuring cup, stir together water and vinegar. With machine running, gradually pour in water mixture through feed tube, using just enough to form ball. Do not overprocess.

Turn out onto lightly floured surface; knead a few times to form soft ball. Roll out and line pie plate. Refrigerate for at least 30 minutes before filling. Makes one 9- or 10-inch (23 or 25 cm) shell.

IRRESISTIBLE ALMOND STREUSEL CHERRY PIE

Fruit pies are always irresistible, and no one will be able to pass up this juicy cherry one with its attractive almond topping. By the way, it travels well if you need something for that family picnic or potluck supper.

1 1/4 cups	granulated sugar	300 mL
1/2 cup	all-purpose flour	125 mL
1/4 cup	ground almonds	50 mL
1/2 cup	cold butter	125 mL
5 cups	pitted fresh or frozen sour cherries*	1.25 L
3 tbsp	*each* quick-cooking tapioca and lemon juice	50 mL
1/4 tsp	almond extract	1 mL
1	10-inch (25 cm) unbaked pie shell	1

In small bowl or food processor, stir together 1/2 cup (125 mL) of the sugar, flour and almonds; cut in butter until mixture resembles coarse crumbs. Set aside.

In large bowl, stir together cherries, remaining sugar, tapioca, lemon juice and almond extract. Arrange cherry mixture in pie shell; sprinkle with flour mixture.

Bake in 425°F (220°C) oven for 10 minutes. Reduce heat to 375°F (190°C); bake for about 40 minutes longer or until topping and pastry are golden brown. Makes 8 servings.

*If using frozen, don't thaw. (You may have to bake pie slightly longer.) If cherries have been frozen with sugar, adjust amount of sugar in cherry mixture accordingly.

CARAMEL APPLE PIE

Nothing emits a more pleasant aroma of fall than a kitchen when an apple pie is baking in the oven. This open-faced pie is special indeed with its caramel coating.

6	tart apples (Spy, Golden Delicious, Spartan, McIntosh or Mutsu 2 lb/1 kg)	6
2 tbsp	fresh lemon juice	25 mL
1¼ cups	granulated sugar	300 mL
2 tbsp	all-purpose flour	25 mL
1 tsp	cinnamon	5 mL
¼ tsp	*each* salt and nutmeg	1 mL
1	9-inch (23 cm) unbaked pie shell	1
¼ cup	butter, cut in bits	50 mL
½ cup	whipping cream	125 mL
½ cup	toasted coarsely chopped walnuts	125 mL

Peel, core and slice apples; place in large bowl and toss with lemon juice. Combine ¼ cup (50 mL) of the sugar, flour, cinnamon, salt and nutmeg; toss with apples.

Spread apple mixture in pie shell; cover with circle of parchment or waxed paper. Bake in 425°F (220°C) oven for 20 minutes. Remove paper and reduce heat to 375°F (190°C); bake for 30 to 35 minutes or until crust is golden and apples are tender, covering with foil if apples or crust become too brown.

In heavy saucepan, heat remaining sugar over medium heat without stirring, shaking pan gently as sugar begins to melt. When sugar is medium-brown caramel color, gradually whisk in butter. Just before butter is all blended, carefully whisk in cream (it will sputter); return to boil. Remove from heat and stir well. Let cool for 5 minutes; pour over hot apples. Sprinkle with walnuts. Let cool before serving. Makes 8 to 10 servings.

DEEP-DISH PEAR PIE WITH SPICED CRUST

A true taste of fall, this spicy pear pie is a cinch to make since you just put the pastry on the top. Choose a dish that's square or round and roll the pastry 1 inch (2.5 cm) bigger than the top. This filling fits perfectly into a 9-inch (23 cm) round dish that's 2 inches (5 cm) deep.

To make the spiced crust, add the cinnamon, nutmeg and ginger to the flour mixture of Food Processor Pastry (page 161) before cutting in the fat.

8 cups	sliced peeled pears (about 8 large)	2 L
2 tbsp	lemon juice	25 mL
⅓ cup	*each* packed brown sugar and granulated sugar	75 mL
3 tbsp	quick-cooking tapioca	50 mL

1 tsp	ground cardamom	5 mL
Pinch	salt	Pinch
2 tbsp	butter, in bits	25 mL
	Pastry for single-crust 9-inch (23 cm) pie	
1 tsp	cinnamon	5 mL
1/2 tsp	*each* nutmeg and ginger	2 mL
	Light cream or milk and additional granulated sugar	

In large bowl, toss pears with lemon juice. Stir together brown and granulated sugars, tapioca, cardamom and salt; toss well with pears. Arrange in baking dish; dot with butter.

When making pastry, add cinnamon, nutmeg and ginger to flour mixture (see above). Roll out pastry 1 inch (2.5 cm) larger than top of baking dish; place over pears and fold edges under. Crimp edges and cut steam vents. Cut out pear and leaf shapes from scraps of pastry if desired. Brush pastry with cream and arrange pastry decoration on top; brush again and sprinkle all with granulated sugar. Bake in 425°F (220°C) oven for 25 minutes; reduce temperature to 375°F (190°C) and bake for 20 to 25 minutes longer or until thick syrup bubbles through vents. Makes 6 to 8 servings.

OPEN-FACED APPLE TART

This simple French-style tart highlights the fresh flavor of crisp, just-picked fall apples. Although very easy to make, the tart looks and tastes sensational, especially served slightly warm with softly whipped cream scented with a touch of cinnamon.

4	tart apples (about 1 1/2 lb/750 g)	4
	Juice and grated rind of 1 lemon	
1/4 cup	butter	50 mL
1/2 cup	granulated sugar	125 mL
Half	pkg (411 g) puff pastry, thawed	Half
1 tbsp	Calvados or apple liqueur	15 mL

Peel apples and cut in half lengthwise. Core and slice each half thinly crosswise, dropping into bowl and tossing with lemon rind and juice as you work.

In large skillet, melt butter over medium heat, cook apples and sugar, stirring often, for 4 minutes. Remove to bowl with slotted spoon.

Bring butter mixture to boil; boil for 5 minutes. Remove from heat; set aside.

On lightly floured surface, roll out puff pastry to 13- x 7-inch (33 x 18 cm) rectangle; transfer to ungreased baking sheet. Straighten edges and pinch up fluted border all around, using first finger and thumb.

Arrange apples in overlapping rows crosswise over pastry; sprinkle with Calvados, syrup from skillet and any juice from bowl. Bake in 400°F (200°C) oven for about 25 minutes or until apples are tender. Let cool slightly or come to room temperature, but do not refrigerate. Makes 6 to 8 servings.

WARM SPICED CRANBERRY AND APPLE PASTRIES

Reminiscent of a good old-fashioned fruit pie, these easy fruit-filled pastry squares take only minutes to make ahead. Reheat while you're finishing your main course.

1/2 lb	puff pastry (thawed if frozen)	250 g
1	egg, beaten	1
4	medium apples	4
4 tsp	fresh lemon juice	20 mL
1	pkg (12 oz/340 g) fresh or frozen cranberries (3 cups/750 mL)	1
1 1/4 cups	packed brown sugar	300 mL
3 tbsp	all-purpose flour	50 mL
1/2 tsp	cinnamon	2 mL
1/4 tsp	allspice	1 mL
	Icing sugar	
	Vanilla ice cream	

On floured surface and working with half of the pastry at a time, roll out pastry to 12- x 4-inch (30 x 10 cm) rectangle. Cut into four 4- x 3-inch (10 x 8 cm) pieces. Transfer to ungreased baking sheet and refrigerate for 15 minutes.

Prick dough evenly all over with fork; brush with egg. Bake in 400°F (200°C) oven for 7 to 8 minutes or until puffed. Reduce heat to 350°F (180°C); bake for 10 minutes longer or until golden brown. Let cool on baking sheet.

Peel apples and cut into 12 slices, tossing with lemon juice in bowl as you work. Stir in cranberries, brown sugar, flour, cinnamon and allspice.

Arrange apple mixture in shallow 8-cup (2 L) baking or gratin dish; cover and bake in 350°F (180°C) oven, gently stirring 2 or 3 times, for about 50 minutes or until apples are just tender and not falling apart and cranberries are bubbling but not bursting. (Recipe can be prepared to this point and set aside at room temperature for a few hours. Warm pastries and fruit mixture in 350°F (180°C) oven for 5 minutes before assembling.)

To serve, split pastries in half horizontally; place bottom halves on 8 dessert plates. Spread each with some of the warm fruit mixture; top with remaining pastry. Sift icing sugar over each. Serve warm with ice cream. Makes 8 servings.

CLASSIC "RUNNY" BUTTER TARTS

Almost the only food specialty that Canada can claim as its very own, butter tarts have had a wide and faithful following in this country for many years. I've seldom met anyone who didn't start to salivate at the mere mention—especially the runny kind. The more set variety has its disciples, too, but the following wonderfully easy-to-make tarts will probably drip down your chin at the first bite. The recipe comes from the farm kitchen of my aunt Lexie Armstrong in Orillia, Ontario. Feel free to add any of those ingredients Canadians have used over the years—

walnuts, raisins, coconut or currants, remembering that you'll need more tart shells.

2 cups	packed brown sugar	500 mL
2	eggs	2
1 tbsp	butter	15 mL
1 tsp	vanilla	5 mL
2 tbsp	hot water	25 mL
18	unbaked pastry-lined medium tart cups	18

Whisk together sugar, eggs, butter, vanilla and hot water. Pour into tart shells, filling each about two-thirds full. Bake in 450°F (230°C) oven for 10 to 12 minutes or until golden brown. Makes 18 tarts.

UPSIDE-DOWN PEAR GINGERBREAD

Serve this old-fashioned soft gingerbread hot with softly whipped cream flavored with chopped candied ginger.

3 tbsp	butter, softened	50 mL
2 tbsp	granulated sugar	25 mL
2	large pears	2
1 cup	butter	250 mL
1/2 cup	packed brown sugar	125 mL
1	egg	1
1 cup	molasses	250 mL
2 tsp	baking soda	10 mL
1 cup	boiling water	250 mL
3 cups	all-purpose flour	750 mL
1 tbsp	ginger	15 mL
1/2 tsp	cinnamon	2 mL
1/4 tsp	*each* salt and cloves	1 mL

Spread soft butter on bottom of 9-inch (2.5 L) square baking dish; sprinkle with granulated sugar. Peel, core and slice pears; arrange in dish and set aside.

In large bowl, cream butter with brown sugar; beat in egg until light and fluffy. Stir in molasses.

Dissolve baking soda in boiling water. Sift or stir together flour, ginger, cinnamon, salt and cloves; add to creamed mixture alternately with soda mixture, stirring just until blended. Pour over pears. Bake in 350°F (180°C) oven for 45 to 60 minutes or until tester inserted in centre comes out clean. Let cool for 15 minutes. Invert onto serving plate. Serve warm cut in squares. Makes 8 servings.

NO-BAKE PEANUT BUTTER COOKIES

Even young children can help make these super-fast cookies, which contain one of kids' favorite flavors.

½ cup	*each* lightly packed brown sugar, chunky peanut butter and corn syrup	125 mL
2 cups	cornflakes	500 mL

In saucepan, combine brown sugar, peanut butter and corn syrup; heat over medium heat, stirring constantly, just until sugar has dissolved. Remove from heat and stir in cornflakes.

Using 2 teaspoons, drop mixture in mounds onto waxed paper, working quickly so mixture doesn't harden. (If it does, reheat gently just until soft enough to spoon.) Let cool and set at room temperature before packing into airtight container. Makes about 3 dozen.

ANNE'S FAMOUS CHOCOLATE CHIP COOKIES

My daughter has been making these cookies ever since she could see over the kitchen counter. They're famous because everyone knows how good they are and that she can make them in a flash. I have no idea where she got the recipe, but her copy is printed in a child's hand with bad spelling, big chocolate chips drawn on the border, a message at the top "very good (Yum)" and a big note on the bottom "Check in oven before turning on." (The latter because of my habit of drying my pans in a warm oven.)

½ cup	butter, softened	125 mL
½ cup	packed brown sugar	125 mL
¼ cup	granulated sugar	50 mL
1	egg	1
1 tsp	vanilla	5 mL
1 cup	all-purpose flour	250 mL
½ tsp	*each* baking soda and salt	2 mL
1	pkg (6 oz/175 g) chocolate chips (1 cup/250 mL)	1
½ cup	coarsely chopped walnuts or pecans	125 mL

In large bowl, cream butter; add brown and granulated sugars and beat well. Beat in egg, then vanilla. Stir in flour, baking soda and salt. Blend in chocolate chips and nuts.

Using 2 teaspoons, drop by spoonfuls, 2 inches (5 cm) apart onto ungreased baking sheets. Bake in 375°F (190°C) oven for 8 to 10 minutes or until golden brown. Remove to let cool on rack. Makes about 4 dozen.

CRANBERRY FILBERT COOKIES

These soft cookies not only taste delicious but they look pretty and are very easy to make. Don't thaw the cranberries if they're frozen.

1 cup	*each* butter and packed brown sugar	250 mL

1	egg	1
1 tbsp	water	15 mL
2 cups	all-purpose flour	500 mL
1/2 tsp	baking soda	2 mL
Pinch	salt	Pinch
1 cup	ground hazelnuts (filberts)	250 mL
1 cup	coconut	250 mL
1 cup	whole cranberries (fresh or frozen), coarsely chopped	250 mL

In large bowl, cream together butter and sugar. Beat in egg and water. Sift or stir together flour, baking soda and salt; stir into creamed mixture. Stir in hazelnuts, coconut and cranberries.

Form into 1-inch (2.5 cm) balls; place about 2 inches (5 cm) apart on lightly greased baking sheets. Flatten with tines of fork or bottom of glass. Bake in 350°F (180°C) oven for 10 to 12 minutes or until golden brown. Remove to racks to let cool. Makes 3½ dozen.

MOCHA-GLAZED COFFEE DROPS

These easy-to-make pretty drop cookies are lightly flavored with coffee.

1/2 cup	butter, softened	125 mL
3/4 cup	packed brown sugar	175 mL
1	egg, beaten	1
1 tsp	vanilla	5 mL
1 1/2 cups	all-purpose flour	375 mL
1/2 tsp	*each* baking powder and baking soda	2 mL
1/4 tsp	salt	1 mL
1/3 cup	hot strong coffee	75 mL
1/2 cup	chopped pecans or walnuts	125 mL
GLAZE:		
1 1/2 cups	icing sugar	375 mL
3 tbsp	cold strong coffee	50 mL
1/4 cup	butter, softened	50 mL
1 tbsp	unsweetened cocoa powder	15 mL

In large bowl, cream butter; beat in sugar until light and fluffy. Beat in egg and vanilla. Sift or stir together flour, baking powder, baking soda and salt; add alternately with hot coffee to creamed mixture, stirring just until mixed. Stir in nuts.

Using 2 teaspoons, drop batter by heaping spoonfuls 2 inches (5 cm) apart onto lightly greased baking sheets. Bake in 375°F (190°C) oven for 8 to 10 minutes or until lightly browned. Remove to let cool on wire racks.

GLAZE: In small bowl, alternately add icing sugar and cold coffee to butter, stirring until smooth; stir in cocoa. Spread liberally on cooled cookies. Let stand at room temperature to air dry for 3 to 4 hours for glaze to harden and set. Store in airtight container. Makes about 4 dozen.

PECAN LACE COOKIES

Crisp and lacy, these delicate cookies are extremely quick to make and go wonderfully well with sorbets. When I need to make elegant cookies in a hurry, I always turn to these winners.

¹⁄₂ cup	*each* unsalted butter, packed brown sugar and corn syrup	125 mL
1 cup	all-purpose flour	250 mL
¹⁄₂ tsp	vanilla	2 mL
³⁄₄ cup	finely chopped pecans	175 mL

In heavy saucepan, combine butter, brown sugar and corn syrup; bring to boil over medium heat, stirring just until sugar is dissolved. Remove from heat; stir in flour, vanilla and nuts.

Drop by scant teaspoonfuls (5 mL) 4 inches (10 cm) apart onto greased baking sheets. Bake in 325°F (160°C) oven for 8 to 10 minutes or until set and lightly browned.

Remove from oven and let cool on pans for 2 minutes. Remove to let cool perfectly flat on finely meshed racks or waxed paper. Store in airtight container with waxed paper between layers. Makes 5 dozen.

OLD-FASHIONED CHEWY DOUBLE GINGER COOKIES

Do you remember your grandmother's kitchen smelling wonderful while old-fashioned cookies like these baked? Old-fashioned maybe, but they're a snap to make and store well.

¹⁄₂ cup	shortening	125 mL
1 cup	granulated sugar	250 mL
2	eggs	2
1 cup	molasses	250 mL
3¹⁄₂ cups	all-purpose flour	875 mL
1 tbsp	ground ginger	15 mL
1¹⁄₄ tsp	baking soda	6 mL
1 tsp	ground cloves	5 mL
¹⁄₂ tsp	cinnamon	2 mL
¹⁄₂ cup	finely chopped crystallized ginger	125 mL
	Granulated sugar	

In large bowl, cream together shortening and sugar until light and fluffy. Beat in eggs one at a time; beat in molasses.

Sift or stir together flour, ground ginger, baking soda, cloves and cinnamon; stir into creamed mixture in three parts. Mix in crystallized ginger until smooth.

Remove dough from bowl and wrap in floured waxed paper; refrigerate for at least 2 hours or overnight. (Dough will be quite soft.)

With floured hands, form dough into 1-inch (2.5 cm) balls; gently roll in granulated sugar. Place about 2 inches (5 cm) apart on greased baking sheets; bake in 350°F (180°C) oven for 10 to 12 minutes or just until set but not overbaked. Remove to wire racks to let cool. Makes about 6 dozen.

OLD-FASHIONED RASPBERRY OATMEAL SQUARES

These delicious squares can be made in a flash with whatever is on hand. If you have no raspberry jam, try apricot, grape or cherry, puréeing it slightly if the fruit is in large pieces.

1 cup	all-purpose flour	250 mL
1/2 cup	packed brown sugar	125 mL
2 tsp	grated lemon rind	10 mL
1/4 tsp	*each* baking soda and salt	1 mL
3/4 cup	butter	175 mL
1 1/2 cups	rolled oats	375 mL
1/3 cup	finely chopped almonds	75 mL
1 cup	raspberry jam	250 mL
1 tbsp	fresh lemon juice	15 mL

In large bowl, stir together flour, sugar, lemon rind, baking soda and salt. With two knives or pastry blender, cut in butter until mixture is crumbly. Stir in rolled oats.

Press two-thirds of the mixture evenly into greased 9-inch (2.5 L) square baking pan. Stir almonds into remaining oat mixture; set aside.

Stir together jam and lemon juice; spread evenly over base. Gently sprinkle with remaining oat mixture; pat lightly down into jam. Bake in 350°F (180°C) oven for 30 minutes or until golden brown. Cut into squares while warm; let cool on rack before serving. Makes about 3 dozen.

RETA'S GINGER BROWNIES

I love getting letters from readers across the country, and one I received from a long-lost cousin was particularly exciting. In Edmonton, Alberta, Reta Price saw my picture in a copy of Canadian Living *and realized I was her cousin. We have been corresponding ever since. The following quick and easy recipe is Reta's own creation. The brownies are thin and fudge-like.*

1/4 cup	unsweetened cocoa powder	50 mL
3 tbsp	boiling water	50 mL
3/4 cup	packed brown sugar	175 mL
1/3 cup	butter, melted	75 mL
1	egg	1
1 tsp	vanilla	5 mL
1/2 cup	all-purpose flour	125 mL
2/3 cup	chopped candied ginger	150 mL
	Chocolate Cream Cheese Icing (see page 185)	

In small bowl, dissolve cocoa in boiling water. Set aside.

In large bowl, cream together sugar and butter; stir in egg, cocoa mixture and vanilla until smooth. Stir in flour and ginger.

Transfer to greased 8-inch (2 L) square cake pan; bake in 300°F (150°C) oven for 20 to 25 minutes or until set. Do not overbake. Ice while still slightly warm with Chocolate Cream Cheese Icing. Makes about 2 dozen.

PLUM GOOD FRUIT

When I was growing up, I remember the most marvellous plum tree beside our house. Its trunk was very dark and gnarled, its branches erratic and the fruit big, dark purple and deliciously warm and sweet.

I have no idea what kind of plums grew on our tree, nor had I thought much about plums at all until I started to notice endless rows of baskets at our local farmers' markets during late summer and fall every year.

Except for knowing that almost every farm harbors at least one old knotted tree, I didn't realize, until I started doing extensive research for a magazine article, that the plum is one of the world's most widely distributed fruit, growing on almost every continent and encompassing more than 2,000 varieties. The fruit itself with its flat seed, can be elliptical, heart-shaped, oblong, ovate or round, making a ripe appearance in a rainbow of colors—purple, blue, scarlet, yellow or green.

There are about eighteen plum species that are horticulturally important. These include two main types—the Japanese varieties and the European varieties. The former, medium to large and famous for their juiciness, are usually more for eating out of hand. A variety of shapes, they are not usually blue or purple or freestone. European varieties (of which there are more in markets) include the most common prune and are always blue or purple. Usually smaller, they are oval or roundish with a milder flavor and firmer texture than Japanese plums.

Plums are always a favorite eaten out of hand, but few people realize how delicious they are in so many other ways. Enjoy them in pies, tarts, cakes, sauces, jams, salads, chutneys, soups, sorbets, shortcakes, crisps or sautéed with meat or poultry. Reine Claude (Greengage), Valor, Burbank (for canning) and the prune varieties are all good for cooking.

To freeze plums when they're in season, merely wash, halve lengthwise and pit. Pack in airtight heavy plastic bags with ³/₄ cup (175 mL) granulated sugar to 4 cups (1 L) fruit. To use, thaw only enough to separate and adjust the amount of sugar called for in the recipe.

NORMAN PLUM SQUARE

This simple elegant dessert is often made with apples in Normandy, France. Plums make a delightful variation. They also are the makings of a wonderful lattice top or open-faced pie using ordinary pie pastry.

30	Italian prune plums (about 3 lb/1.5 kg)	30
1	pkg (14 oz/397 g) frozen puff pastry, thawed	1
¹/₂ cup	granulated sugar	125 mL

2 tbsp	fresh lemon juice	25 mL
	Whipped cream, crème fraîche (see page 29) or	
	Remarkable Low-Fat Cream (see page 185)	

Halve and pit plums; cut lengthwise into quarters. Set aside.

On lightly floured surface, roll out pastry to 12-inch (30 cm) square. Place on greased baking sheet, crimping up edges slightly. Arrange plums over pastry in slightly overlapping rows. Sprinkle with sugar and lemon juice.

Bake in 450°F (230°C) oven for 20 minutes or until pastry is golden and plums are tender. Serve warm with whipped cream. Makes about 6 servings.

CHERRY NANAIMO BARS

Popular Nanaimo bars satisfy even the sweetest sweet tooth.

2 cups	graham cracker crumbs	500 mL
1 cup	flaked coconut	250 mL
1/2 cup	toasted chopped pecans	125 mL
2/3 cup	butter	150 mL
1/3 cup	sifted unsweetened cocoa powder	75 mL
1/4 cup	granulated sugar	50 mL
1	egg, beaten	1

CHERRY LAYER:

1/2 cup	quartered maraschino cherries	125 mL
2 cups	icing sugar	500 mL
1/4 cup	butter, softened	50 mL
2 tbsp	maraschino cherry liquid	25 mL
Dash	almond extract	Dash
2 tsp	grated orange rind	10 mL

CHOCOLATE TOPPING:

1/4 lb	semisweet chocolate	125 g
1 tbsp	butter	15 mL
	Maraschino cherries, chopped	

In bowl, stir together crumbs, coconut and pecans. In small saucepan, gently heat together butter, cocoa and sugar until butter melts. Remove from heat; whisk in egg. Blend into crumb mixture. Press into greased 9-inch (2.5 L) square cake pan; bake in 350°F (180°C) oven for 10 minutes. Let cool on rack.

CHERRY LAYER: Pat cherries dry. In bowl, blend half of the icing sugar with butter; mix in cherry liquid, almond extract, remaining icing sugar, orange rind and cherries. Spread over base.

CHOCOLATE TOPPING: Melt chocolate; stir in butter. Spread evenly over cherry layer; let cool. Cut into bars; garnish each with small piece of maraschino cherry. (Bars can be covered and refrigerated for up to 2 weeks or frozen for up to 2 months. Let bars soften slightly at room temperature before slicing.) Makes about 4 dozen.

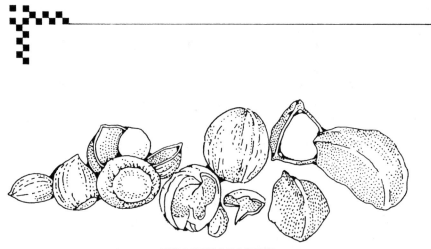

TOASTING NUTS

In most of my recipes calling for nuts or coconut, I suggest that they be toasted first. Toasting brings out the oils that highlight their flavor. It also helps bring back to life any nuts that are slightly stale. By the way, always taste any nuts, especially walnuts and Brazils, before incorporating them into a recipe, because rancid ones can render a whole dish less than palatable.

To toast nuts, spread out on a baking sheet and bake in 350°F (180°C) oven until golden brown and fragrant, 5 to 12 minutes depending on size and kind of nut.

Just one word of warning about toasting any nut. Watch them carefully! There's a little demon inside my oven (very much like the one in the dryer that demolishes one sock of any given pair) that will seize every opportunity to make a whole pan of sliced almonds totally black one second after they're toasted.

TRIPLE DECKER SQUARES

No matter what else appears at a potluck supper, everyone raves over these simply made but delightful and rich morsels that my friend and helper Mary Lou Ruby Jonas makes.

2 cups	all-purpose flour	500 mL
¼ cup	granulated sugar	50 mL
2 cups	butter	500 mL
1 cup	packed brown sugar	250 mL
¼ cup	corn syrup	50 mL
1	can (300 mL) sweetened condensed milk	1
1 tsp	vanilla	5 mL
2 cups	semisweet chocolate chips (350 g or 300 g pkg)	500 mL

In large bowl, stir together flour and granulated sugar; cut in 1 cup (250 mL) of the butter until mixture is crumbly. Press evenly into greased 13- × 9-inch (3.5 L) baking pan. Bake in 350°F (180°C) oven for about 25 minutes or until lightly colored.

Meanwhile, in saucepan, combine remaining butter, brown sugar, corn syrup and condensed milk; stir over low heat until sugar is dissolved. Bring to boil over medium heat, stirring constantly; boil gently for 5 minutes, stirring to prevent sticking.

Remove from heat; add vanilla and beat well. Pour over warm base and spread evenly. Let cool on rack.

Melt chocolate chips and spread over cooled squares. Let chocolate set before cutting into squares. Makes 5 dozen.

SENSATIONAL TURTLE BROWNIES

A very easy brownie batter is not quite baked, covered with pecans and a quick caramel sauce, baked a few minutes longer and sprinkled with chocolate chips for a decadent treat no one will be able to resist. For a sundae, use as a base with chocolate, coffee or vanilla ice cream and chocolate sauce.

1 cup	butter, in pieces	250 mL
4 oz	unsweetened chocolate, coarsely chopped	125 g
1 3/4 cups	granulated sugar	425 mL
4	eggs, well beaten	4
1 tsp	vanilla	5 mL
1 1/4 cups	all-purpose flour	300 mL
1/2 tsp	salt	2 mL

TOPPING:		
1/2 cup	whipping cream	125 mL
1/2 cup	packed brown sugar	125 mL
1/4 cup	butter	50 mL
1 1/2 cups	pecan halves	375 mL
1 cup	chocolate chips	250 mL

In top of double boiler over simmering water, melt butter with chocolate. Stir in sugar until well combined. Stir in eggs and vanilla. Gradually add flour and salt, stirring well after each addition.

Pour into greased 13- × 9-inch (3.5 L) baking pan; bake in 400°F (200°C) oven for 10 minutes. (Batter will not be totally cooked but will be set enough to add topping.)

TOPPING: Meanwhile, in saucepan, combine cream, brown sugar and butter; bring to boil and boil for 2 minutes.

Sprinkle partially baked base with pecans; drizzle evenly with caramel syrup. Bake for 8 to 10 minutes or until golden but not browned.

Remove from oven; sprinkle with chocolate chips. Let melt slightly for 1 to 2 minutes; swirl with knife so that some caramel and nuts show through. Let cool on rack. Cut into squares. Makes 16.

ALMOND SHORTBREAD BARS

Simple to make and easy to pack, these delightful bars are perfect for lunch boxes or potluck suppers.

³/₄ cup	butter	175 mL
¹/₂ cup	icing sugar	125 mL
1 cup	all-purpose flour	250 mL
Pinch	salt	Pinch
¹/₂ cup	packed brown sugar	125 mL
1 tsp	fresh lemon juice	5 mL
³/₄ cup	sliced almonds	175 mL
¹/₂ tsp	almond extract	2 mL

In large bowl, cream together ¹/₂ cup (125 mL) of the butter and icing sugar. Stir together flour and salt; gradually mix into creamed mixture.

With floured hands, pat into ungreased 9-inch (2.5 L) square pan. Bake in 350°F (180°C) oven for 12 to 15 minutes or until lightly colored.

Meanwhile, in small saucepan, melt remaining ¹/₄ cup (50 mL) butter. Stir in brown sugar, 1 tbsp (15 mL) water and lemon juice; bring to boil, stirring constantly. Remove from heat; stir in almonds and almond extract.

Spread over base; bake for 12 to 15 minutes longer or until golden brown. Cut into bars while still warm but not hot. Makes 2 dozen.

RHUBARB CUSTARD PIE

If my family knew they could have only one pie all year, this is the one they'd choose...reason enough for nicknaming rhubarb "pie plant." This was my mother's recipe and the very first thing I ever demonstrated on television almost twenty years ago.

3 cups	coarsely chopped (1-inch/2.5 cm pieces) rhubarb	750 mL
1 cup	granulated sugar	250 mL
3 tbsp	all-purpose flour	50 mL
2 tbsp	butter	25 mL
2	egg yolks, beaten	2
1	unbaked 9-inch (23 cm) pastry shell	1

MERINGUE:

2	egg whites	2
¹/₄ tsp	cream of tartar	1 mL
¹/₄ cup	granulated sugar	50 mL
2 tbsp	water	25 mL
¹/₂ tsp	vanilla	2 mL
¹/₄ tsp	salt	1 mL

In large bowl, stir together rhubarb, sugar, flour and butter; stir in egg yolks. Arrange in pastry shell. Bake in 425°F (220°C) oven for 10 minutes; reduce heat to 350°F (180°C) and bake another 30 minutes. Remove pie and let cool to lukewarm.

MERINGUE: Meanwhile, in bowl, beat egg whites and cream of tartar until soft peaks form; very gradually beat in sugar. Add water, vanilla and salt; beat until very stiff, shiny peaks form.

Spread meringue over pie, sealing right to pastry rim. Swirl into decorative peaks. Bake in 375°F (190°C) oven for 12 to 15 minutes or until tips of meringue become golden. Let cool slowly. Makes 6 servings.

RHUBARB

Every spring, I recall the long row of vigorous green leaves that marked the rhubarb patch running along the garden's edge on our farm. And I never think of rhubarb without remembering a teaching colleague of mine who loved it with such a passion that she nibbled on long stalks right from the patch.

Although everyone may not love it to this extent, the tart, refreshing "fruit" is generally regarded as a "spring tonic," the harbinger of other good seasonal fruit to come.

Actually, this "fruit" is botanically a "vegetable," but don't let that deter you from using the celery-like stalks in a wonderful array of welcome desserts and sweets. Its tart flavor is good on its own or teamed with other fruits in sauces, jams, chutneys, cakes, crisps, sorbets, soufflés, drinks and; of course, pies—that confection from which rhubarb gets its nickname; "pie plant."

Because rhubarb freezes so well, you don't have to restrict your "taste of spring" to this season. Simply prepare as you would for immediate use. Choose firm, crisp stalks; trim off the thick bottom end of each and all leaves (which are toxic, by the way). Wash and dry well; cut into 1-inch (2.5 cm) pieces. Either pack immediately into plastic freezer bags and freeze, or spread in single layer on cookie sheet to freeze then package to keep pieces separate.

If you wish to freeze with sugar, add 1 cup (250 mL) to 4 cups (1 L) chopped rhubarb and label clearly with amount.

For most recipes like pies, stewed rhubarb and jam, do not thaw, but you may have to adjust cooking time. For baked goods like muffins, thaw the rhubarb almost completely (leaving some ice crystals) and pat dry with paper towels otherwise the extra moisture will make muffins heavy.

RHUBARB CRISP

Fruit crisps are always favorites with everyone, and this easy rhubarb version is particularly good with its crunchy topping of oats and toasted walnuts. Serve warm with whipped cream, vanilla ice cream or a custard sauce.

5 cups	coarsely chopped (1-inch/2.5 cm pieces) rhubarb	1.25 L
³/₄ cup	granulated sugar	175 mL

TOPPING:

¹/₃ cup	walnut pieces	75 mL
¹/₂ cup	*each* all-purpose flour, rolled oats and packed brown sugar	125 mL
1 tbsp	granulated sugar	15 mL
¹/₄ tsp	*each* cinnamon and nutmeg	1 mL
¹/₄ cup	butter, softened	50 mL

TOPPING: Spread walnuts on baking sheet; toast in 375°F (190°C) oven for 5 minutes. Let cool and chop finely.

In bowl, combine walnuts, flour, rolled oats, brown sugar, granulated sugar, cinnamon and nutmeg; work in butter until crumbly. Set aside.

Toss rhubarb with ³/₄ cup (175 mL) granulated sugar; arrange in even layer in buttered 8-inch (2 L) glass baking dish. Sprinkle with walnut mixture and bake, uncovered, in 375°F (190°C) oven for 35 to 40 minutes or until rhubarb is tender and top golden brown. Makes 6 servings.

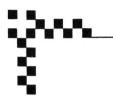

Finishing Touches

Sometimes simply cooked meat, fish or poultry can take on great new dimensions with the addition of an easy sauce. In this chapter, there are just such embellishments. They are primarily for main courses, but a few will bring extra life to fruit or desserts.

LEMON-YOGURT DRESSING

This simple low-cal dressing is delicious on salads of sliced cucumbers, assorted greens, shredded red or green cabbage with raisins, cooked sliced beets or raw spinach. Or use it as a marinade for chicken or fish before broiling.

⅓ cup	low-fat plain yogurt	75 mL
¼ cup	light mayonnaise	50 mL
1 tbsp	fresh lemon juice	15 mL
½ tsp	grated lemon rind	2 mL
2	green onions, thinly sliced	2
1 tsp	dried dillweed	5 mL

In small bowl, whisk together yogurt, mayonnaise, lemon juice and rind until blended. Stir in onions and dill. Cover and refrigerate for up to 5 days. Makes ¾ cup (175 mL).

LEMON-APRICOT BUTTER

This butter is great on toast as well as Fresh Mint Quick Bread (see page 37).

½ cup	butter	125 mL
1 tsp	finely grated lemon rind	5 mL
2 tsp	lemon juice	10 mL
¼ cup	finely chopped dried apricots	50 mL

In small bowl, cream butter; beat in lemon rind and juice. Blend in apricots. (Butter can be covered and refrigerated for up to 5 days. Bring to room temperature before serving.) Makes ¾ cup (175 mL).

QUICK CHOCOLATE SAUCE

For a special company sauce, add 2 teaspoons (10 mL) brandy or liqueur after the butter.

¾ cup	whipping cream	175 mL
5 oz	semisweet chocolate, broken up	150 g
1 tbsp	butter	15 mL
2 tsp	brandy or nut liqueur	10 mL

In small heavy saucepan, bring cream to boil; remove from heat. Whisk in chocolate until melted. Whisk in butter. Let cool slightly before using. (Sauce can be covered and refrigerated for up to 1 week. Reheat over low heat and serve warm.) Makes 1 cup (250 mL).

PLUM CHUTNEY

Serve this dark purple, rich and spicy chutney with pork, poultry or cold cuts. It's also good spread over cream cheese on bagels.

4 lb	purple prune plums (about 4 quarts/4 L)	2 kg
2 lb	apples (about 8)	1 kg
1½ cups	white vinegar	375 mL
4 cups	packed brown sugar	1 L
1 tbsp	pickling salt	15 mL
1½ tsp	*each* ground allspice, ginger, cloves and cinnamon	7 mL

Wash and pit plums; cut into eighths and place in large nonaluminum heavy kettle. Peel, core and coarsely chop apples; add to plums along with vinegar. Bring to boil; reduce heat and simmer, uncovered, for 1 hour, stirring occasionally.

Stir in sugar, pickling salt, allspice, ginger, cloves and cinnamon; bring to boil. Reduce heat and simmer, uncovered and stirring often, until thickened, about 1 hour. Ladle into hot sterilized jars to within ⅛-inch (3 mm) from top and seal immediately. Cool and store in cool, dark, dry place. Makes about 8 cups (2 L).

QUICK CHILI SAUCE

This quick condiment is boiled for only 20 minutes rather than the usual three hours. Part of the secret is in salting the vegetables and letting them stand overnight. Don't forget to use your food processor for chopping.

8 lb	very ripe tomatoes	3.5 kg
6	onions, finely chopped	6
1	bunch celery, chopped	1
⅓ cup	pickling salt	75 mL
3 cups	granulated sugar	750 mL
2½ cups	cider vinegar	625 mL
1	large sweet green pepper, finely chopped	1
1 tsp	*each* pepper, cinnamon, ground cloves and allspice	5 mL
½ tsp	ginger	2 mL

In large pot of boiling water, blanch tomatoes for 15 to 30 seconds; immediately plunge into cold water. Remove skins; core and chop coarsely.

In large glass or stainless steel bowl, combine tomatoes, onions, celery and salt; cover and refrigerate overnight.

Drain all liquid from vegetables. In large stainless steel kettle, combine vegetables with sugar, vinegar, green pepper, pepper, cinnamon, cloves, allspice and ginger. Bring to boil; boil, uncovered, for 20 to 30 minutes or until thickened.

While still hot, pour sauce into hot sterilized jars, leaving ½-inch (1 cm) headspace and seal. Let cool. Wipe jars and store in cool, dark, dry place. Makes about 16 cups (4 L).

SALSA

Salsa means sauce in Spanish, but it is unlike most other sauces we know. There is nothing hidden in a salsa, which is a combination of finely diced fruit or vegetables with herbs, spices and flavorings like lime juice or rice vinegar. Salsas are fresh, adding interest to the simplest of grilled fish or chicken, even plain tacos.

I like salsas, too, because they're quick and easy. You don't even have to worry about measuring accurately; nor do you need any special cooking techniques—just chop and stir.

I also like their flavors and textures. They can be sharp and sweet, hot and cool all at once—usually a little crunchy and a little smooth, too.

The other lovely appeal salsas have right now is their lightness and freshness—lots of flavor without using a mountain of butter or cream.

FRESH TOMATO-CUCUMBER SALSA

Instead of using heavy cream sauces or butters, serve this fresh, zesty salsa with Lime-Grilled Salmon (see page 90) or with grilled chicken.

1	tomato, seeded and finely chopped	1
¹/₂ cup	finely chopped cucumber	125 mL
¹/₄ cup	chopped red onion	50 mL
1 tbsp	finely chopped fresh coriander	15 mL
1 tbsp	minced jalapeño pepper	15 mL
1 tbsp	fresh lime juice	15 mL
Pinch	granulated sugar	Pinch
	Salt and pepper	

In small bowl, toss together tomato, cucumber, onion, coriander, jalapeño pepper, lime juice, sugar, and salt and pepper to taste. Cover and refrigerate for up to 2 days. Makes about 1 cup (250 mL).

CITRUS-CRANBERRY SALSA

I love the refreshing tartness of raw cranberries. Although a raw cranberry relish is not new, it has a new name here because I think of salsas as fresh, light sauces. Enjoy this one with not only turkey, but also chicken, duck or goose. If using frozen cranberries, do not thaw before chopping.

1	large orange	1
1 cup	finely chopped cranberries	250 mL
2 tbsp	fresh lime juice	25 mL
1/4 cup	packed brown sugar	50 mL
4	green onions, finely chopped	4
Pinch	*each* salt and hot pepper flakes	Pinch
2 tbsp	dried currants	25 mL

Grate 1 tsp (5 mL) rind from orange; peel and finely chop pulp, reserving juice.

In bowl, combine orange pulp, juice and grated rind.

Stir in cranberries, lime juice, sugar, green onions, salt and hot pepper flakes until sugar is dissolved. Stir in currants. Cover and refrigerate for up to 1 day. Makes 1½ cups (375 mL).

FRESH PEACH SALSA

The only true peach is one ripened on the tree. It is one yearning you just can't satisfy in the winter, because those peaches grown in other countries, picked green and shipped here from miles away have the texture of sponge and absolutely no flavor or juice. But a true peach, ripened on the tree, has a sinfully smooth texture and juice that drips right down to your elbow—and a flavor worth the year's wait.

Serve this light, fresh sauce with grilled veal, pork, chicken or fish.

3	peaches	3
1 tbsp	white wine vinegar or lime juice	15 mL
1/4 cup	diced red onion	50 mL
1 tbsp	chopped fresh coriander	15 mL
1 tsp	minced jalapeño pepper	5 mL
	Salt and pepper	

Peel and finely dice peaches to make 1½ cups (375 mL), placing in small bowl and sprinkling with vinegar as you work.

Stir in onion, coriander, jalapeño pepper; season with salt and pepper to taste. Cover and refrigerate for up to 8 hours. Makes about 1¾ cups (425 mL).

ALL-PURPOSE COOKED TOMATO SAUCE

This versatile sauce can be the basis for many good meals. Try it as is over pasta, or add browned ground beef, mushrooms and Parmesan cheese for a hearty meat sauce for spaghetti or lasagna. Use for homemade pizza or with chicken, veal or grilled fish. Store in small containers.

2 tbsp	olive oil	25 mL
2	cans (each 28 oz/796 mL) tomatoes, (preferably plum), chopped	2
1	can (5½ oz/156 mL) tomato paste	1
½ cup	chopped fresh parsley	125 mL
3	cloves garlic, minced	3
2 tbsp	freshly grated Parmesan cheese	25 mL
1 tbsp	granulated sugar	15 mL
2 tsp	dried basil	10 mL
1 tsp	dried oregano	5 mL
½ tsp	*each* salt and pepper	2 mL
¼ tsp	hot pepper flakes	1 mL

In large stainless steel saucepan, heat oil; combine tomatoes, tomato paste, one tomato paste can of water, parsley, garlic, cheese, sugar, basil, oregano, salt, pepper and hot pepper flakes; bring to boil.

Reduce heat to very low; simmer, uncovered, for about 1 hour or until thickened and fairly smooth. Taste and adjust seasoning. (Sauce can be cooled and refrigerated in small containers for a few days or frozen for several months; taste and adjust seasoning if frozen for more than 2 months.) Makes 6 cups (1.5 L).

ZESTY HOMEMADE BARBECUE SAUCE

This spicy sauce will keep for several days in the refrigerator or it can be frozen for longer storage. Use it for basting meat on a barbecue or in oven-barbecued chicken or spareribs. For oven-barbecued chicken, pour over pieces and bake, uncovered, in 350°F (180°C) oven for 60 minutes, turning once. For ribs, roast, uncovered, in 400°F (200°C) oven for 30 minutes; pour on sauce, cover and roast at 350°F (180°C) for 1 hour.

1 tbsp	vegetable oil	15 mL
1	large onion, finely chopped	1
¼ cup	packed brown sugar	50 mL
¾ cup	ketchup	175 mL
¼ cup	fresh lemon juice	50 mL
1 tbsp	*each* Worcestershire sauce and Dijon mustard	15 mL
1 tsp	chili powder	5 mL
Pinch	cayenne pepper	Pinch

In small saucepan, heat oil; cook onion until softened but not browned. Stir in sugar; cook over low heat, stirring constantly, until sugar has dissolved.

Remove from heat; stir in ketchup, lemon juice, Worcestershire, mustard, chili powder and cayenne. Makes 1¾ cups (425 mL), enough for 4 lb (2 kg) spareribs or 3 lb (1.5 kg) chicken.

MICROWAVE OLD-FASHIONED SALAD DRESSING

One of my favorite uses for the microwave oven is to make sauces and creamy cooked dressings. If you made this old-fashioned salad dressing in a double boiler, it would take 10 minutes of constant stirring. The dressing is wonderful on shredded cabbage or cooked potatoes for those salads you remember from years ago.

½ cup	granulated sugar	125 mL
3 tbsp	all-purpose flour	50 mL
1 tbsp	dry mustard	15 mL
1 tsp	salt	5 mL
2	eggs	2
1 cup	*each* milk and water	250 mL
¾ cup	white vinegar	175 mL

In 8-cup (2 L) microwaveable measuring cup, combine sugar, flour, mustard and salt; beat in eggs. Stir in milk, water and vinegar.

Microwave at Medium-High (70%) for 6 minutes. Stir and microwave at High for 5 minutes or until bubbly and thickened, stirring halfway through.

Let cool at room temperature for a few minutes, stirring often. (Dressing can be stored in covered jar in refrigerator for up to 2 weeks.) Makes 2¾ cups (675 mL).

MURIEL'S BLUE CHEESE DRESSING

My sister, Muriel Barbour, who lives in Delta, B.C., is a great cook and specializes in crisp green salads. She calls this tangy dressing her "House Dressing," and I think you'll probably want to keep a jar on hand, too. Although I normally wouldn't suggest using dried chives or onions, do so in this recipe since the dressing will keep for days, but it won't if you use raw onions.

1 cup	*each* light sour cream and light mayonnaise	250 mL
¼ cup	lemon juice	50 mL
2 tbsp	Worcestershire sauce	25 mL
2 tsp	dried onion or chive flakes (optional)	10 mL
1 tsp	dry mustard	5 mL
½ tsp	salt	2 mL
6 oz	blue cheese, crumbled	175 g

In small bowl, whisk together sour cream, mayonnaise, lemon juice and Worcestershire sauce until smooth. Whisk in dried onion (if using), mustard and salt. Mash cheese with fork and stir in. Cover and refrigerate overnight before using or for up to 1 week. Makes 2⅔ cups (650 mL).

PICKLED CHERRIES

Set a little bowl of these easy-to-make cherries inside the Food Processor Gougère Ring (page 23) for an unusual and tantalizing treat. Or, serve them with a selection of cheeses. Make these when black cherries are in season so that you have a year-round supply.

2 quarts	sweet black cherries (with stems)	2 L
2 cups	water	500 mL
1 cup	cider vinegar	250 mL
1/2 cup	packed brown sugar	125 mL
2 tbsp	pickling salt	25 mL

Wash cherries and do not pit; set out on paper towels to dry.

In heavy nonaluminum saucepan, bring water, vinegar, sugar and pickling salt to boil, stirring until sugar is dissolved.

Meanwhile, pack cherries carefully into sterilized jars. Cool syrup to temperature of jars, pour over cherries and seal immediately. Cool and store in cool, dark, dry place. Makes 20 cups (2.5 L).

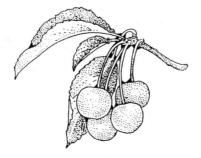

PICKLED GARLIC

A Chinese specialty, these tangy, crisp pickles are perfect with pâté and melba toast or roast beef. Everyone fights over the last one in the dish.

2 cups	garlic cloves (3/4 lb/375 g or about 14 heads)	500 mL
1 1/4 cups	white vinegar	300 mL
1/4 cup	granulated sugar	50 mL
1/2 tsp	coarse pickling salt	2 mL
1/2 tsp	*each* whole black peppercorns and mustard seeds	2 mL
1	bay leaf	1

Peel garlic cloves; cut very thick cloves lengthwise.

In large saucepan, stir together vinegar, sugar, salt, peppercorns, mustard seeds and bay leaf; bring to boil over high heat, stirring, until sugar dissolves.

Drop in garlic and return to boil; cook, uncovered and stirring occasionally, for 1 minute. Let cool.

Transfer garlic and liquid to clean sterilized jar; cover and refrigerate for at least 24 hours or up to 2 months. Makes 2 cups (500 mL).

REMARKABLE LOW-FAT CREAM

This is not a new idea, in fact it's an ancient one from the Mediterranean. However, at a time when we are watching our fat intake, draining the whey from yogurt to make ''yogurt cheese'' (actually more like a heavy cream) will provide a very satisfying substitute for whipped cream or savory cream sauces with main courses.

4 cups	natural plain yogurt (low-fat or nonfat), 750 g container	1 L

SWEET VERSION:

3 tbsp	granulated sugar (or to taste)	50 mL
1 tsp	grated lemon rind	5 mL

SAVORY VERSION:

	Salt	
	Chopped herbs or spices	

Line sieve with several layers of dampened cheesecloth; place over bowl. Place yogurt in sieve; cover and refrigerate for at least 2 hours (for thinner sauce) or overnight (for thicker sauce). To serve, scrape cheese from cloth and place in separate bowl.

SWEET VERSION: Stir in sugar and lemon rind to accompany desserts.

SAVORY VERSION: Season with salt and herbs or spices to taste to accompany savory dishes.

Makes 2 cups (500 mL) if allowed to drain overnight.

CHOCOLATE CREAM CHEESE ICING

This easy icing, which is not overly sweet, can be the crowning glory on white or chocolate cakes. It's particularly wonderful on Reta's Ginger Brownies (see page 169).

1/4 lb	light cream cheese	125 g
3 tbsp	sour cream	50 mL
1/2 cup	icing sugar	125 mL
2 tbsp	unsweetened cocoa powder	25 mL

In bowl or food processor, cream together cheese and sour cream until fluffy. Sift together sugar and cocoa; beat into cheese mixture until thickened. Makes enough icing for 8 or 9-inch (20 to 23 cm) cake or torte.

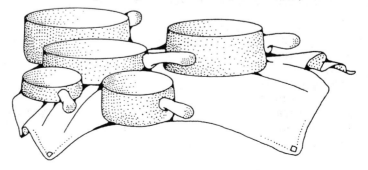

STOCKING THE PANTRY

Besides the essentials like flour, sugar, eggs, butter and milk, most cooks have their personal lists of ingredients without which they would feel lost in the kitchen. My own list includes a hunk of real Parmesan cheese (which keeps for ages ready to be grated when I need it), a good-size chunk of fresh ginger, candied ginger, hot pepper sauce, fresh garlic, fresh lemons, Dijon mustard, Worcestershire sauce, soy sauce, cans of chicken and beef broth, bittersweet or semisweet chocolate, chocolate chips, rice and wine vinegars and a vast selection of herbs and spices.

The following is a list of handy ingredients that are easy to use and give lots of flavor to a dish. Many of them may also help out in the case of unexpected company.

Cans, Jars and Tubes:
- salmon, tuna and anchovy paste
- artichoke hearts
- beans of all kinds (kidney, white, chickpeas, etc.)
- several can sizes of tomatoes, tomato sauce and tomato paste (a tube is handy if you can find one)
- jams and jellies, such as red currant, apricot, peach and orange marmalade for glazes and sauces
- horseradish
- hot pepper sauce (Tabasco), soy sauce and Worcestershire sauce
- jalapeño peppers and olives
- regular prepared and Dijon mustard, dry mustard
- white and cider vinegar, rice and wine vinegars
- canned chicken and beef broth (instant stock mixes for emergency tablespoonfuls, but not for few cups, since they tend to be very salty and often contain msg)
- good-quality olive oil, vegetable oil
- honey, molasses and corn syrup

Refrigerator and Freezer Staples:
- Parmesan and Cheddar cheese
- lemons and oranges for zest and juice
- apples
- nuts and coconut in the freezer.

Index